POSTCARD HISTORY SERIES

# *Port Huron*
## *1880–1960*

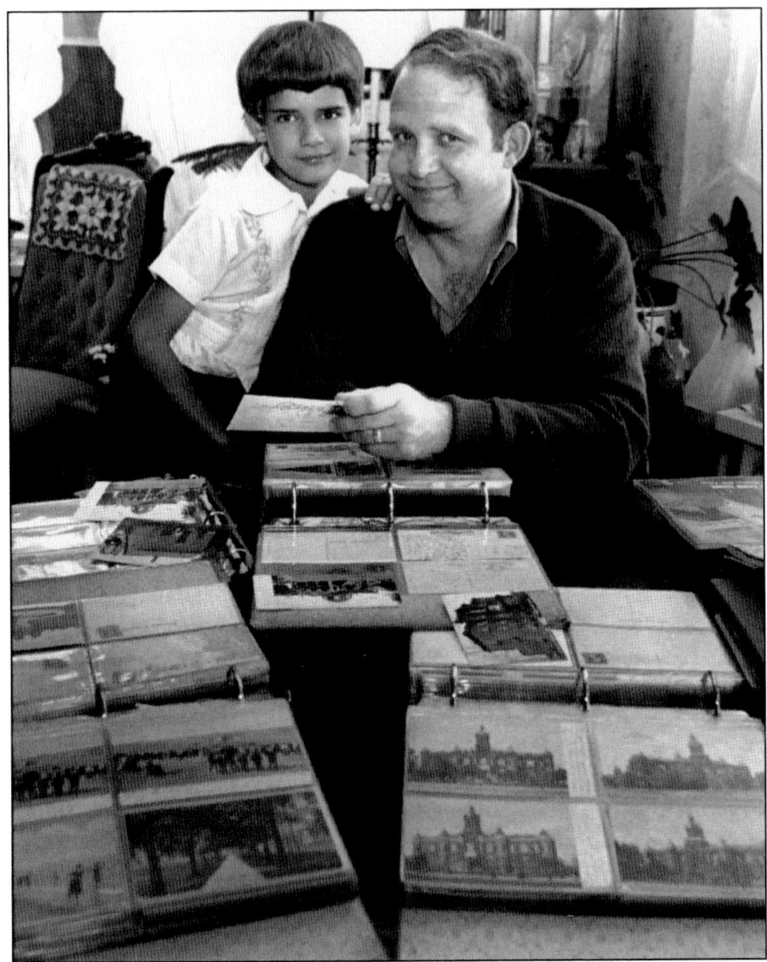

This 1984 photograph of the author, Thomas Jay "T. J." Gaffney, at the age of nine and his father, Thomas John Gaffney, was taken for a *Port Huron Times Herald* article about the elder Gaffney's postcard collection. Some of the postcard views in this book can be seen in the binders in the photograph. The elder Thomas Gaffney collected postcards for nearly 40 years, starting in his college days at the University of Michigan and continuing until his death in October 2003. At the time of his death, he had amassed a collection of nearly 10,000 postcards of the Thumb Region of Michigan alone.

*On the front cover*: Produced sometime prior to 1900, this postcard shows the second Military Street Bridge, used from the 1870s until it was replaced due to age in 1913. Like many of Port Huron's early bridges, it was mounted on a pedestal in the middle of the Black River and swung parallel with the river when open. "You'll Like Port Huron" was a popular advertising slogan at the time. (Author's collection.)

*On the back cover:* This *c.* 1939 souvenir postcard tells the reader "Greetings from Port Huron, Michigan." The main background image shows the *J. T. Wing*, the last commercial schooner on the Great Lakes, passing beneath the first Blue Water Bridge. This image has become of the more iconic in Port Huron-era tourism. Within the letters one can also see images of Port Huron and the Port Huron Post Office/Customs House; the Mackinac Race; the Fort Gratiot Lighthouse; the Military Street Bridge; the Women's Benefit Association Building; and interestingly enough, the Sanilac County Petroglyphs. (Author's collection.)

POSTCARD HISTORY SERIES

# *Port Huron*
## *1880–1960*

*T. J. Gaffney*

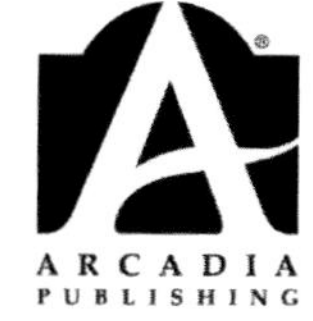

ISBN 978-0-7385-4119-8

Published by Arcadia Publishing
Charleston, South Carolina

Printed in the United States of America

Library of Congress Catalog Card Number: 2006930979

For all general information contact Arcadia Publishing at:
Telephone 843-853-2070
Fax 843-853-0044
E-mail sales@arcadiapublishing.com
For customer service and orders:
Toll-Free 1-888-313-2665

Visit us on the Internet at www.arcadiapublishing.com

*To Heather, Phoebe, T. W., and Mom. I love you guys.*

# Contents

# Acknowledgments

Since I first began putting this book together, there have been many who have supported me through the process. While it is impossible to thank everyone who has offered his support, there are a few who have gone out of their way to keep me on the right track.

I wish to thank Stephen Williams, former director of the Port Huron Museum, for his unfailing support and guidance on this project. His willingness to review and honestly critique my work was invaluable, and for that and many other reasons, I will be forever grateful.

I am grateful to the Thursday Morning Ladies Genealogy Group members: Amy Banker, Suzette Bromley, Chris Gaffney, Marian Greig, Kay Korth, Kay Mitchel, Jack Radike, Lynn Secory, Fran Thomas, Lois Wedge, and Helen Whiting. The enthusiasm they have shown and given me every Thursday toward a seemingly never-ending task means more than they will ever know.

In addition, I wish to thank my editor at Arcadia Publishing, Anna Wilson, for her guidance, expertise, and most importantly, her patience, as my occasional tongue-in-cheek comments and constant e-mails early on probably pushed her a bit.

There are many who, though they may not know it, have paved the way for this book through their research, writing, and passion for local history. Specifically, I wish to thank the following: Jim Acheson, Jeanne S. Bottomley, Mary and Walter Brooks, Harry and Rose Burgess, Alan Carlisle, Bill Duff, Katherine Duffy-Houghton, Mino Duffy and Gerry Kramer, Helen Endlich, Paulla Gaffney, Bob Hanford, Marsha Haynes, Kristi Hazard, Bill Pierce, and Capt. Ted Richardson, for their many efforts towards promoting and preserving our community's heritage. I also thank George "Sandy" Y. Duffy Jr., who is retired from the Port Huron and Detroit Railroad and collects Michigan cards of Belle Isle canoes and Tawas Beach.

And though they both passed away long before I was born, I am grateful to William Lee Jenks and D. B. Harrington. Jenks's *History of St. Clair County* set the benchmark for all of us who wish write about the past. Without Harrington, there would have been no Port Huron, as he named it so in 1849.

Finally, my dad, Thomas John Gaffney, purchased a shoebox full of postcards one day in Ann Arbor in the summer of 1966, which started him on a life-long love of collecting, one that he in turn passed to his son. It is, in a very real sense, *his* book that you are now reading.

# Introduction

The book you are about to enjoy includes just a small part of the Thomas Gaffney Collection of postcards, begun nearly 40 years ago. When I met Tom in the mid-1960s, card collecting was not the huge hobby it is today. Back then, he was among a small handful of collectors going to estate sales, roaming paper shows, and searching antique shops. Once, he mentioned obtaining a shoebox full of cards, and at the time, it did not occur to me that old postcards could be of any value.

Decades later, by the time I had been bitten by the same postcard bug, Tom's collection had grown to dozens of three-ring binders, sorted by state and subject, stored neatly on shelves. He liked them all, from the now highly sought-after real-photo cards of Louis Pesha to the chrome cards of the 1950s and 1960s. He especially liked cards from early Port Huron, and those that you will find here are rare and wonderful to study.

As most of us know, postcards were created with an image on one side and a message/address on the reverse, to be mailed and sent to a friend or relative. By its nature and design, the message side gave the sender an opportunity to personalize, explain, or add to the image. To me, an old card gains intrinsic value when someone writes about the very scene the card displays.

These old postcards of Port Huron never age because they are timeless: the men, women, and subjects in them will always appear exactly as they were. When we hold a postcard and look into that small, perfectly captured window of time, for one brief moment, we can relive the delight of the original recipient in exactly the same way as the sender had hoped. The image and the message of an old postcard can still produce their magic, decades later.

Here, then, are the Port Huron–area postcards from the collection of Thomas Gaffney—scenes from a simpler time, meant to bring the same pleasure and contentment as they did long ago. Tom would have been very pleased to have you linger over each.

—George Duffy Jr.

# *One*

# Memories of Downtown

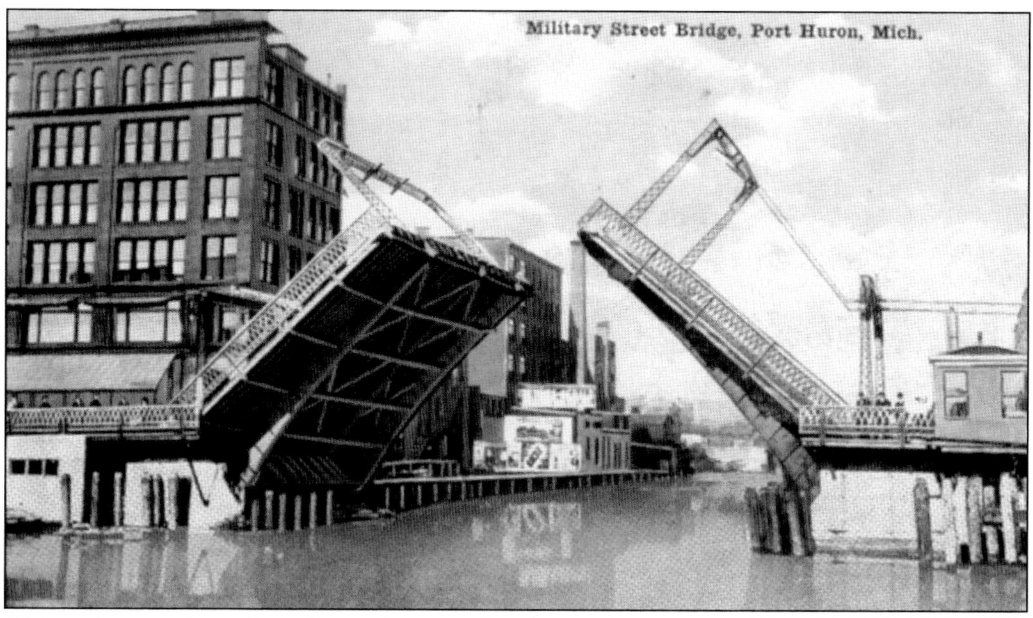


Although not unique, Port Huron is unusual in that its downtown area has always been split by water. To further confuse matters, the main thoroughfare has different names on either side: Military Street to the south and Huron Avenue to the north. Replacing the structure seen on the cover of this book, this third incarnation of the bridge connecting the downtown area was completed in 1913. A double-span lift bridge, it gave water traffic access to the center of the Black River for the first time, allowing even larger ships to pass beneath it. The two raised towers seen on either side were for carrying the electric lines used by the streetcars of the day, and were removed shortly after this service was abandoned in 1926.

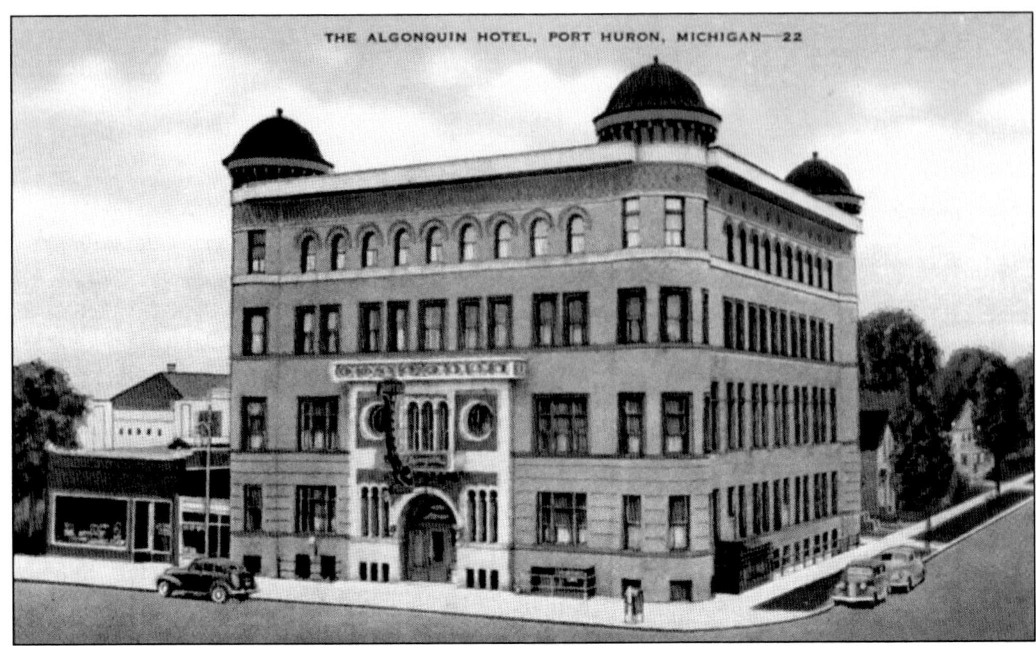


This early-1940s view shows the Algonquin Hotel on Huron Avenue. Originally constructed as the home of the Maccabees fraternal order in 1892, it later served as a hotel and apartments. An effort was made to turn the building into a long-term care facility, but a devastating fire on January 28, 2000, damaged the structure beyond repair, and it was torn down soon after.

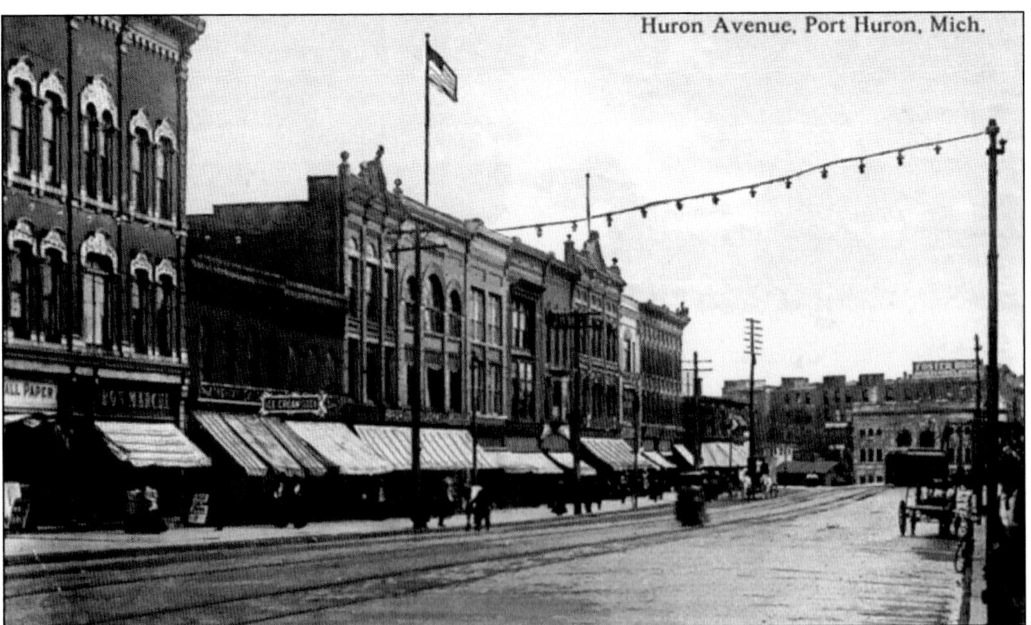


Taken about 1910, this photograph of Huron Avenue reveals a once-prominent part of the downtown business district: awnings. It is said that at this time one could walk an entire city block in a rainstorm without fear of getting wet. Most of the awnings were removed during the 1920s, although some longtime businesses continued to use them as late as World War II.

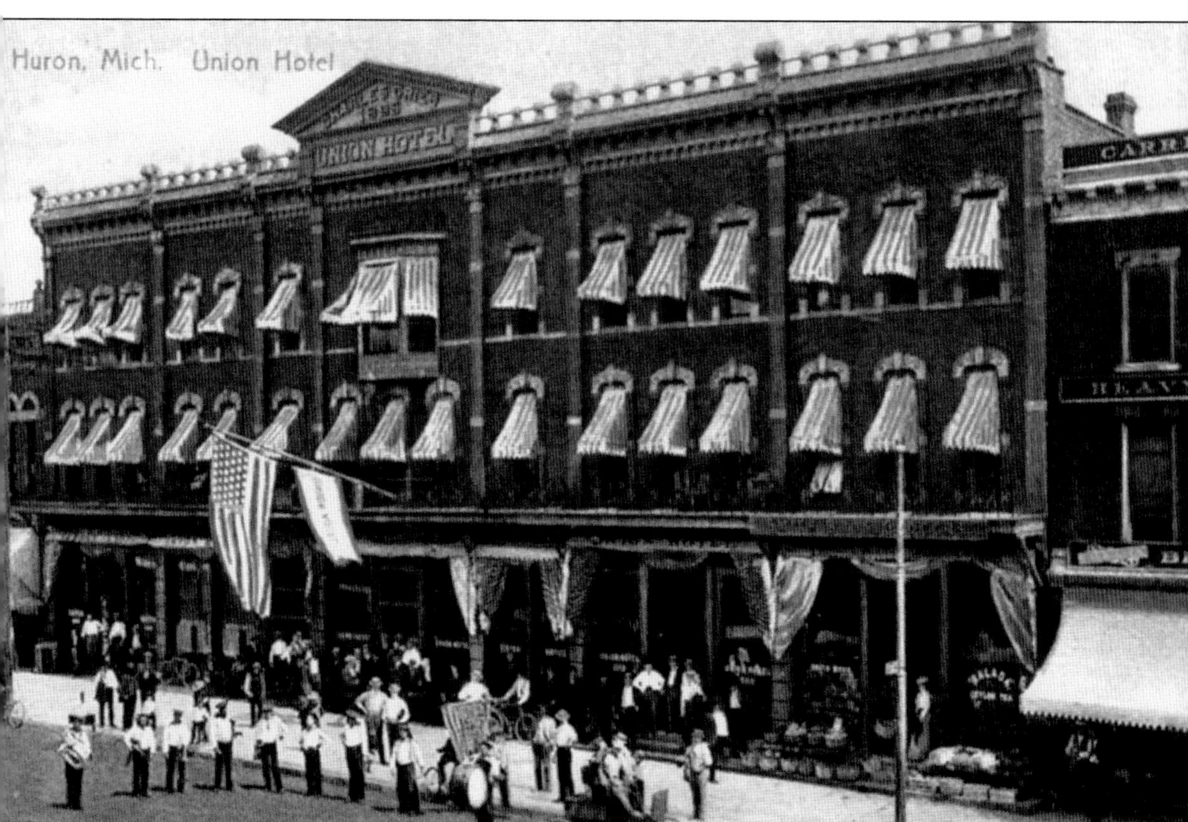


Located between 318 and 322 Huron Avenue, the Union Hotel was opened in 1895 by Charles Gries. In 1900, Phillip Eichorn acquired the business and remained its owner until it finally closed in the 1920s. For most of its early history, the Union Hotel was advertised as "the place to stop," and was considered one of the premier accommodations in the region. After its closure, the lower level held several small businesses, most memorably the Detroit Tea Store, the Port Huron Paint Company, and the Port Huron Coney Island. The building was removed in the mid-1960s during urban renewal and replaced by the modern, single-story ACE Hardware, now Gilroy's. Sadly, the hole left amidst the several surrounding historic structures remains a jarring reminder of how ill-advised urban renewal can sometimes devastate a city.

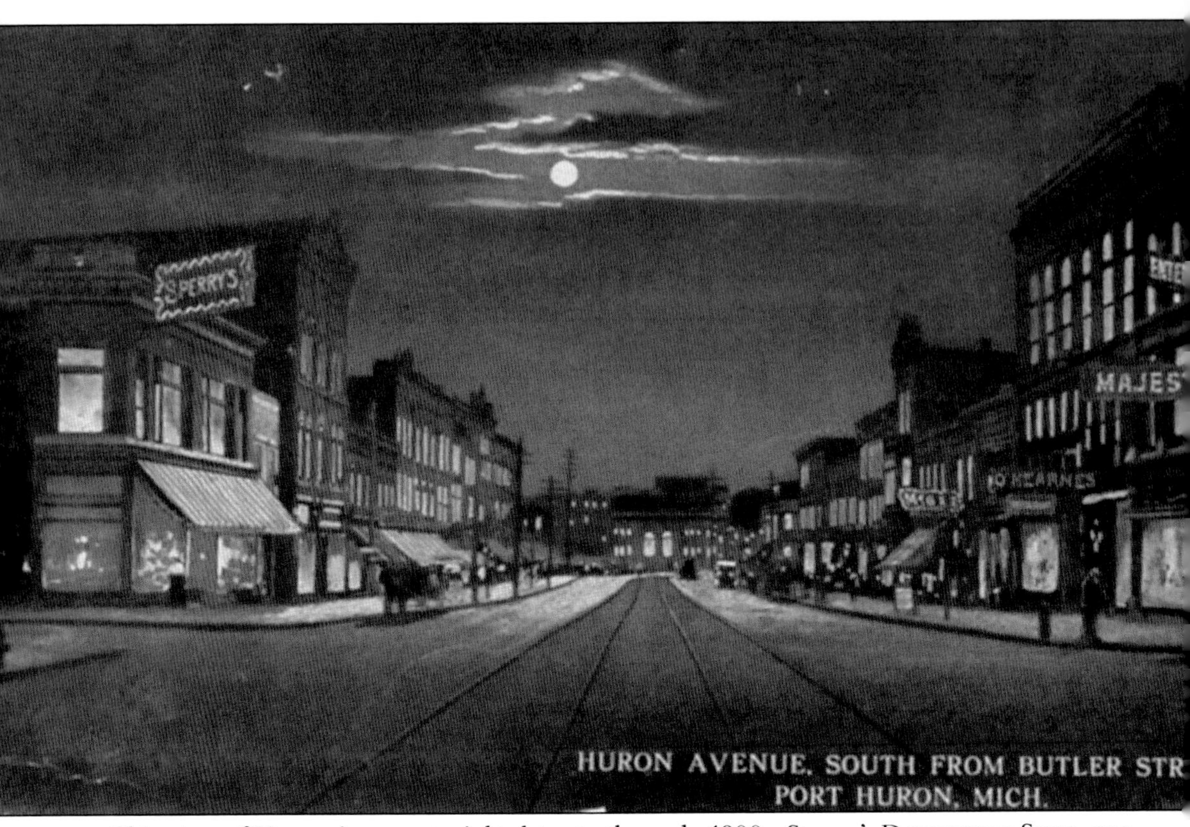


This view of Huron Avenue at night dates to the early 1900s. Sperry's Department Store, one of the longest-running downtown Port Huron businesses, is in a location most residents would remember as the S. S. Kresge Company's store. Founded in 1893 by J. B. Sperry, the department store relocated across the intersection of Butler Street (now Grand River Avenue) in 1923. It remained under the management of the Sperry family until 1969, when it was sold to a series of conglomerates. It was finally closed under the Stage Company in 2000, ending 108 years of continuous service to the community. The book *Sperry's: The First Hundred Years*, written in 1993 by Bernie P. Lyons, gives an excellent history of this fine company.

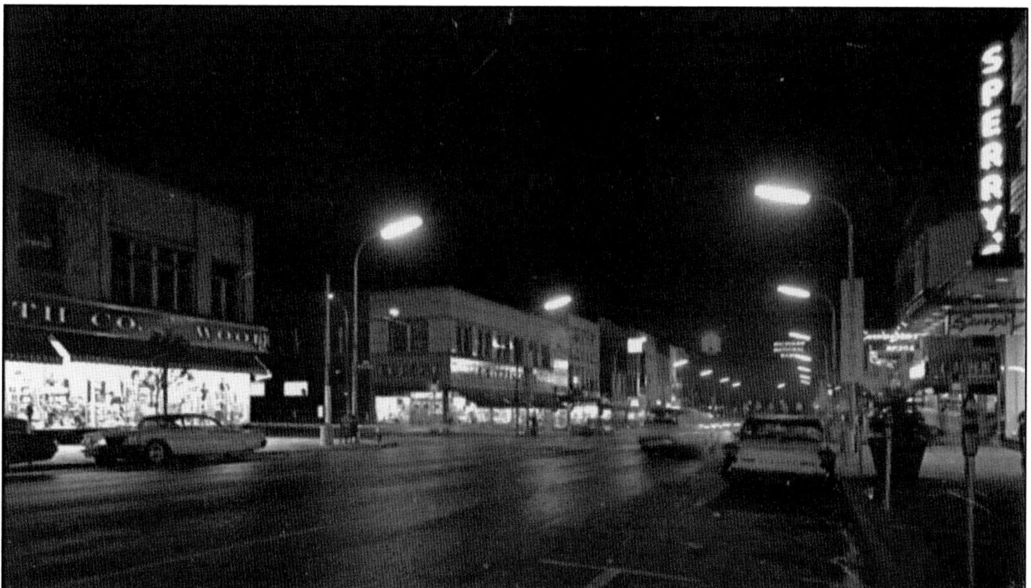


Taken around 1960, this photograph shows the famous Sperry's neon sign, which still exists today. The S. S. Kresge Company, founded in Detroit in 1897, opened its second store in Port Huron in 1901 in order to compete with the locally owned Ballentine Dry Goods Company. When Sperry's moved across the street in 1923, Kresge's expanded into its former space. Even after the Kresge name changed to K-Mart and two new stores opened on the northern and western edges of the city in the 1960s, the shop remained open. The downtown site finally closed in 1983, but it was not the end of the K-Mart presence in the community. The two edge stores were consolidated into a Super K-Mart in the 1990s, making Kresge's one of the area's oldest continually operating businesses.

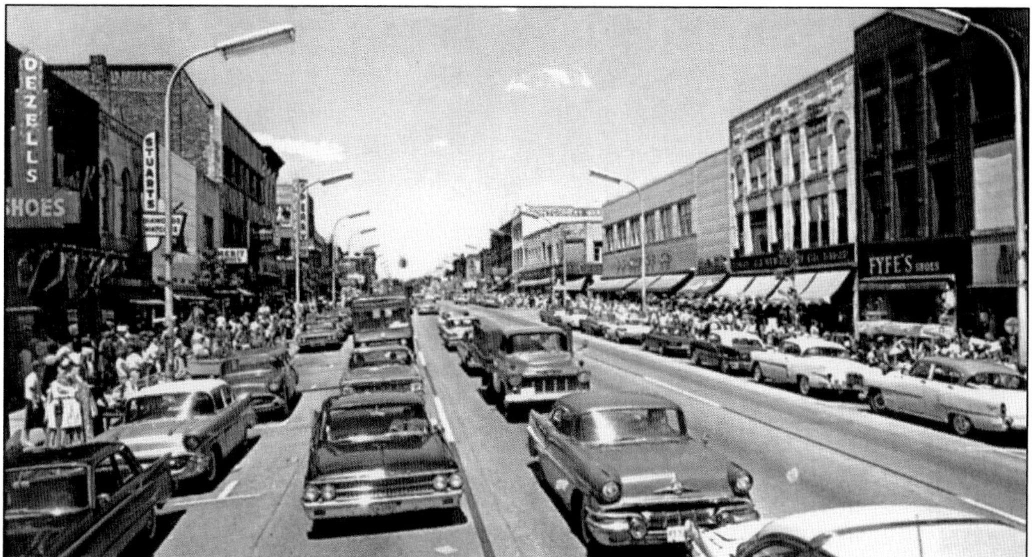


Sidewalk sale days occur on Huron Avenue in this *c.* 1960 northward view. The overcrowded sidewalks and parking spaces indicate just how popular an event this was. It was once such a defining part of their yearly income that downtown merchants would often prepare weeks or months in advance for this event.

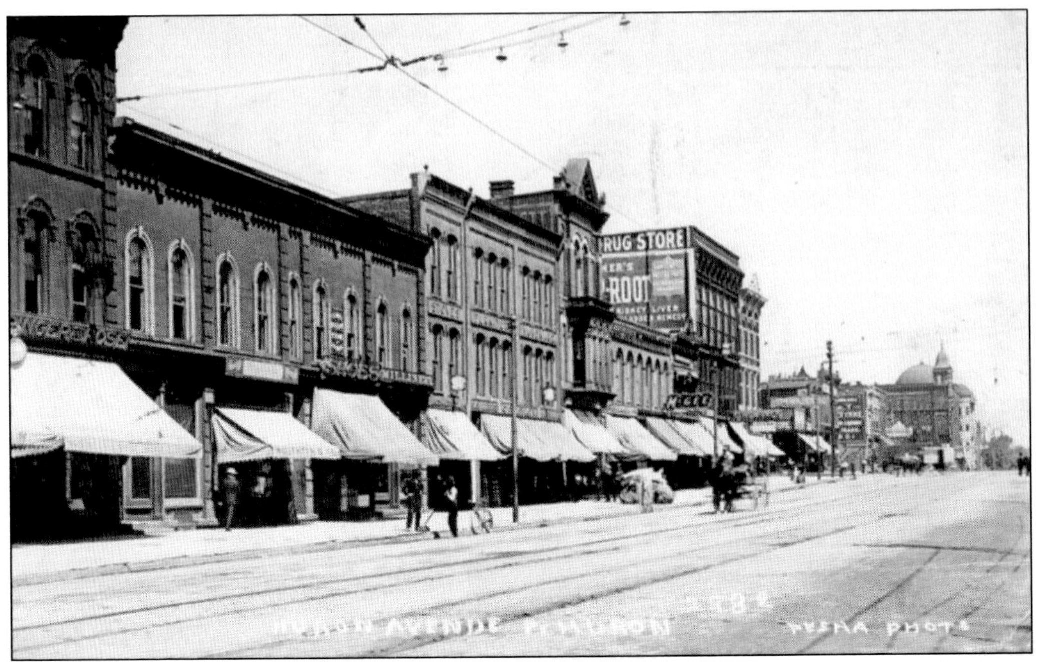


This view of the west side of Huron Avenue, looking toward Butler Street (now Grand River), was taken by the famous photographer Louis Pesha about 1905. Many of the buildings seen here were already 25 years old or more at the time. Even more amazing is how many of these structures survive over 100 years later—a testament to the active role of preservation in the community.

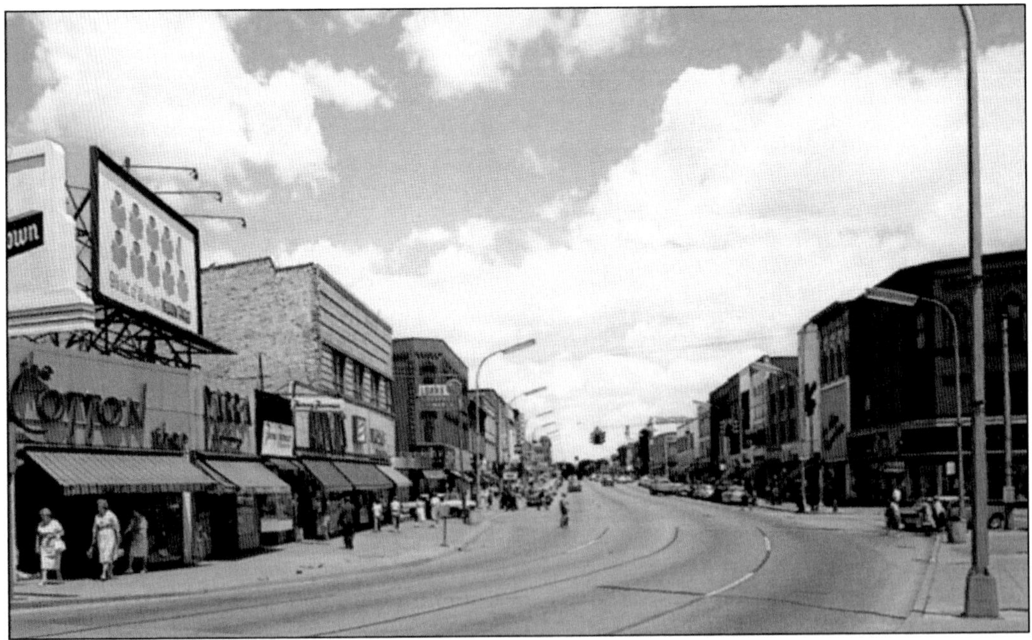

Huron Avenue is seen from the Military Street Bridge around 1955. Visible here is the heart of the central business district, including such stores as, from left to right on the left side of the street, Cotton Shop clothing store, Parra Millinery, Arden's, Marx Jewelers, and Ballentine Dry Goods.

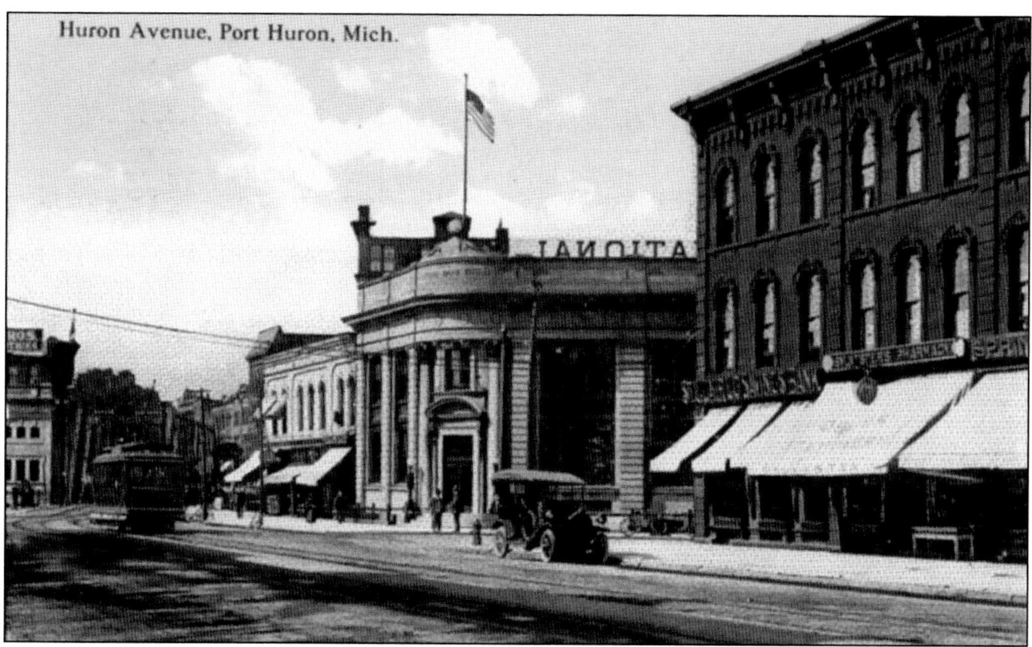


The reverse of the previous view, this photograph was taken roughly 50 years earlier. Note the car parked on the street: an unusual site at this time. This particular one was manufactured by the Northern Motor Car Company, which produced automobiles in Port Huron from the 1890s until about 1905.

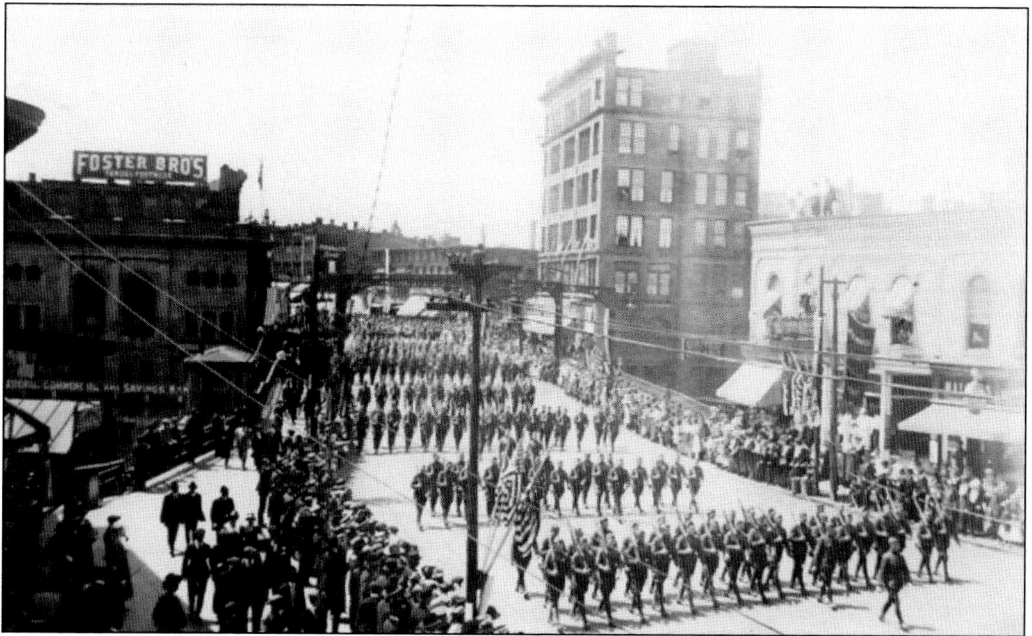


A World War I doughboy parade marches through downtown in 1917. Note the previously mentioned "new" Military Street—barely four years old at the time this was taken—and the crowds, nearly four deep in places. Citizens from outlying communities would routinely come to Port Huron for parades in the days before television and organized sports.

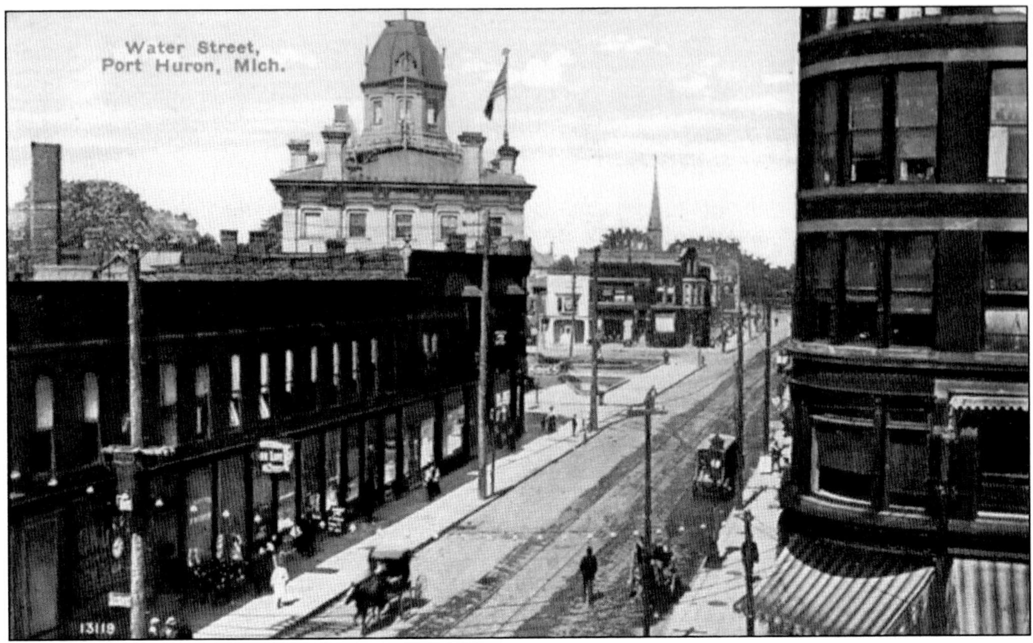

This view looks west up Water Street around 1900. On the left and at a slight angle is the customs house and post office, the only building in this image still standing today. The structure on the right is the Bon Marche Department Store, later home to Peoples Bank.

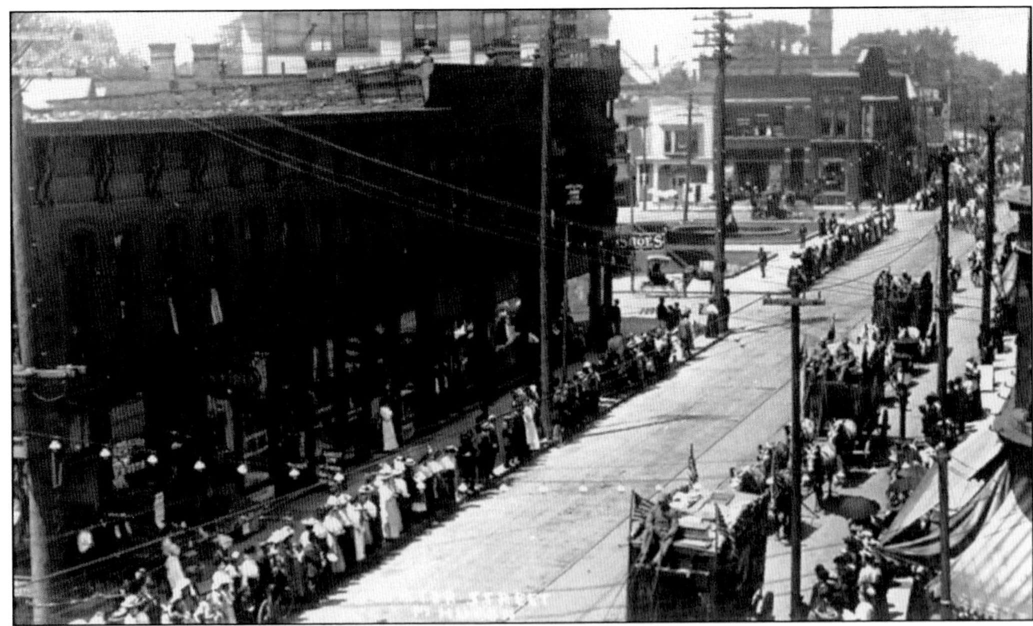
The circus comes to town! Taken by Louis Pesha about 1905, this photograph shows the arrival of the Cole Brothers Circus down Lapeer Avenue and Water Street. Although at one time an annual sight, it has been many years since a circus parade has been held in Port Huron.

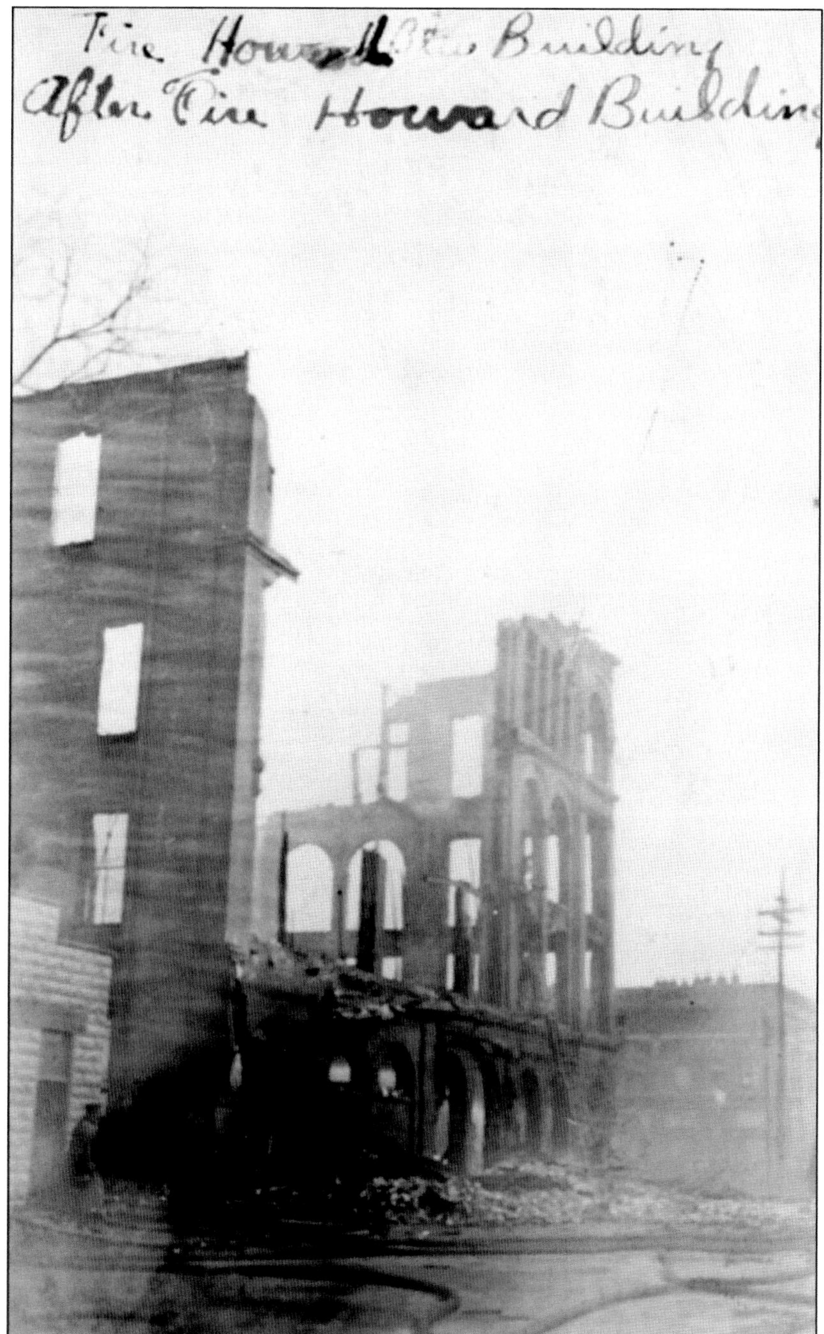


Fire was a common occurrence in early Port Huron, due in part to the large number of wooden structures in the city. As building techniques changed, so did the construction materials, and brick began to be used in an effort to make some buildings more fire safe. This *c.* 1905 view of a fire shows that this did not always work. The structure is believed to be the Howard building at 525 Water Street. However, the Henry Howard building and the Howard Furniture Company were located at several sites throughout the city over the firm's 90-year history, so there is some question if this is the correct location.

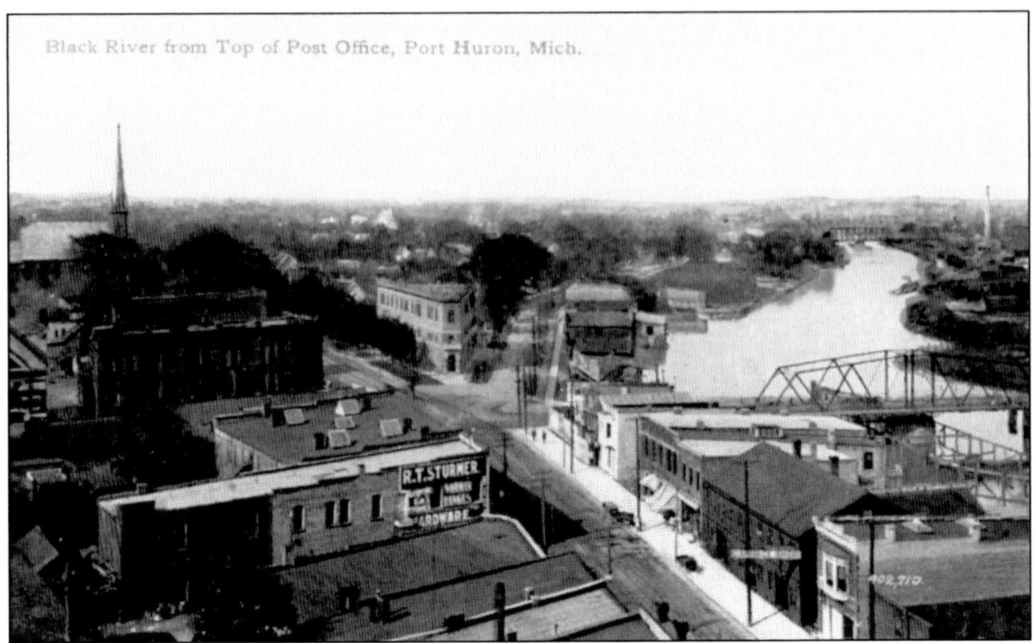


This *c.* 1910 image, taken from the post office and customs house, shows the Black River and Seventh Street area. This view would seem strange to many of today's citizens because much has been altered, including the streets. Water Street, at the right of the "wye" in the center, was eliminated between Seventh and Tenth Streets to make way for condominiums in the late 1980s.

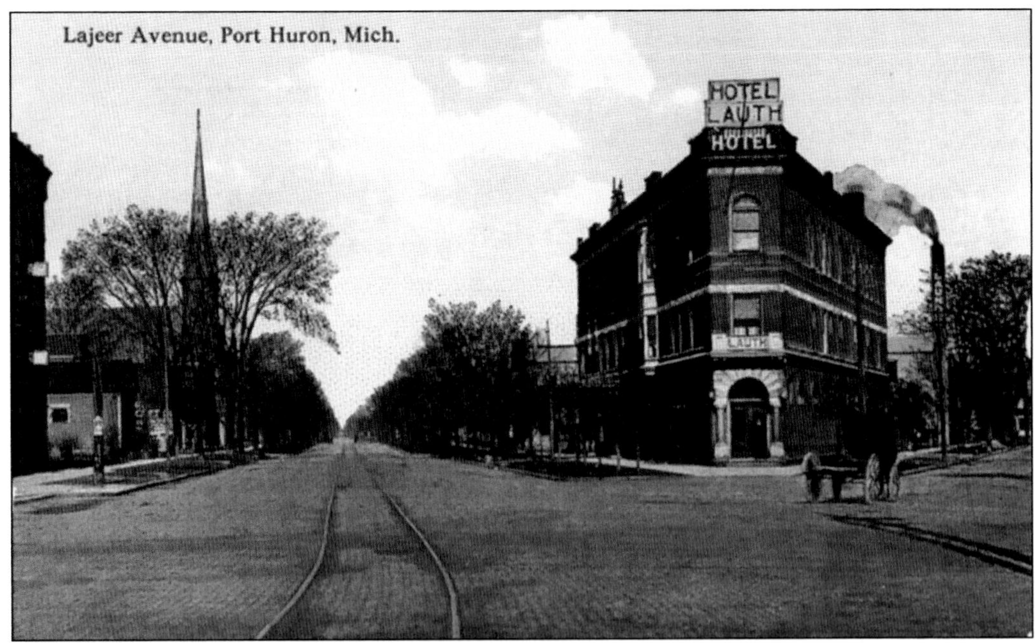


Built in 1900 by Christian Lauth, the Lauth Hotel was a defining building in this section of Port Huron. At one point, Lapeer (misspelled Lajeer) Avenue had its own business district, including a laundry, hotel, A&P, bathhouse, and saloon. Sadly, this building was torn down in 1980.

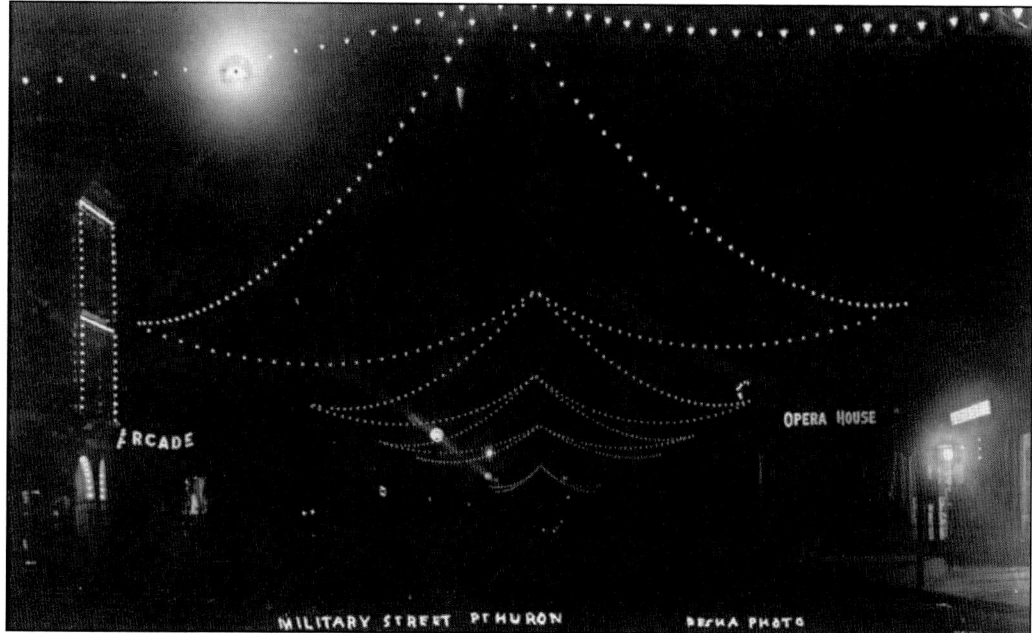


In this real-photo Louis Pesha view, Military Street bears "Christmas tree" lights around 1900. Strung between gas street lamps, these lights became the first example of electric illumination on city streets, and foreshadowed the electrified street lamps to come.

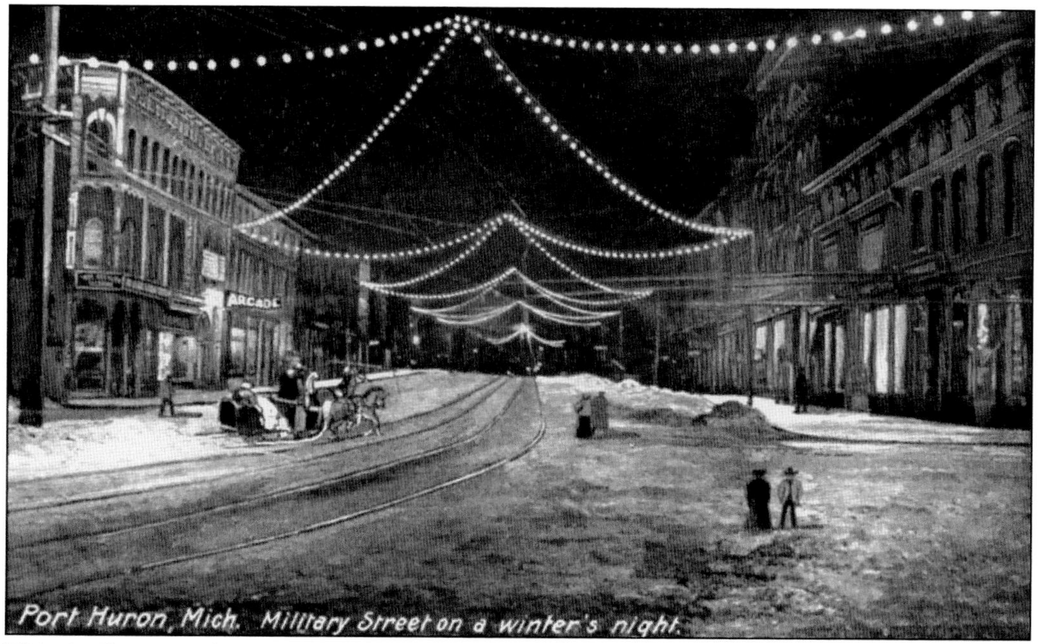


This similar view shows the same light strings with a small snowfall. Being the boyhood home of Thomas Edison definitely had its advantages in the early days of electricity!

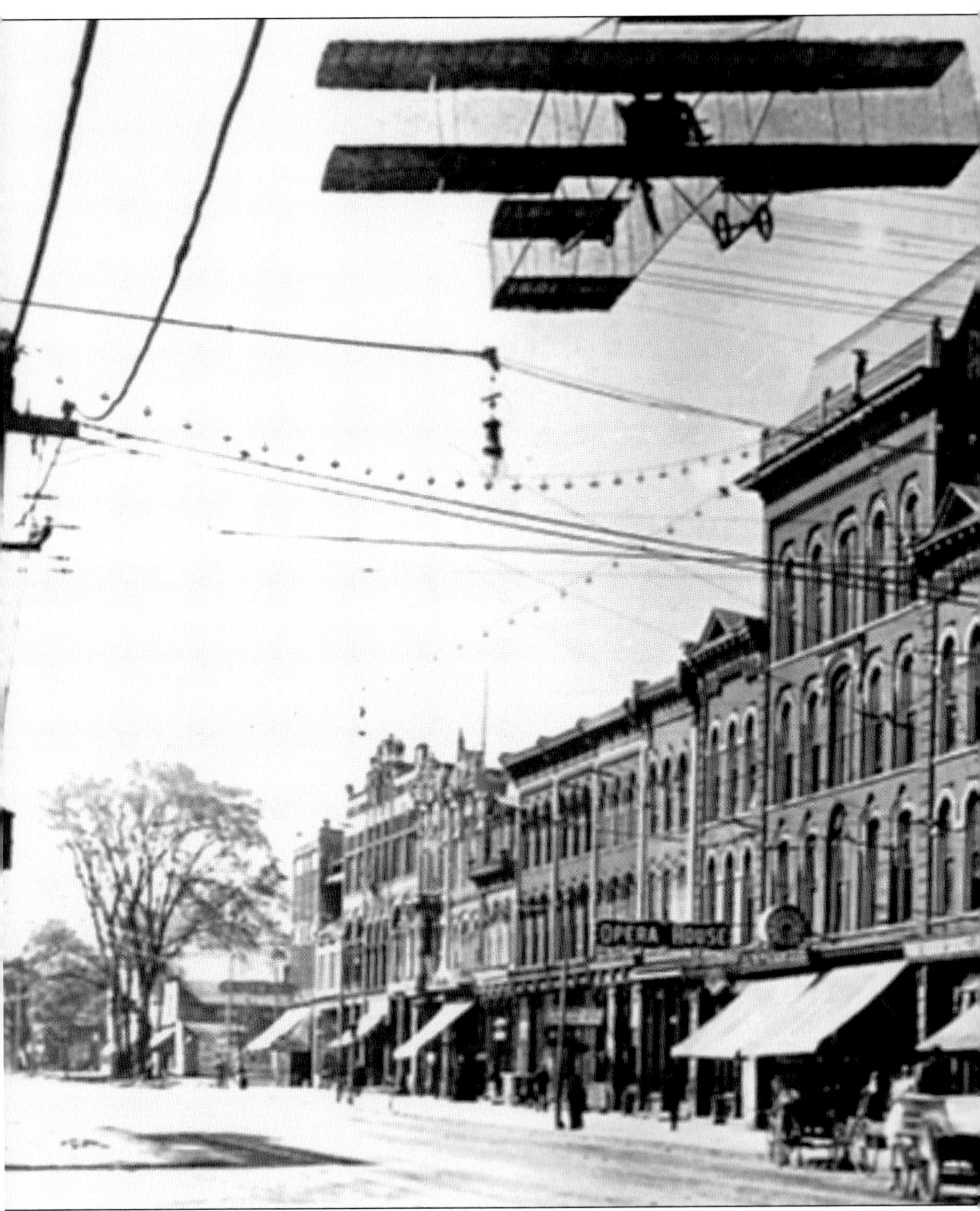


Could this be Orville and Wilbur doing a fly-by? No, it is a carefully crafted "trick" postcard by photographer Louis Pesha. He became somewhat famous for producing this kind of postcard, which was particularly difficult given that it was achieved with glass plates. Other existing Pesha

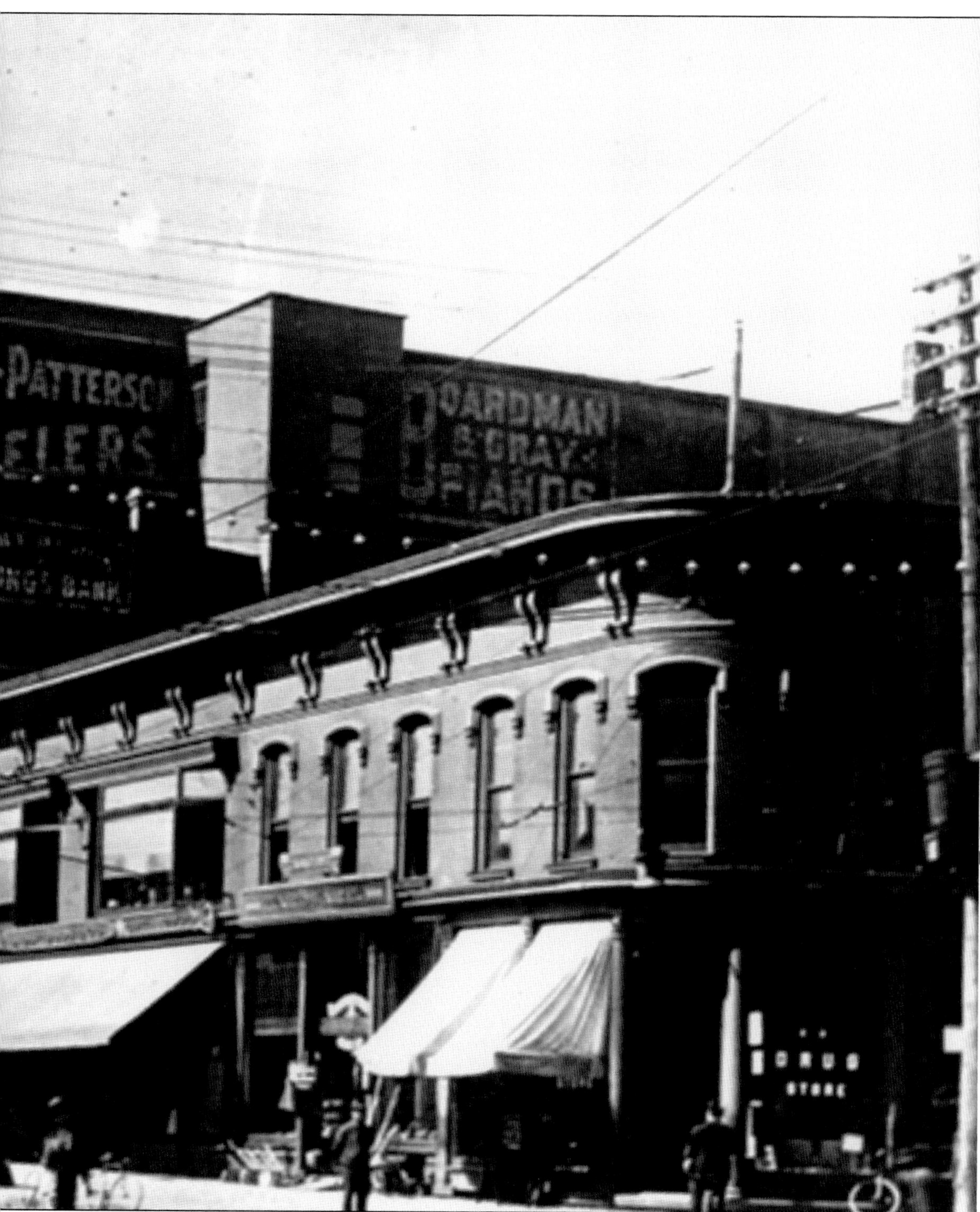


trick cards show freighters sailing down city streets, locomotives running on water, and other oddities, proving that anything was possible in a postcard with a little effort.

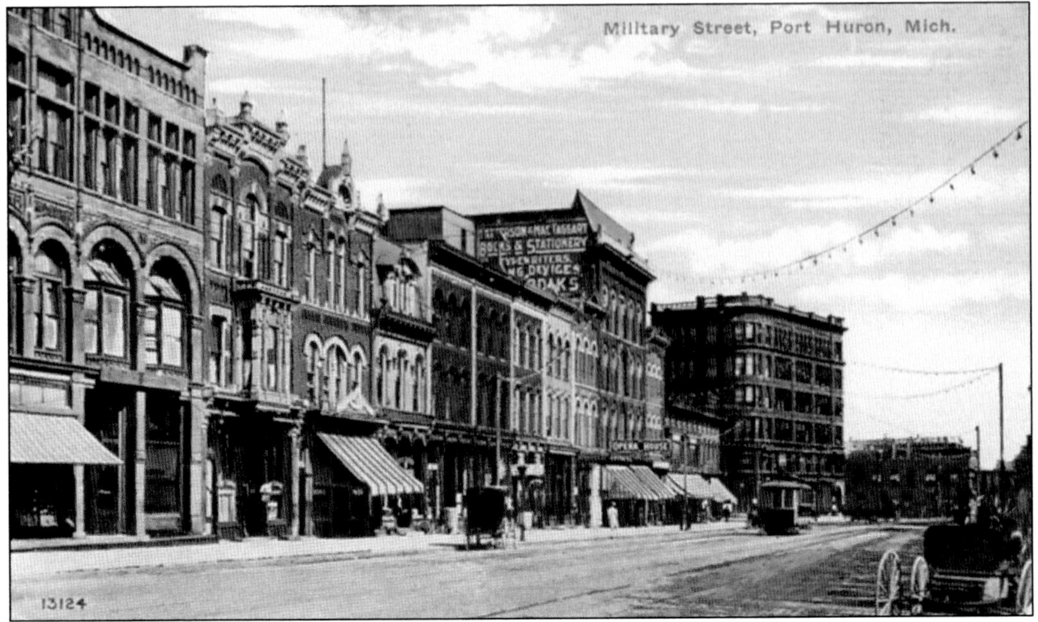


This postcard shows the west side of Military Street around 1910. The Patterson-McTaggart Bookstore advertisement can be seen on the Port Huron Opera House building on the left. Later known as McTaggart-Hoffman, this business occupied different buildings on the block for nearly 80 years.

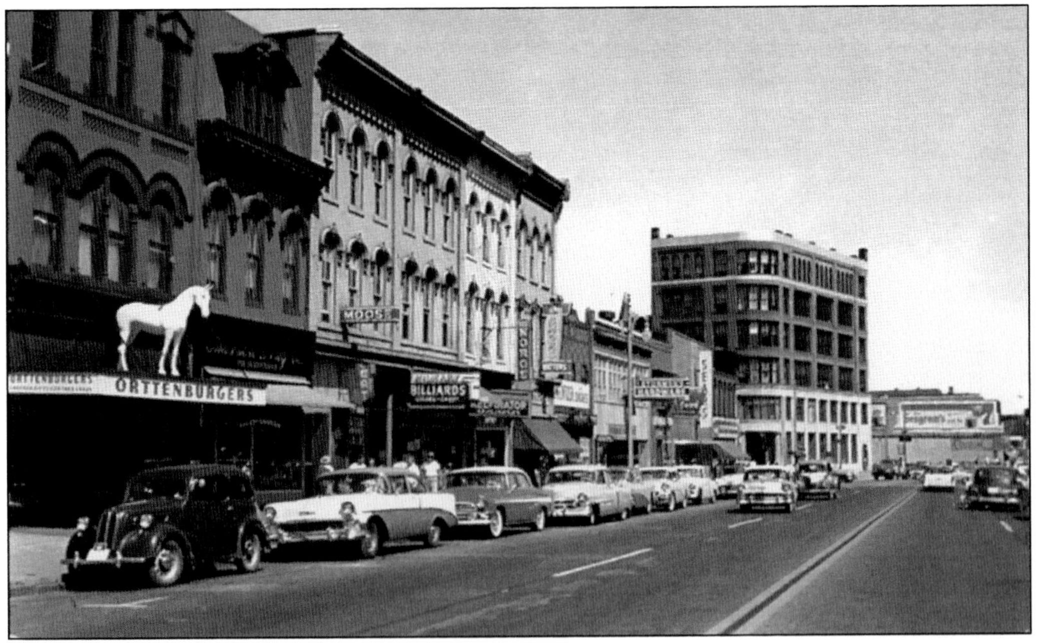


Equally long lasting, the Ortenburger Luggage and Leather Goods store and its infamous horse can be seen in this mid-1950s view of the same buildings. The horse was replaced three times, the last after some Mackinac Race revelers decided to "ride" it not long after this photograph was taken. This entire block, which held buildings dating back to the city's incorporation in 1857, was destroyed to make way for the new offices of the *Times Herald* between 1975 and 1980.

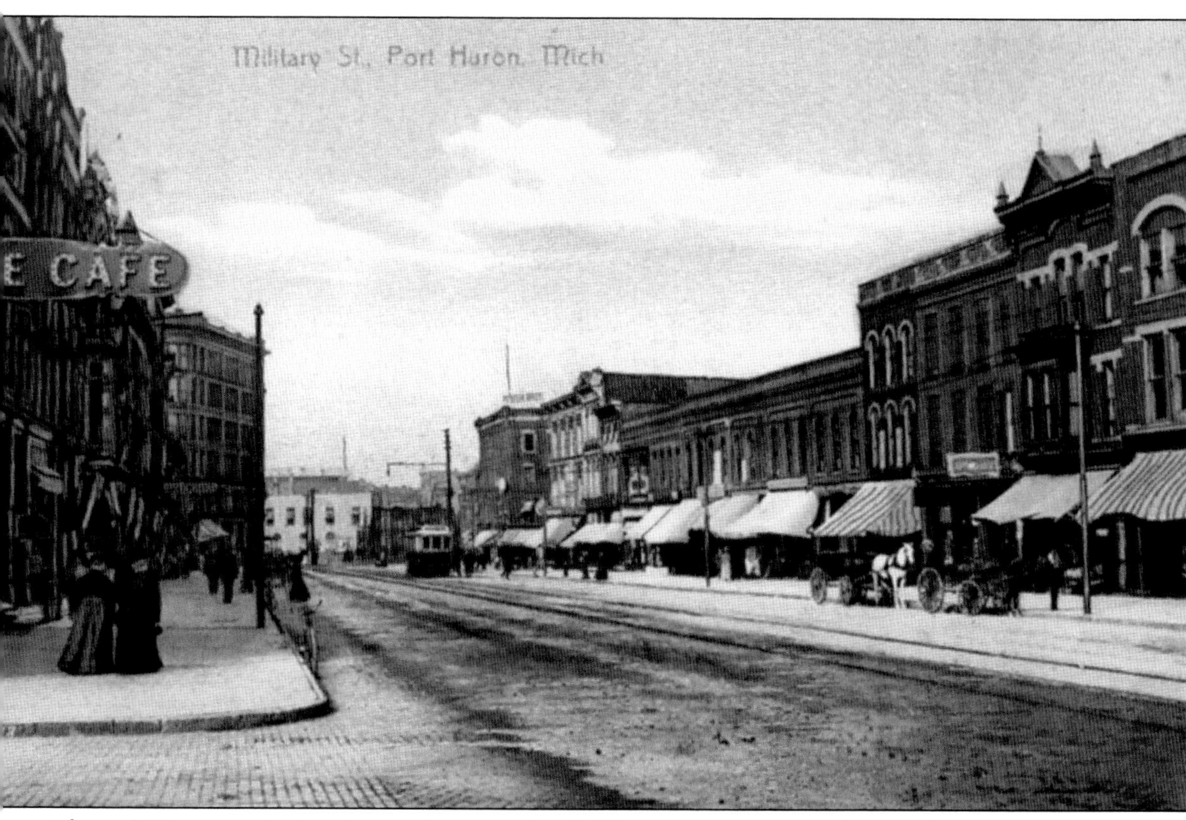


This *c.* 1900 postcard view depicts the east side of Military Street. Although this side of the street survived urban renewal during the 1970s, very few historic images exist. The building that now houses the popular Raven Coffee House and studio lofts is visible on the far right. Gerry Edson, a retired lawyer, spent nearly 10 years and countless dollars restoring this structure from a gutted shell into the magnificent eating establishment it has become.

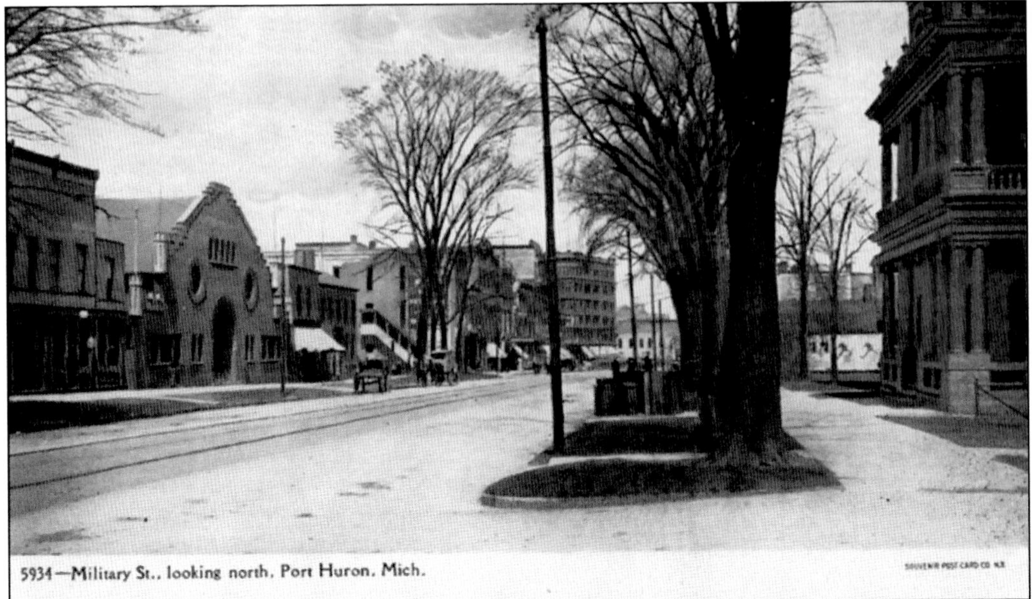


This scene of Military Street reveals one of the more unique buildings in Port Huron: the Huron Cycle And Electric Company, second from the left. Later Yokum Motor Sales, it was one of the first automobile retailers in the area. Seen on the right side is the famous porch of the Harrington Hotel.

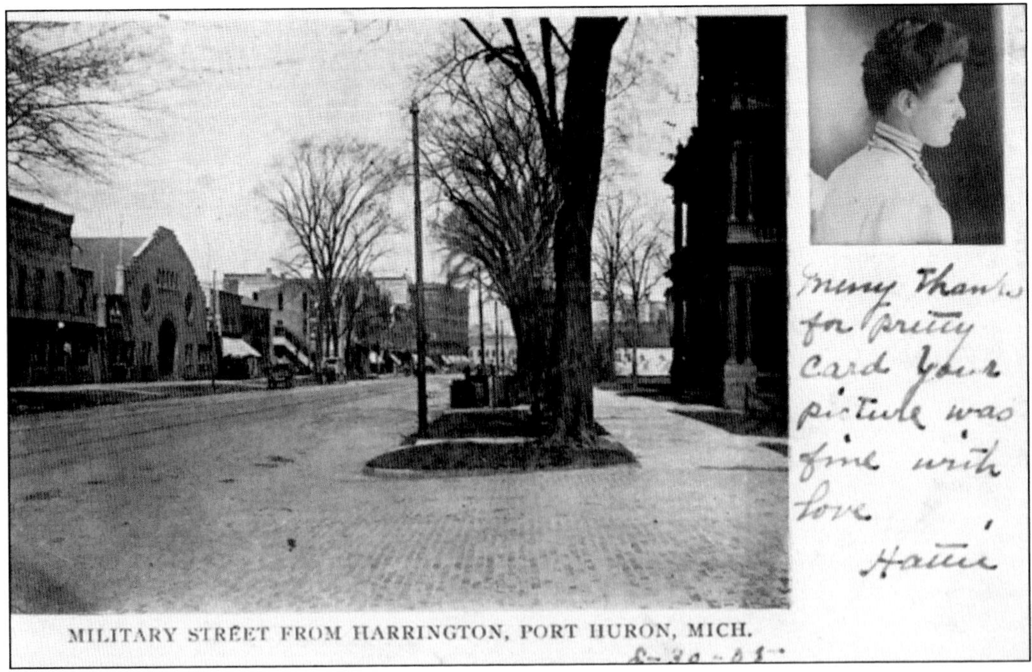


Although similar to the image above, this unique view shows an inset of the sender, most likely a visitor to the community. She notes, "Many thanks for pretty card. Your picture was fine. With love Hattie." While not a trick image, it allowed a more personal way for photographers and printers to sell their wares.

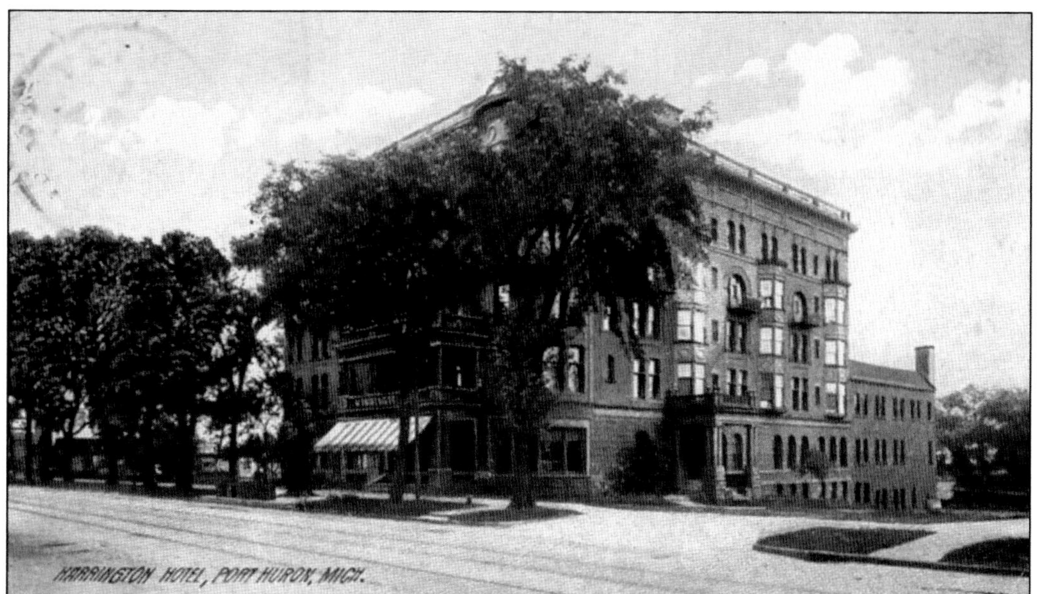


For years the Harrington Hotel, pictured here about 1910, was the epitome of fine service in the area. Opened in 1896 by Charles Harrington, son of the man who gave Port Huron its name, it remained an active hotel for nearly 80 years. Its coffee shop and tavern were almost as well known as it dining room. Due to the rise of the motel, the Harrington became more of an apartment house. Threatened with demolition in the 1980s, it was rescued and restored and is now home to a senior living center.

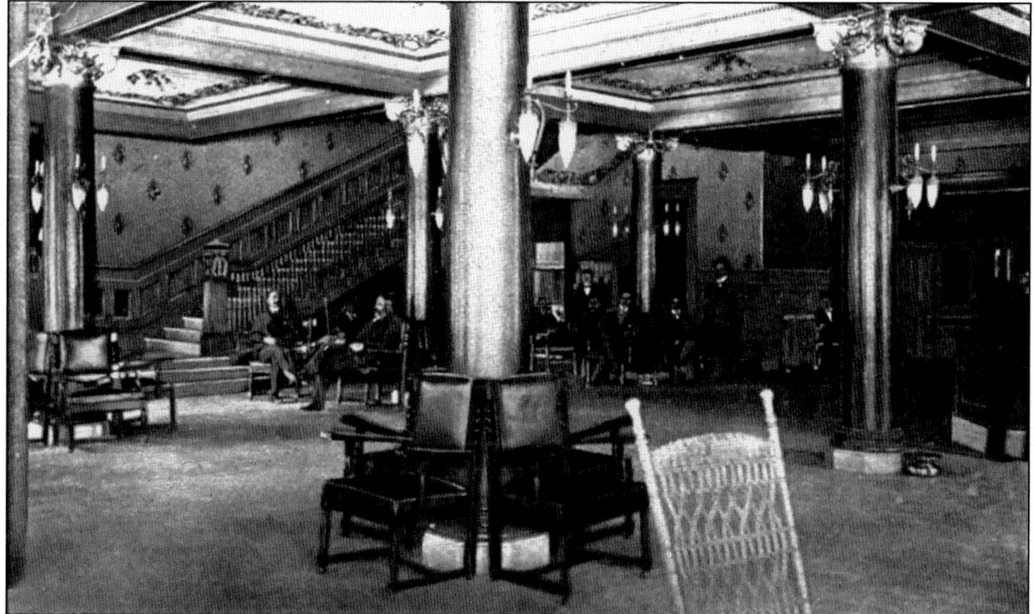

Seen here around 1915, the Harrington Hotel lobby has greeted many famous visitors—Henry Ford, Thomas Alva Edison, William Howard Taft, Harry S. Truman, and Mickey Rooney to name but a few. Of particular note, Harry and Bess Truman stayed here during their honeymoon in 1919. The two remembered their time so fondly that in the later years of his presidency, the two only had to mention the name Port Huron to bring a smile to their faces.

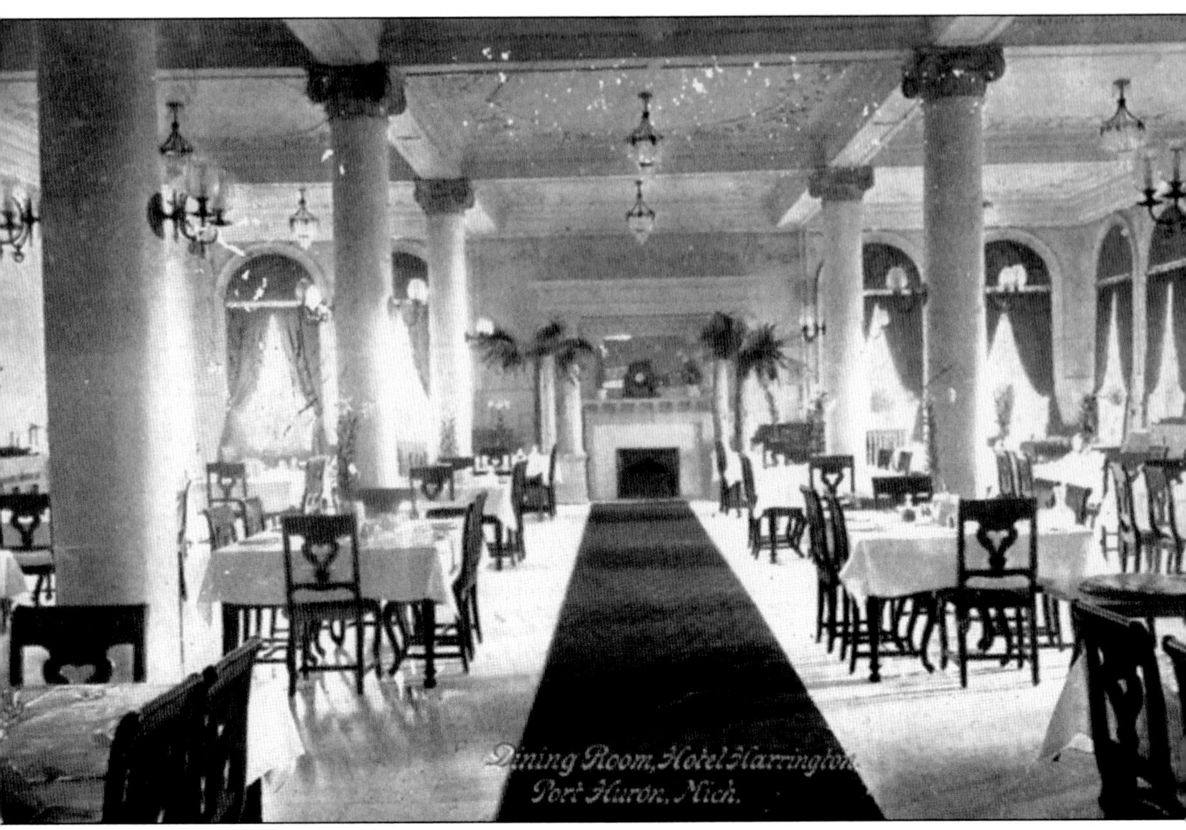


The Harrington Hotel dining room is seen in this *c.* 1910 image. Although many notable occasions have taken place here, one of the most famous was the grand reception dinner for the movie premiere of ***Young Tom Edison*** in February 1940. Dignitaries included Mickey Rooney, Louis B. Mayer, and Edison's wife, Mina. In the 1940s, the pillars were boxed in and topped with mirrors to update the space.

# *Two*

# Port Huron on the Move

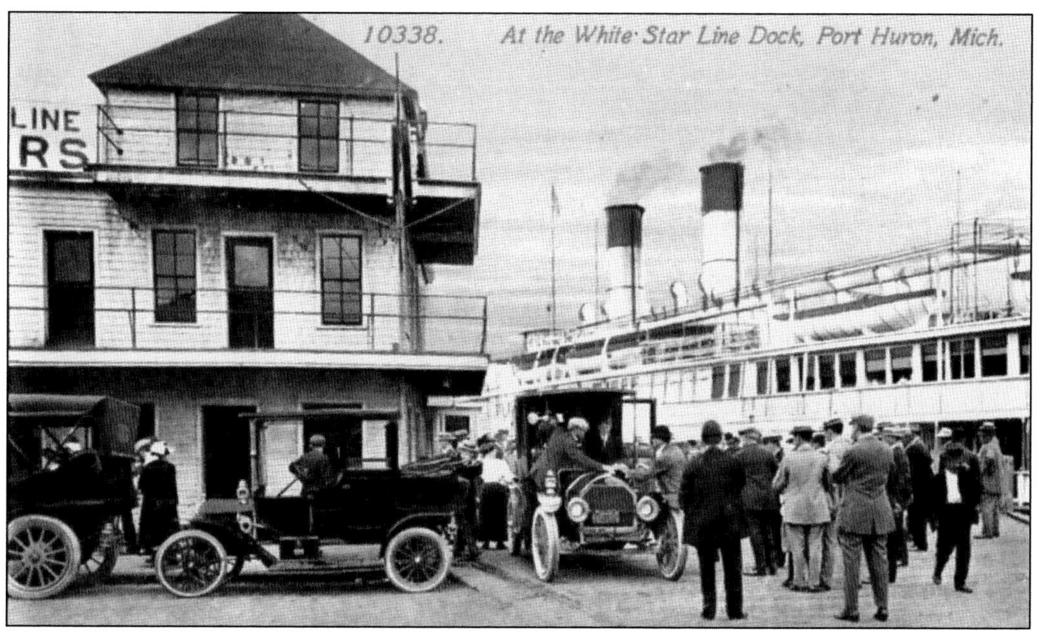


Taxis line up at the White Star Line dock about 1905. Located at the foot of Butler Street (now Grand River Avenue), this dock welcomed many visitors arriving from Detroit and other areas of the Great Lakes into the Port Huron area. The famous steamer *Tashmoo* waits to make one of its many trips to Detroit.

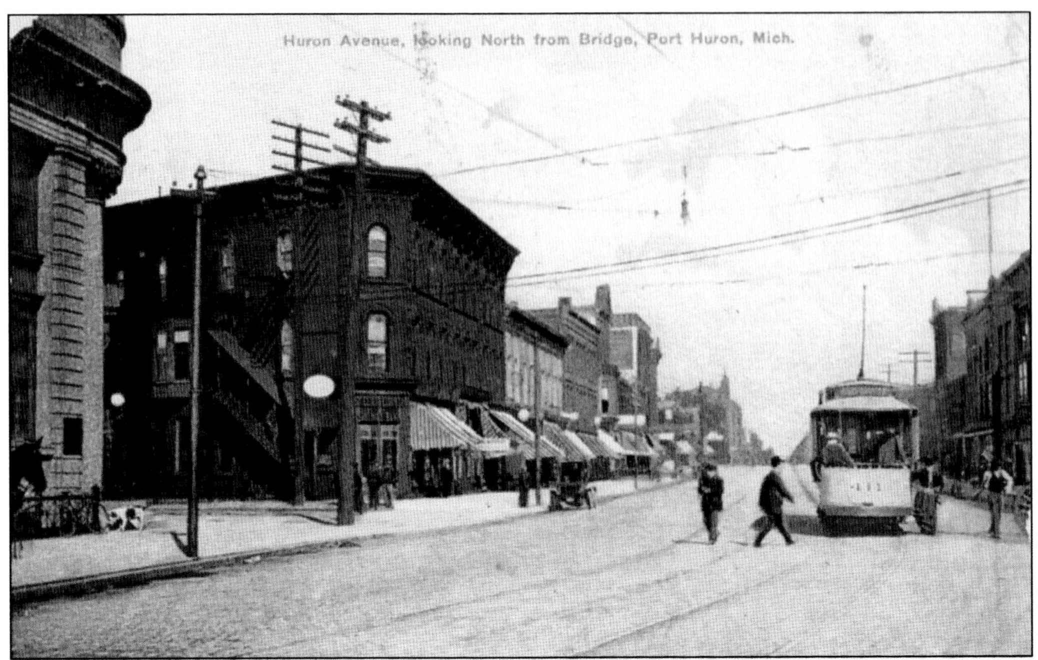


Huron Avenue is alive with streetcars and pedestrians around 1895. Note the single electric light hanging from the overhead wire, a then-newfangled invention by Port Huron's own Thomas Alva Edison.

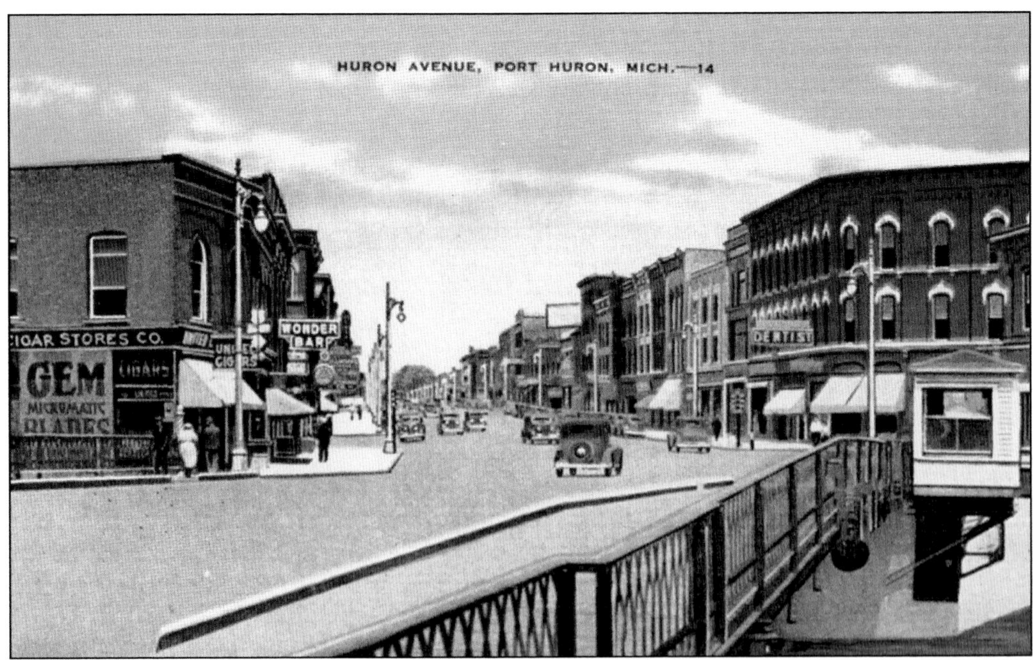


This similar view of Huron Avenue was taken in the 1930s. Note the art deco–inspired cars, a far cry from the streetcars and drovers of just a few years earlier.

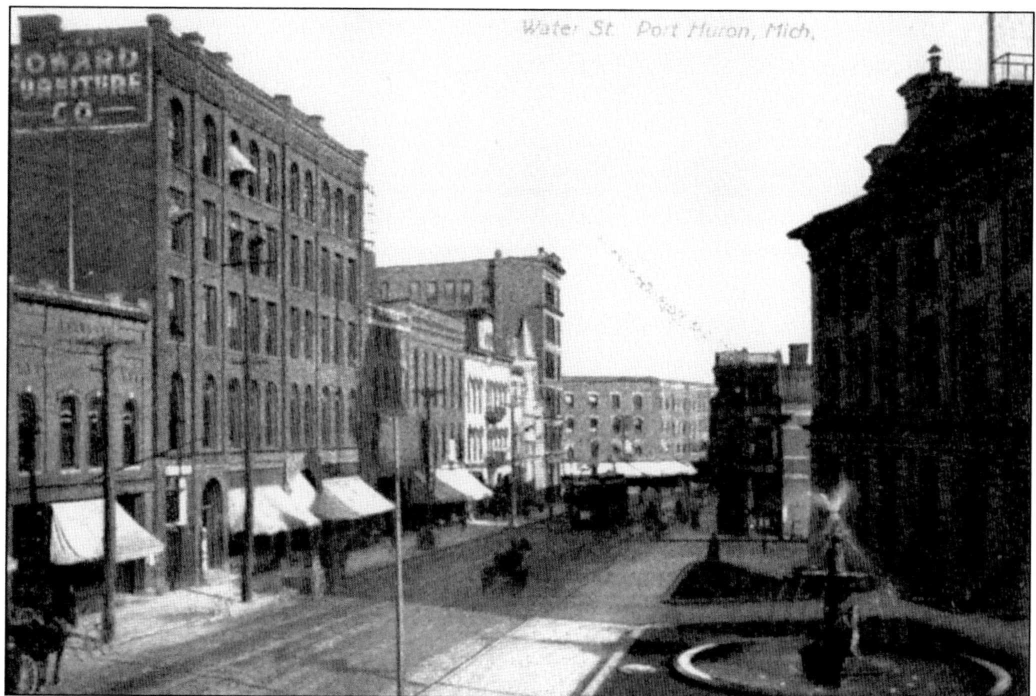


It is not clear who has the right-of-way, the horses or the streetcars, in this *c.* 1900 image of the Water Street business district. Motormen had to be very careful when passing horses on the road, as the speed of the streetcars would often cause a skittish horse to bolt.

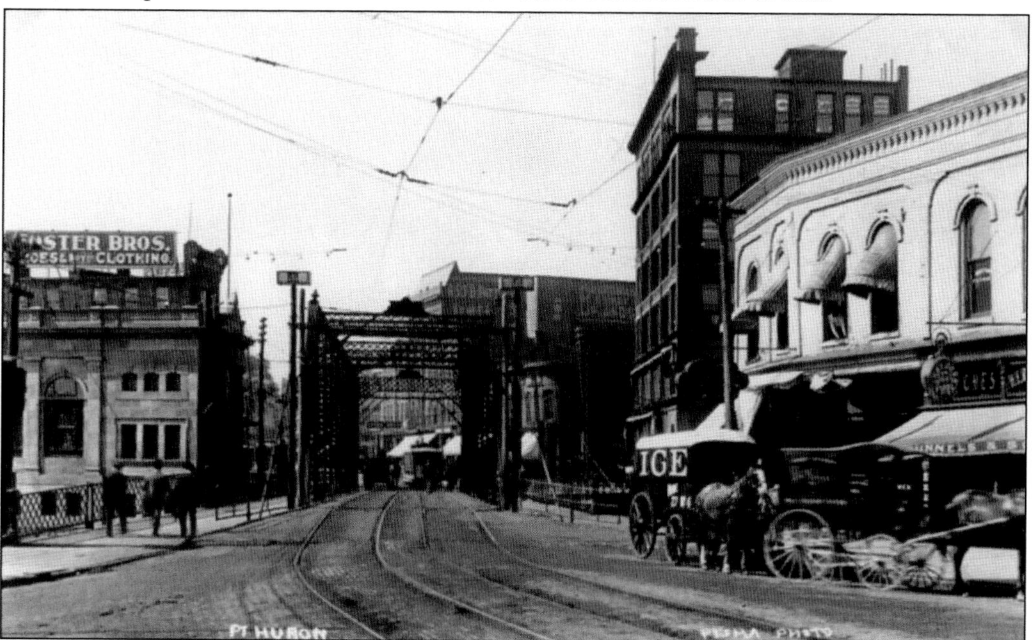


This classic image of the second Military Street Bridge area was created by photographer Louis Pesha around 1910. Note the ice delivery wagon parked in front of Runnels and Son, a jeweler of the time. In just a few years, the horse-drawn delivery wagon would be no more, replaced by a new invention: the gasoline-powered truck.

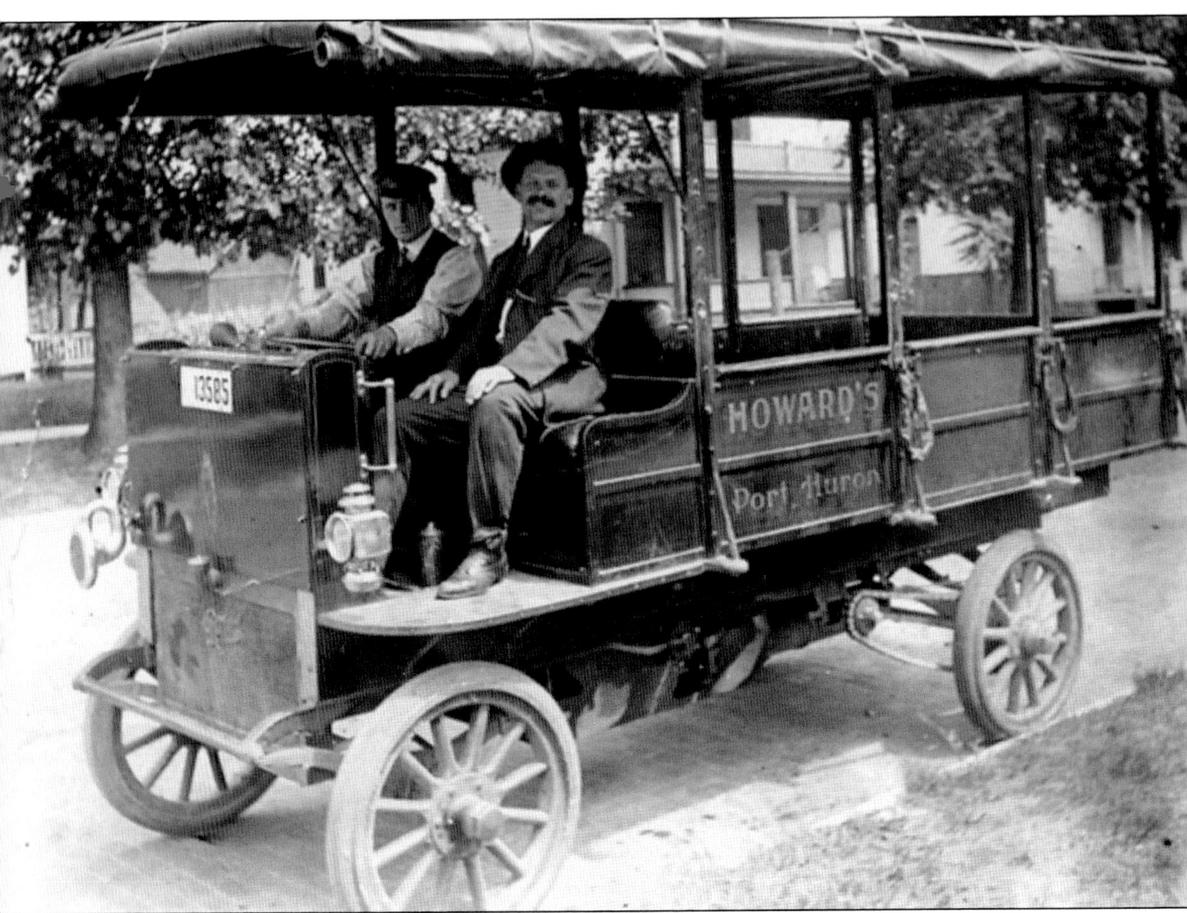


Pictured about 1905 is the first delivery truck of Howard's Furniture, which was one of the oldest furniture stores in Port Huron before it finally closed in the early 1990s. Note the chain drive mechanism—a step up from your average bicycle. Port Huron businesses found the ease of delivery by truck to be a great way to extend their customer bases, allowing them to deliver to smaller surrounding communities in St. Clair County.

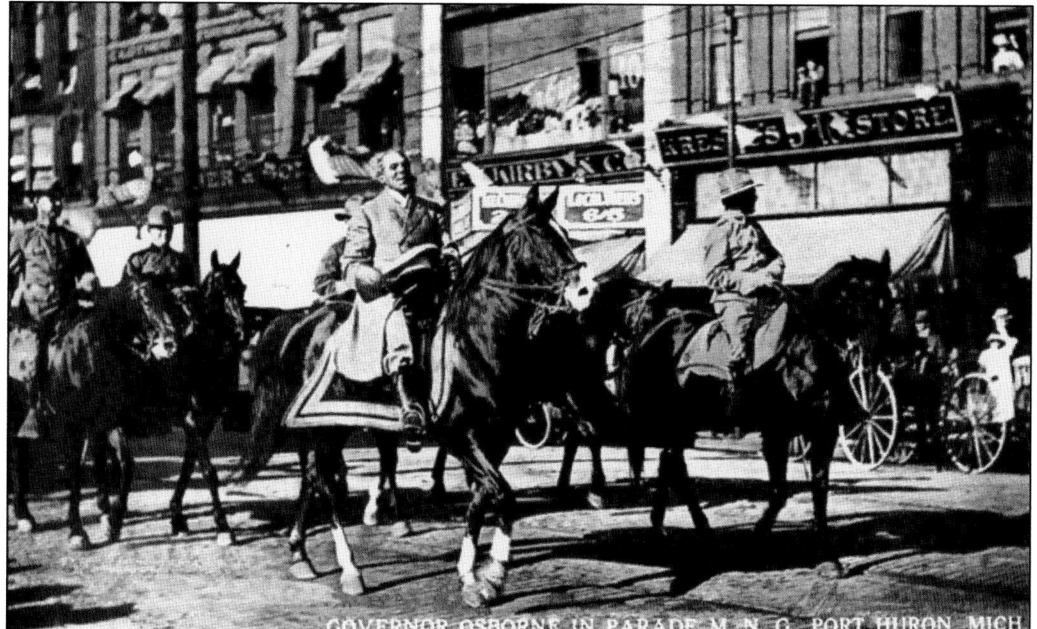


Governor Osborne marches in the Michigan National Guard parade in this *c.* 1914 view. Note the pomp and circumstance associated with the event; even the most junior officers of the guard are impeccably dressed.

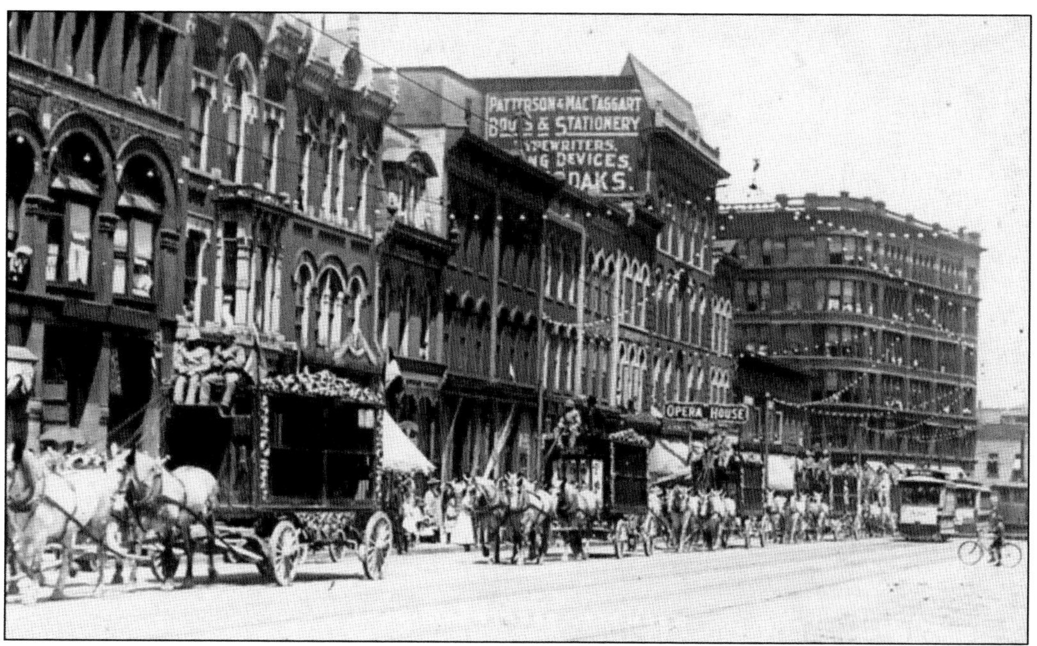


A veritable traffic jam has developed on Military Street due to the circus coming to town. No less than three streetcars, four horse-driven wagons, and a bicycle can be seen in this 1900s-era view.

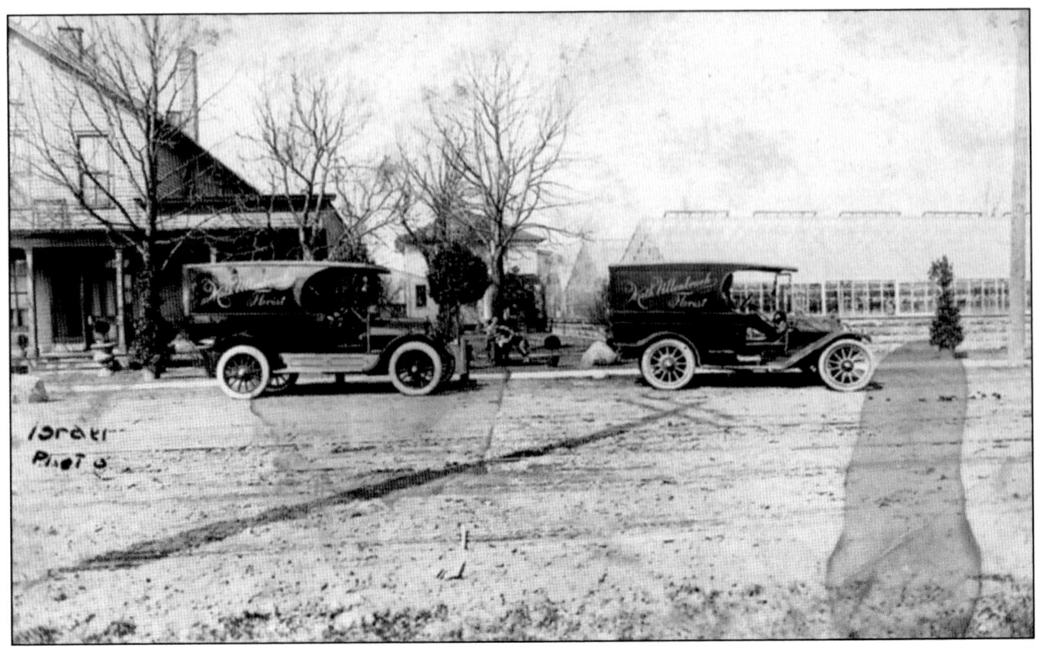

The first two delivery trucks of Mathew Ullenbruch, a local florist, can be seen in this 1912 photograph taken on Lapeer Avenue. Although no longer owned by the same family, Ullenbruch's Flowers continues in business at the same location on Lapeer Avenue nearly 100 years later.

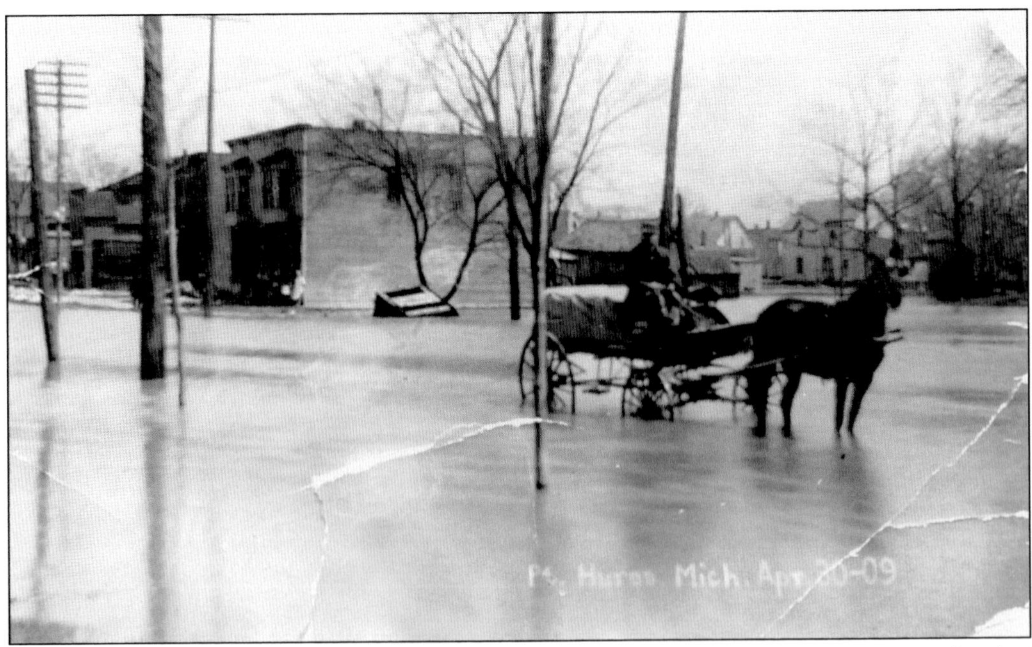


This photograph was taken at an unidentified location in Port Huron during the spring flood of April 30, 1890. Before the land was raised along the Black River in the downtown area, floods were fairly frequent occurrences.

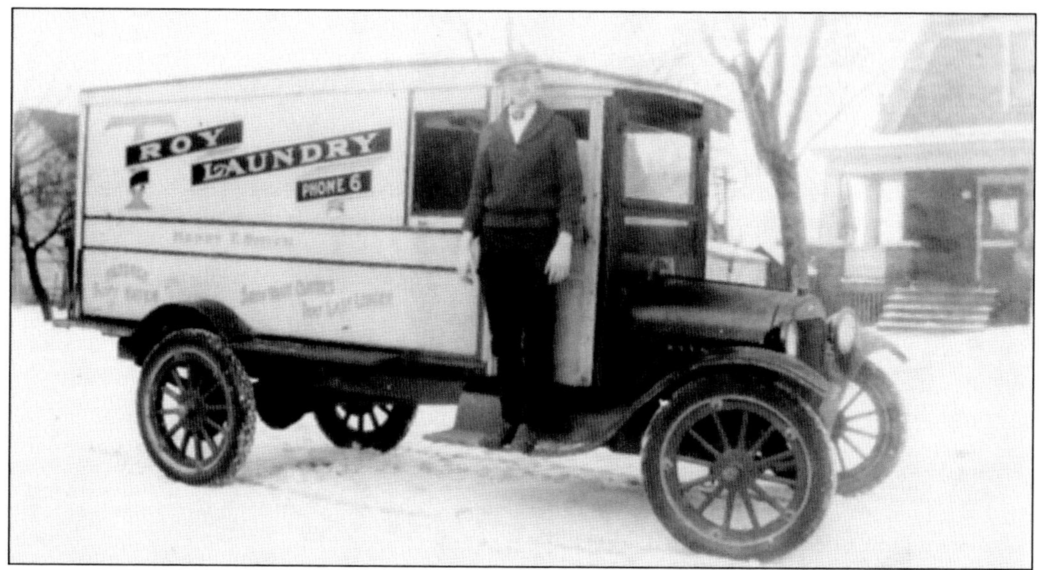


Henry T. Smith of Troy Laundry appears with his delivery truck about 1920. A long-standing business still operating today in Port Huron, Troy Laundry was so named for Troy, New York, where the dry-cleaning process reportedly originated.

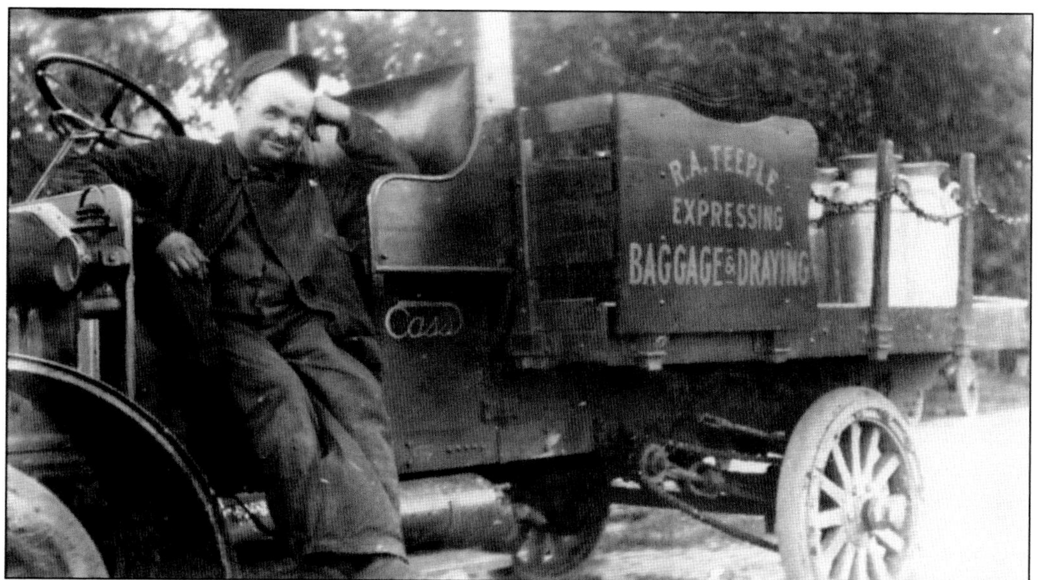


R. A. Teeple poses with his Cass truck around 1915. The Cass Motor Truck Company built trucks on Lapeer Avenue from 1910 to 1915. The site was later purchased by the Mueller Brass Company.

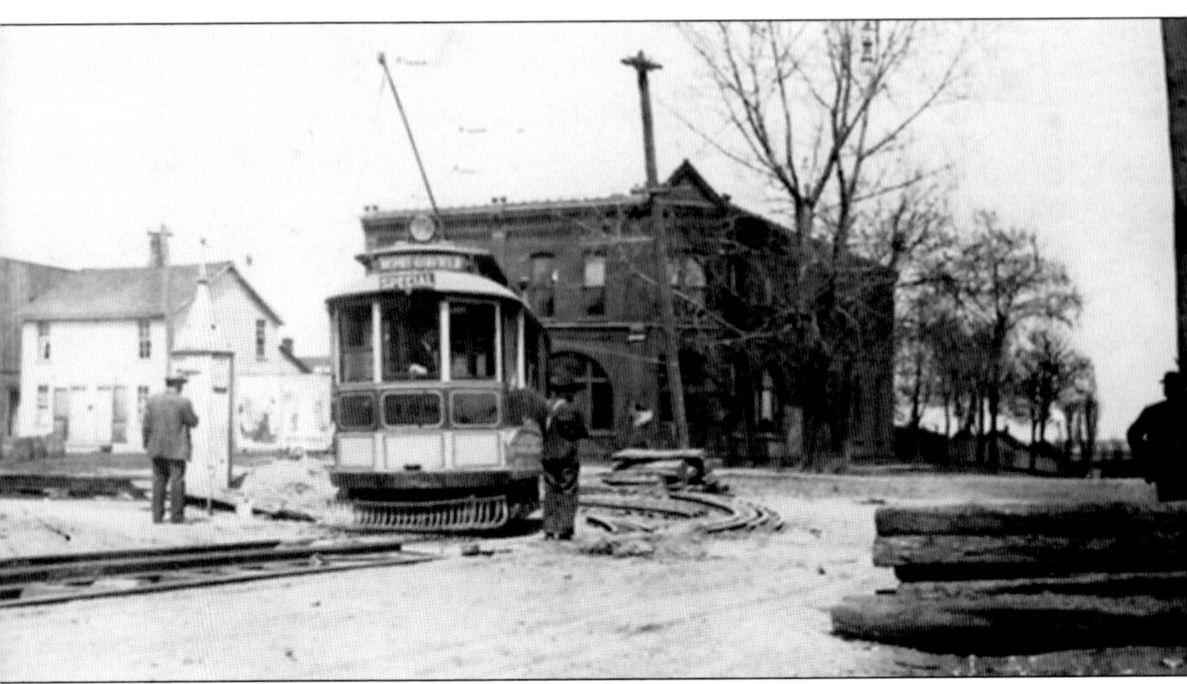

In this J. M. White photograph, a Port Huron city electric streetcar takes the corner at Gratiot and Elmwood Avenues about 1900. This streetcar is most likely headed to the Elmwood Driving Park, located about eight blocks behind the photographer. Originally designed as a horse-racing field, the park later became an early venue for automobile racing, even hosting famous early race car driver Barney Oldfield. This scene remains remarkably the same in many respects. The building behind the streetcar, then the Grand Trunk Hotel, still exists and is now occupied by Michigan Industrial Controls.

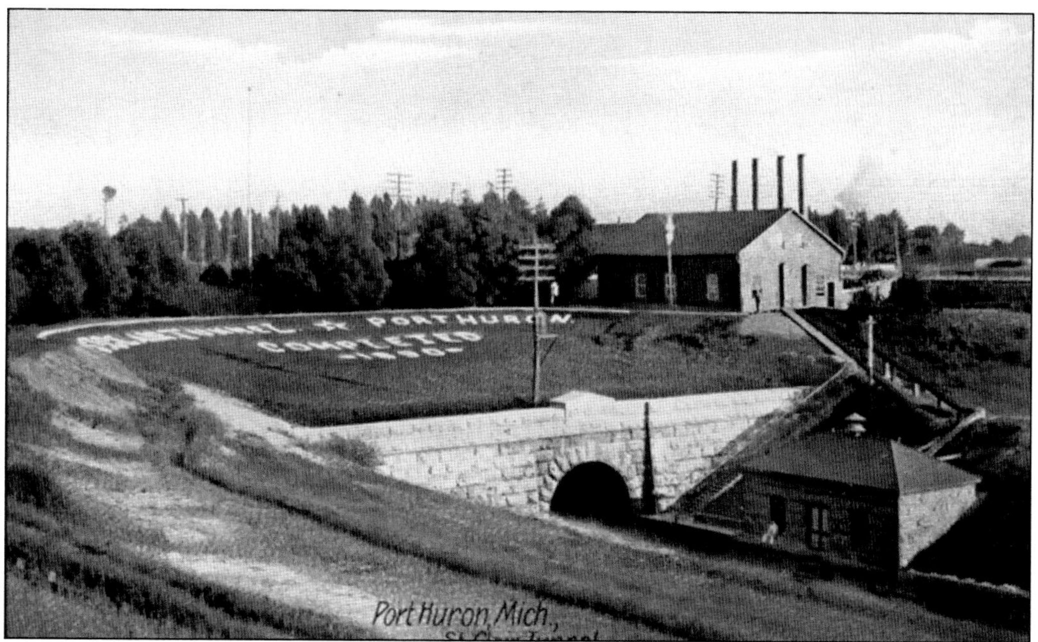


Looking toward Tenth Street, this view shows the St. Clair River Tunnel approach about 1910. Completed in 1890, the tunnel was an engineering marvel: the first railroad tunnel to connect two countries beneath water.

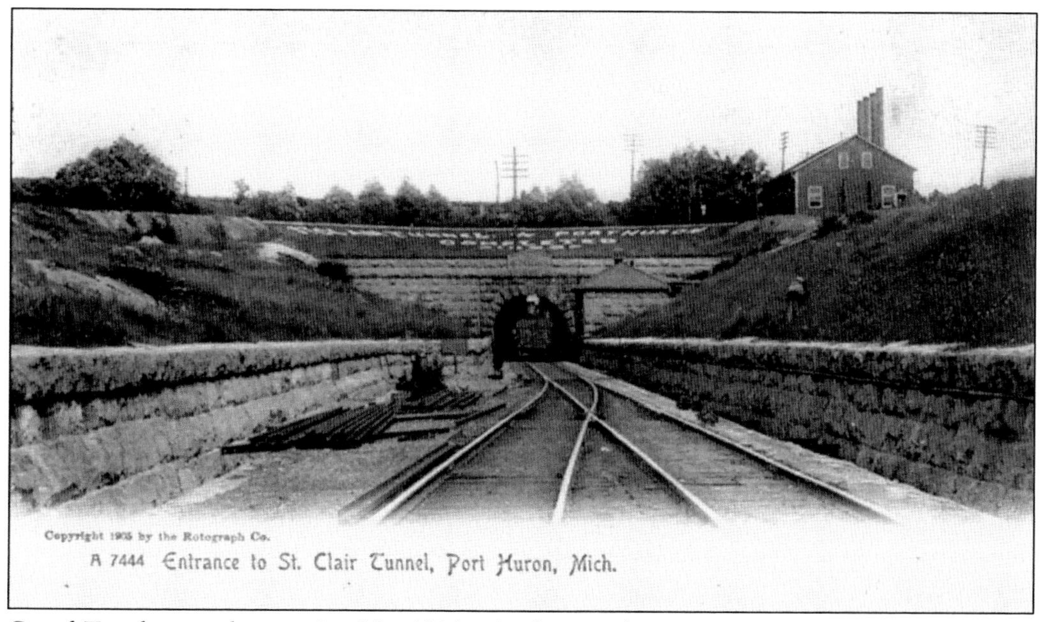


Grand Trunk steam locomotive No. 1304 exits the St. Clair River Tunnel prior to 1908. Note the well-groomed gardens and landscaping; the Grand Trunk believed in maintenance.

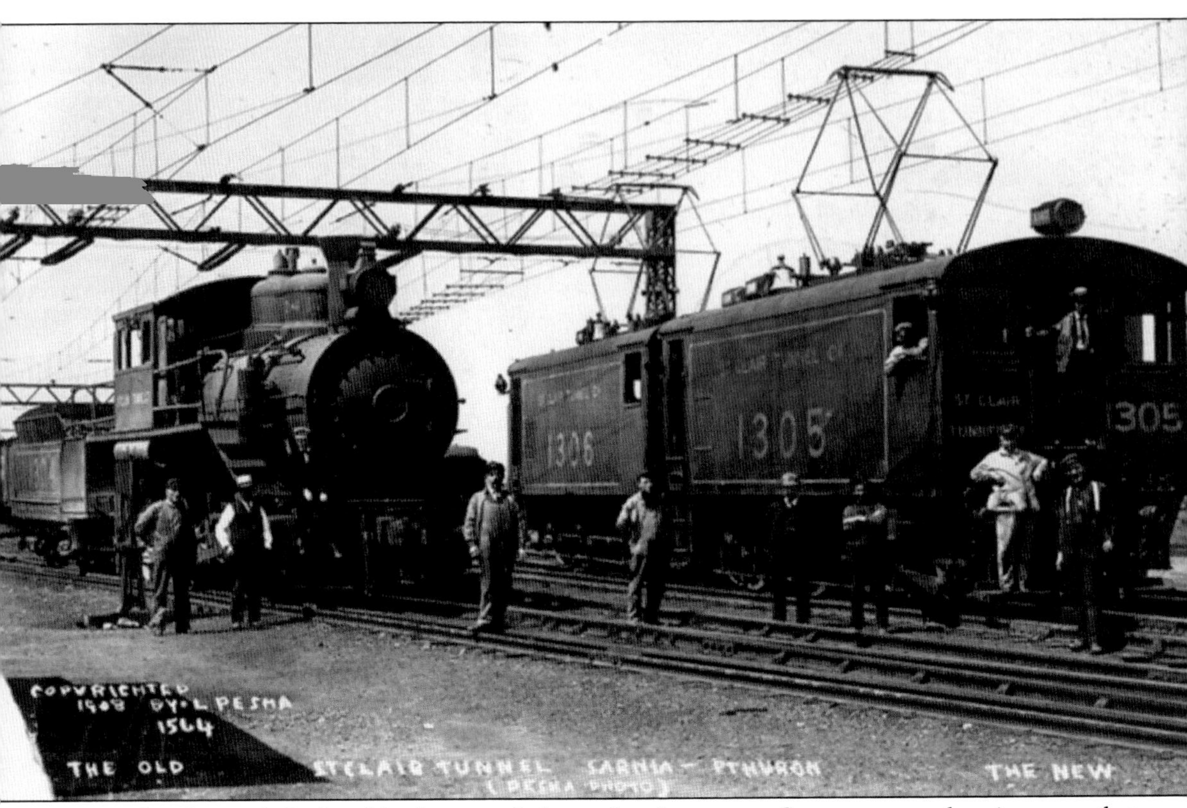


Taken by Louis Pesha, this photograph shows the changeover from steam to electric power that occurred in 1908. Although steam power was initially used to transport passengers and goods through the tunnel, it quickly became clear that if problems occurred while in the tunnel, the danger of being overcome by fumes was great. There was a reason to be concerned; three separate asphyxiation accidents between 1892 and 1904 had killed 10 men. Because of these accidents, the tunnel was electrified between 1906 and 1908 and remained so until 1958, when electric locomotives were replaced by diesels.

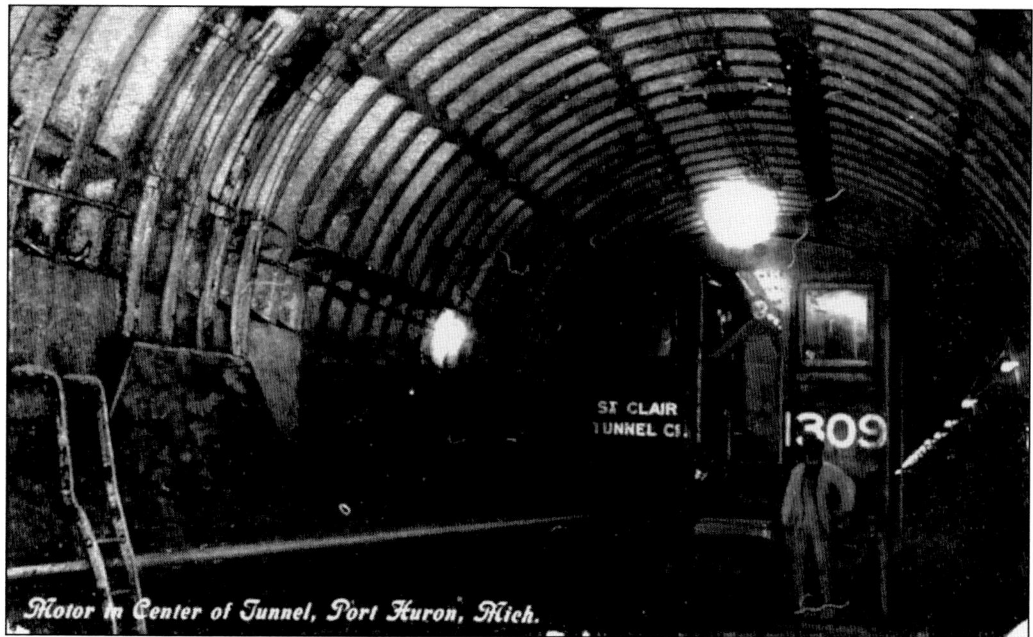


Motor in Center of Tunnel, Port Huron, Mich.

St. Clair Tunnel Company electric locomotive No. 1309 and its crew are pictured inside the tunnel around 1910. The coming of the "Tunnel Electrics" allowed this photograph to be taken, as asphyxiation dangers would have previously deemed it impossible.

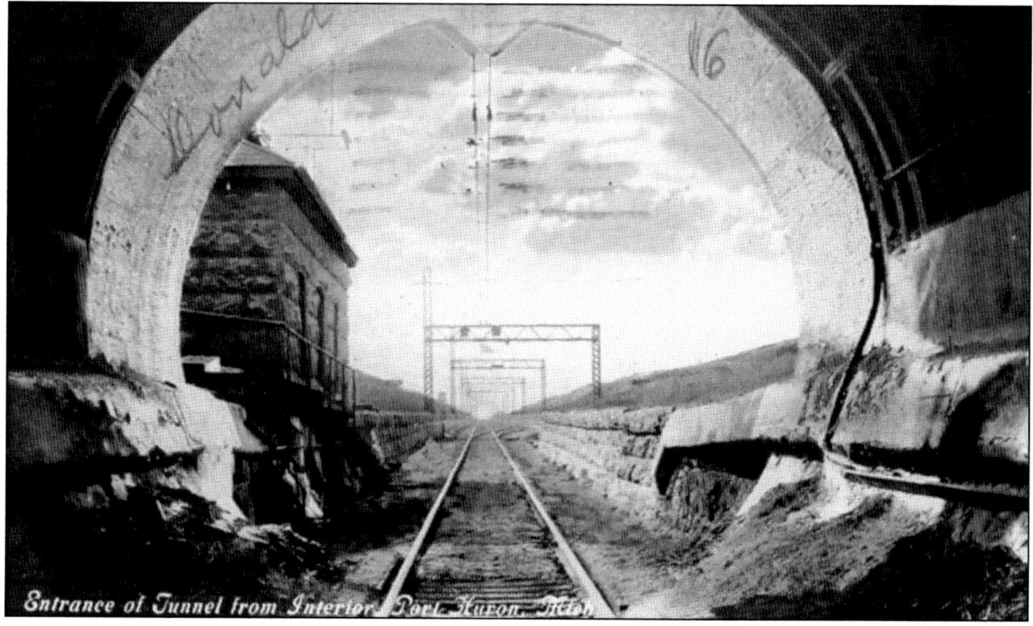

Entrance of Tunnel from Interior, Port Huron, Mich.

This *c.* 1910 view was taken from the mouth of the tunnel looking toward Sixteenth Street. Note the large iron towers, which were necessary to carry the electrical wires for the new locomotives.

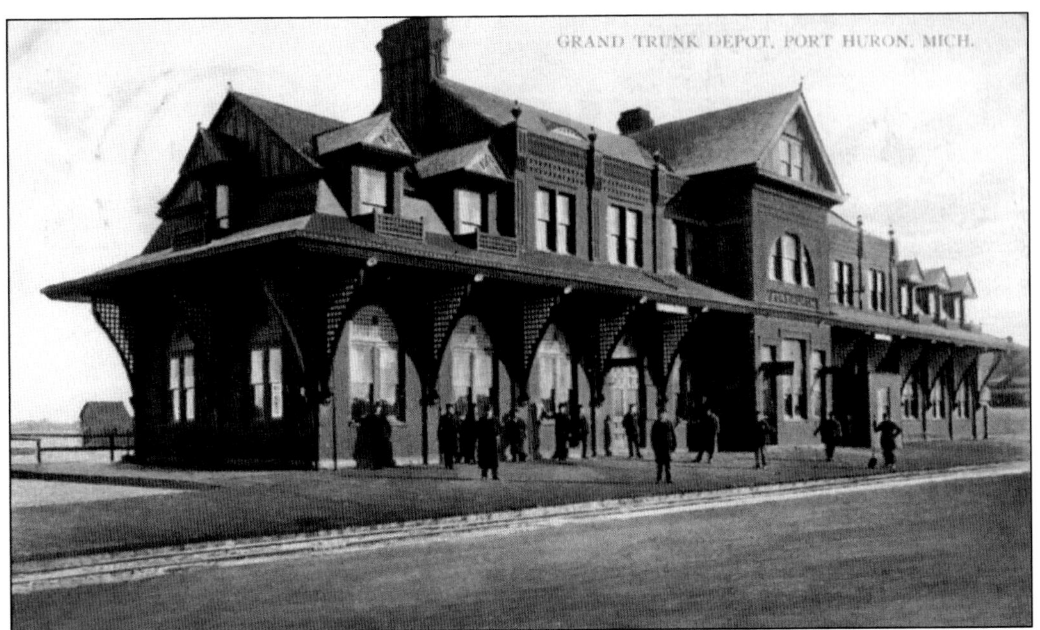


The new Tunnel Depot was constructed in 1891 by the Grand Trunk Railway. It replaced the 1859 Fort Gratiot station, which Thomas Edison had worked out of as a news butcher. These views, taken around 1920, show the depot from track side and look toward Sixteenth Street and the St. Clair River Tunnel. Although Amtrak was formed in 1971 to take over the nation's passenger service, the passenger trains of the Grand Trunk Western Railway were not included. With its days as a passenger station over, the Tunnel Depot was torn down in 1975. Passenger trains returned to Port Huron in 1977—but to a drab building with none of the character of this proud structure.

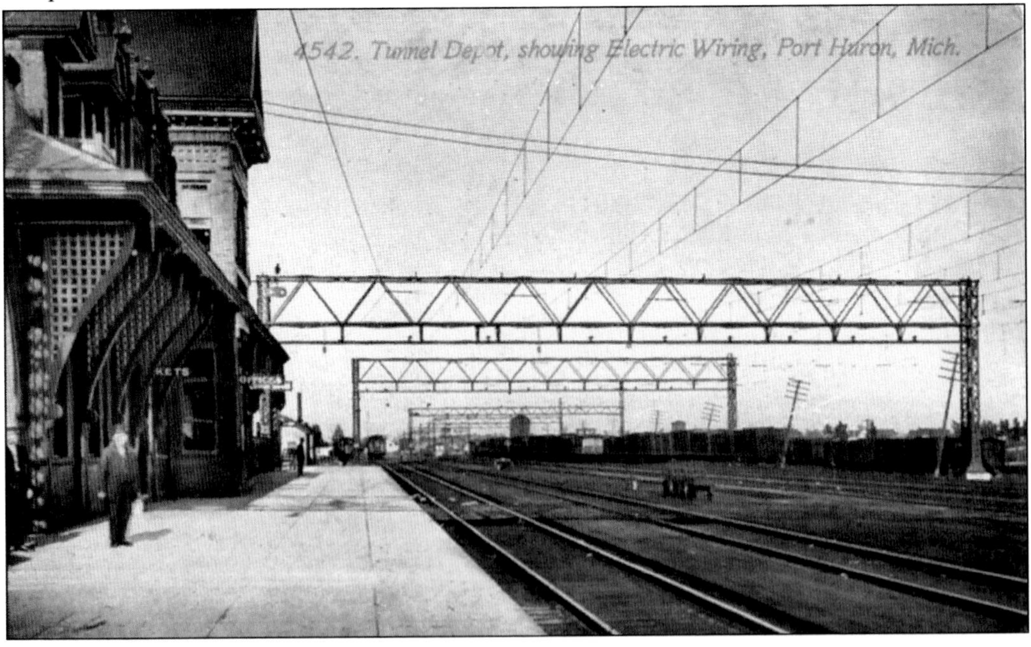

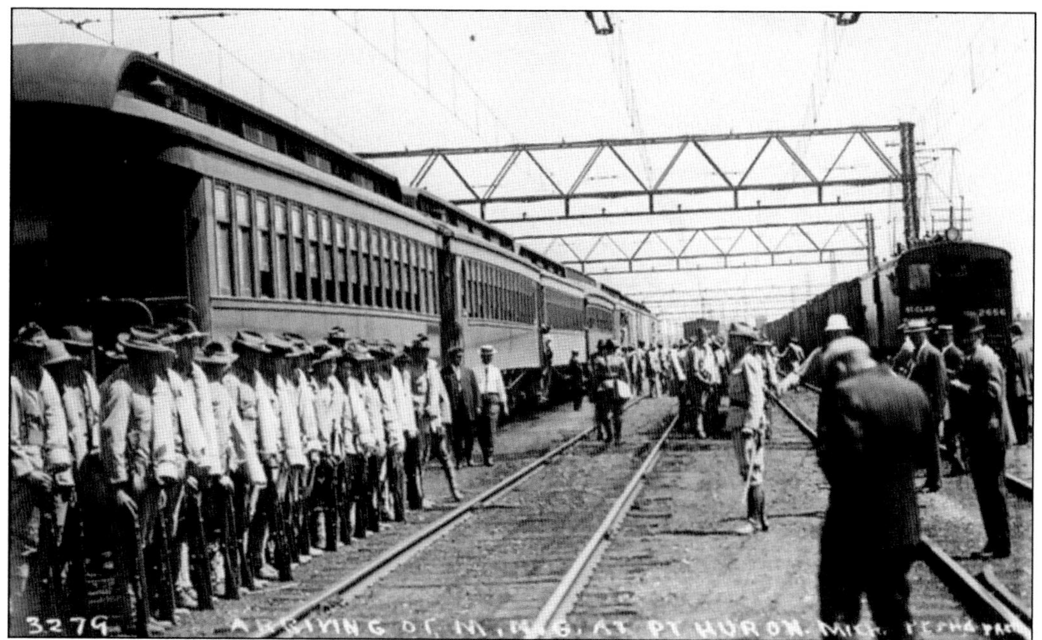


The Michigan National Guard arrives at the Tunnel Station in this *c.* 1910 Louis Pesha photograph. The uniforms indicate a Spanish-American War heritage far removed from the doughboy attire of World War I, less than five years away.

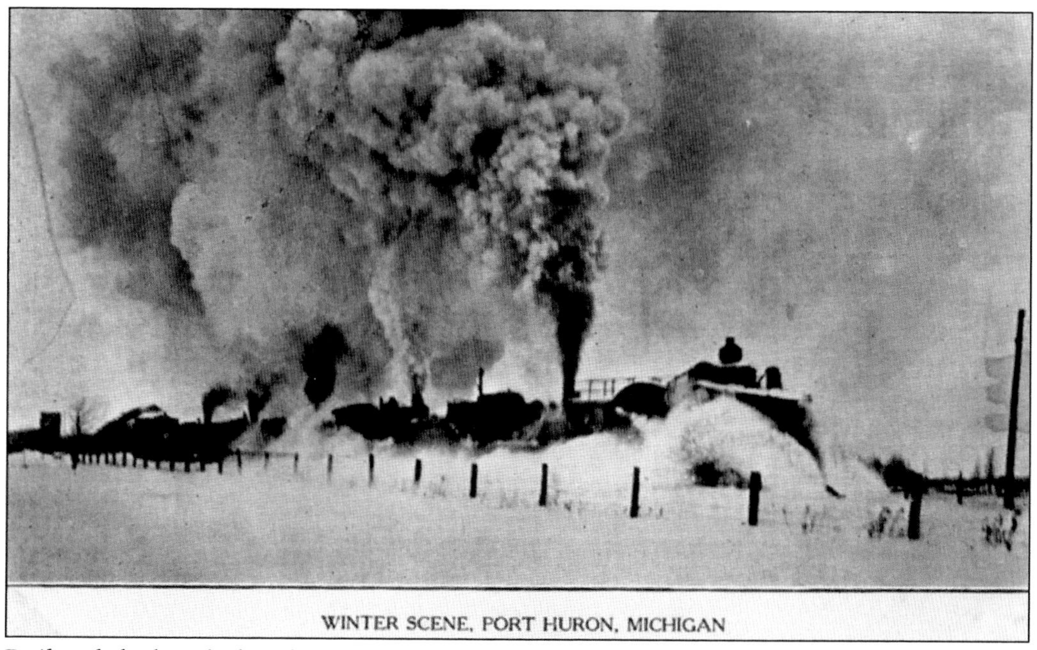

WINTER SCENE, PORT HURON, MICHIGAN

Railroads had to deal with winters of heavy snow in the Port Huron area. Here, nearly five separate steam locomotives push a railroad snow plow around 1910.

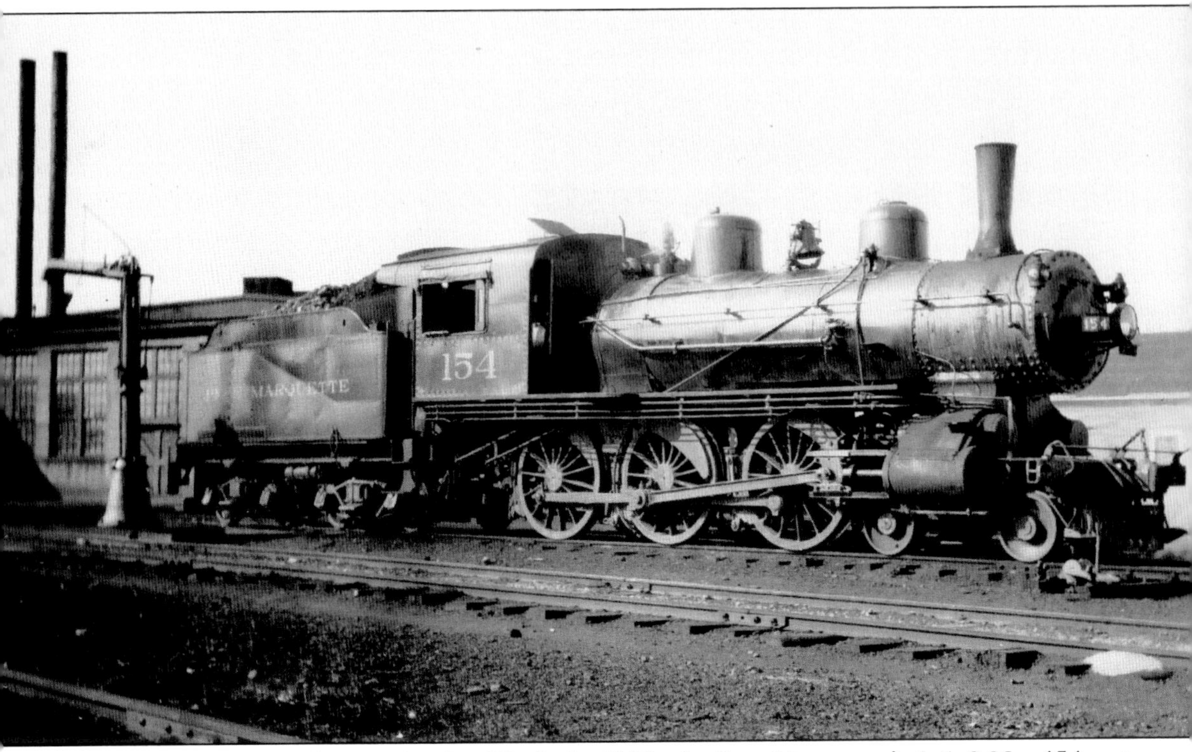


Built by the Brooks Locomotive Works in 1902, the Pere Marquette's 4-6-0 No. 154 rests near the water plug in this October 21, 1928, view at the Port Huron Roundhouse. The Pere Marquette constructed this roundhouse at Sixteenth and Beard Streets around 1912 to replace its aging engine facilities at Second and Wall Streets, which had been built by the Port Huron and Northwestern in the late 1870s. The roundhouse was torn down in 1978, but the turntable was not removed until 1999, when a collector in Mayville purchased it. The site is now occupied by the Southeastern Michigan Gas Company's maintenance garage.

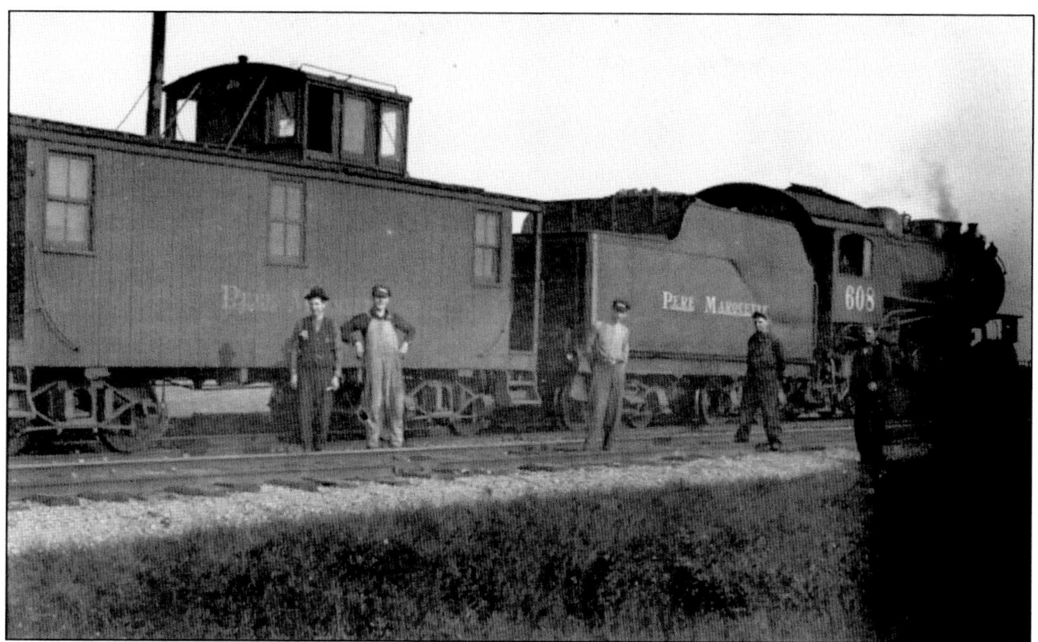


In this *c.* 1915 view, a train crew in the Port Huron "boatyard" readies to put its train together for Saginaw. This locomotive, 2-8-0 No. 608, was purchased by the railroad in 1910 from the American Locomotive Company and was retired by the Pere Marquette's successor, the Chesapeake and Ohio, in 1952.

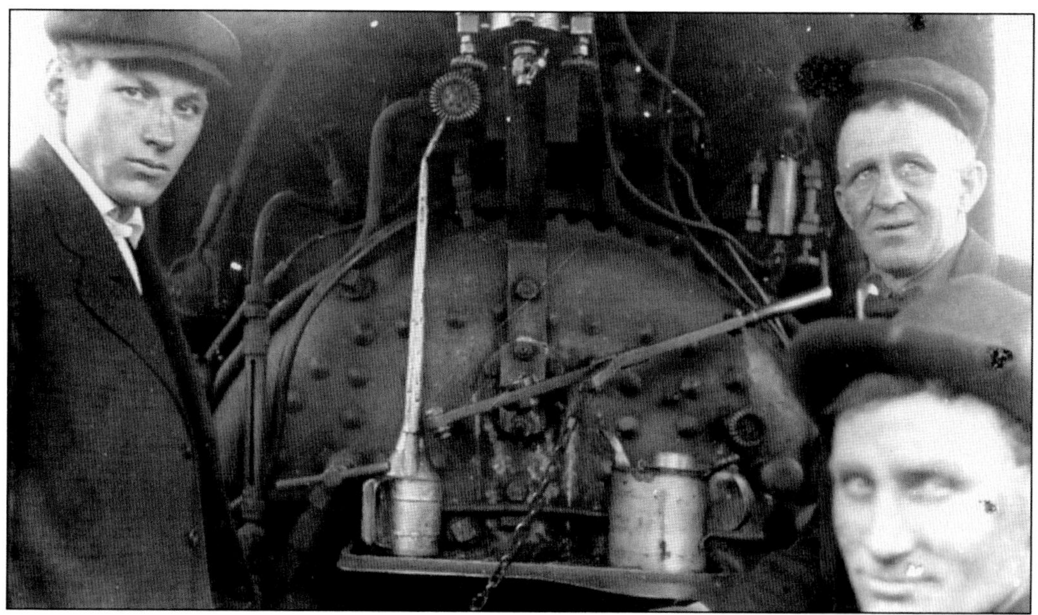

An unidentified Pere Marquette Railway crew takes a break from duties to pose around 1910. Note the long spouted oil can, used for oiling in hard to reach areas of the steam locomotive, and the engineer, who is wearing a somewhat uncharacteristic bow tie.

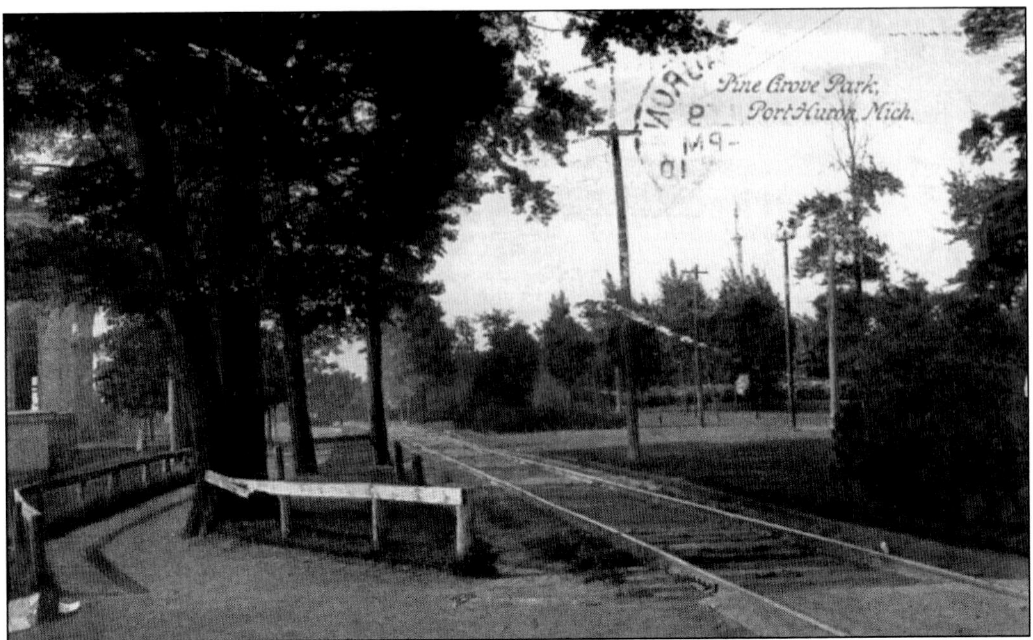


Why yes, Virginia, trains did once run in Pine Grove Park! The Pere Marquette's railroad tracks through Pine Grove Park are shown in this *c.* 1890 view. They were removed with the abandonment of the line between Croswell and Port Huron in the 1970s. The porch to the left is that of Port Huron's first water treatment plant.

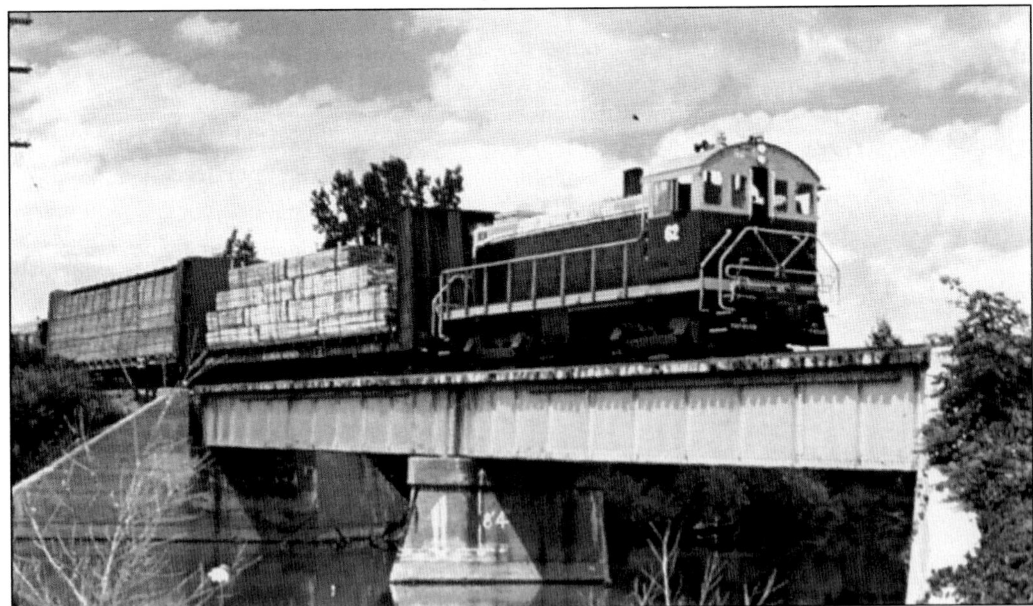

A typical Port Huron and Detroit Railroad train hauls loads of lumber during the 1960s. Built originally as the Port Huron and Southern Railway, the line was purchased by the Handy Brothers of Bay City and renamed about 1915. Although the railroad had dreams of reaching Detroit, it never made it, ending instead at a connection with the Algonac Transit Company in Marine City. This railroad was one of the first in the nation to completely dieselize, doing so in 1951 with three ALCOs: the 52, 60, and later the 62, pictured here.

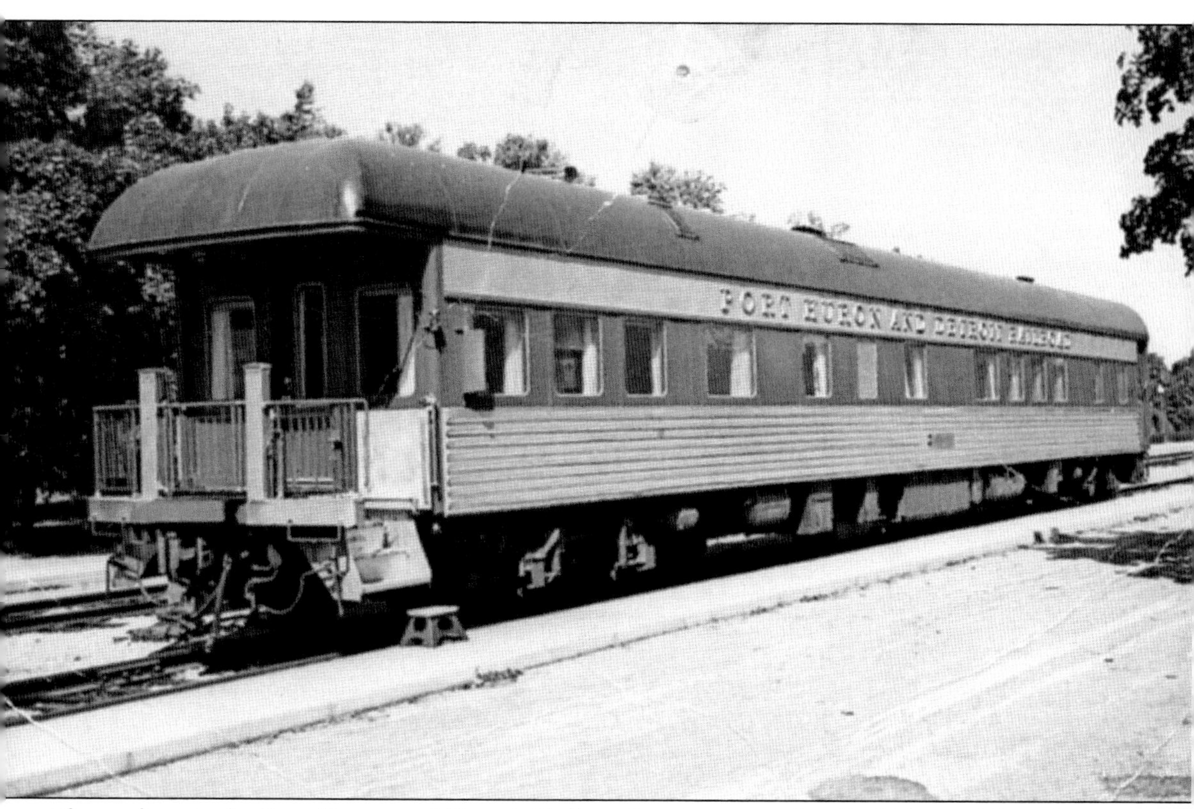

Shown here is the Port Huron and Detroit Railroad's private car, the *Castleblaney.* When the Handy Brothers empire folded, its lawyer, James Duffy, took the railroad as back payment. His heirs continued to run the railroad until 1984, when it was sold to CSX Transportation Systems. The *Castleblaney*, a former Chesapeake and Ohio Railway observation car, was retained by the family for many years, finally being donated to the Florida Gulf Coast Railroad Museum in the early 1990s.

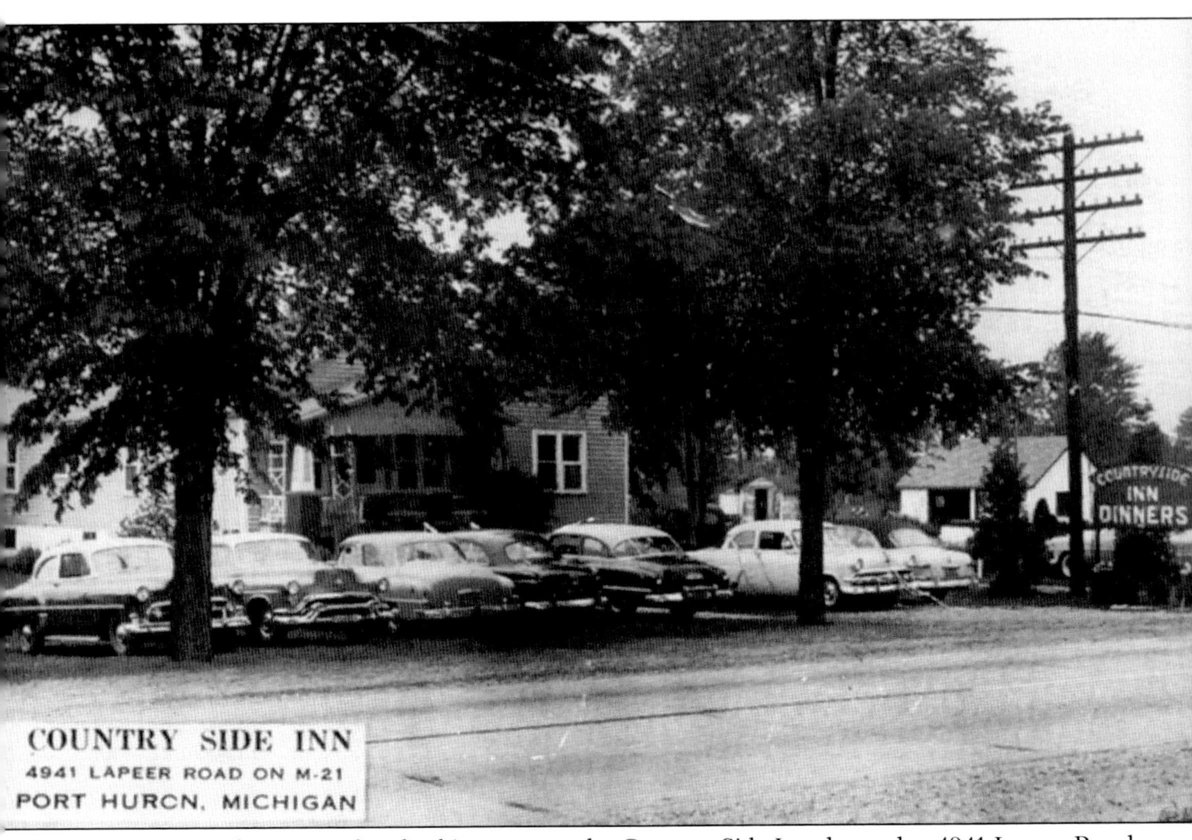


Tired travelers rest and grab a bite to eat at the Country Side Inn, located at 4941 Lapeer Road, also known as Michigan 21. Judging by the age of the automobiles, this photograph was likely taken sometime in the early to mid-1950s. The two-lane Michigan 21 was the main thoroughfare between Port Huron and Flint until being replaced by Interstate 69 in the 1980s.

*Three*

# Working in Port Huron

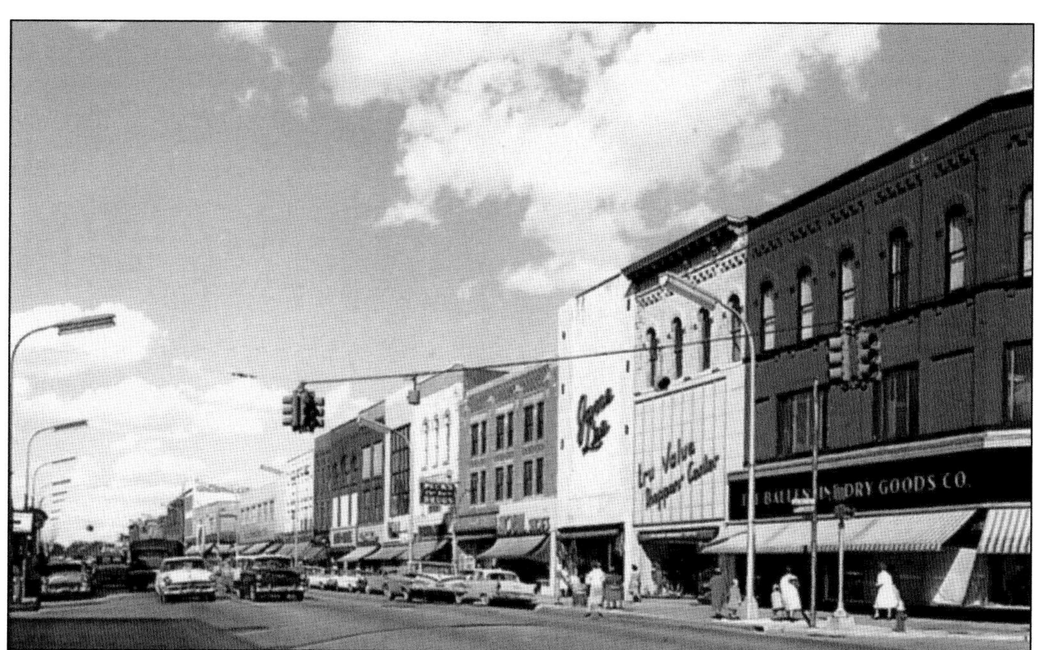


This *c.* 1960 view shows the Huron Avenue business district, and specifically Ballentine Dry Goods. A much greater percentage of people worked downtown at this time, as compared to today. The S. S. Kresge Company opened its second store in Michigan to compete with Ballentine's.

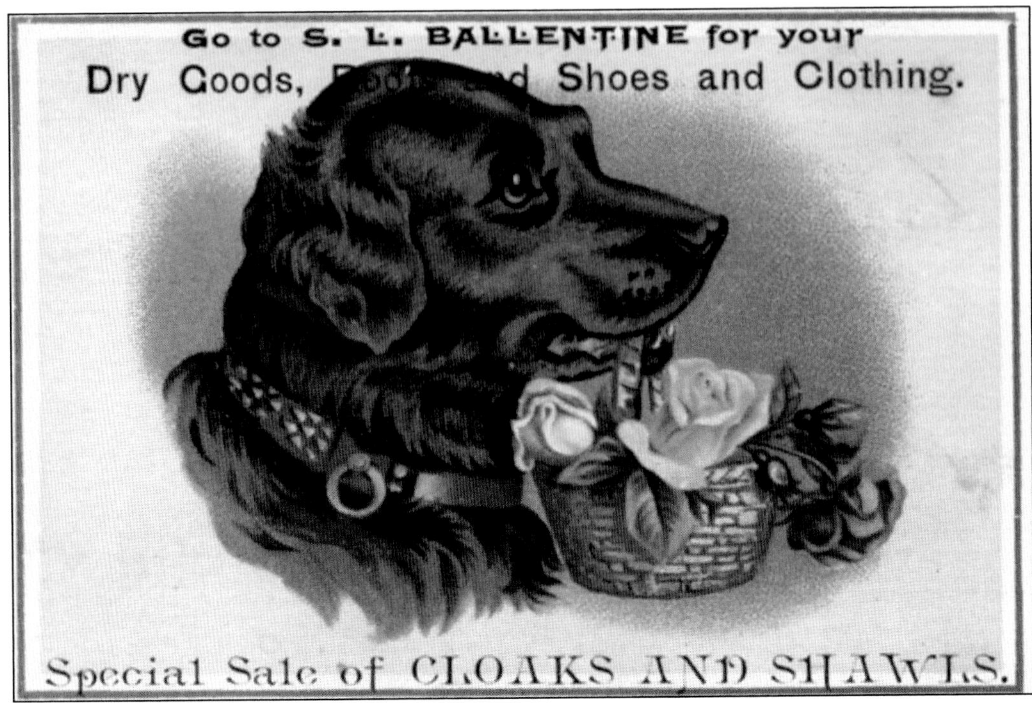


An 1870s advertising postcard from Ballentine Dry Goods depicts a dog carrying a basket of flowers. Founded in the 1860s by Silas L. Ballentine, the shop once boasted of being the largest dry goods store in Michigan's Thumb. Amazingly, it remained in business until 1961, long after similar stores had shut down.

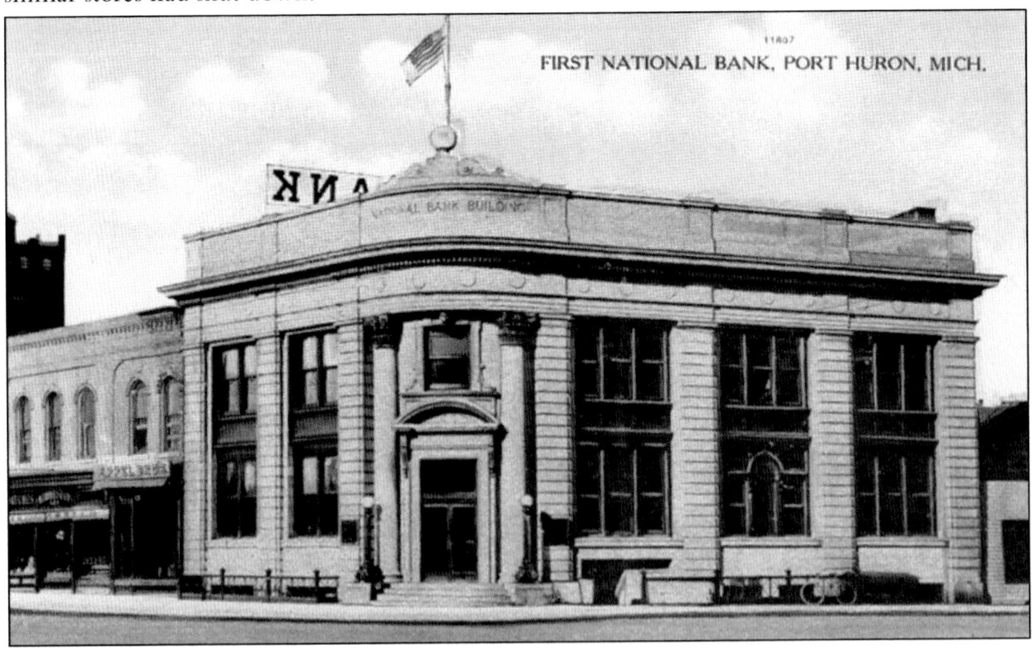


The First National Bank, pictured about 1920, would later be the home of Fox's Jewelry. It was removed in the mid-1990s for the reconstruction of the Military Street Bridge, and Port Huron's Heritage Park now occupies the site.

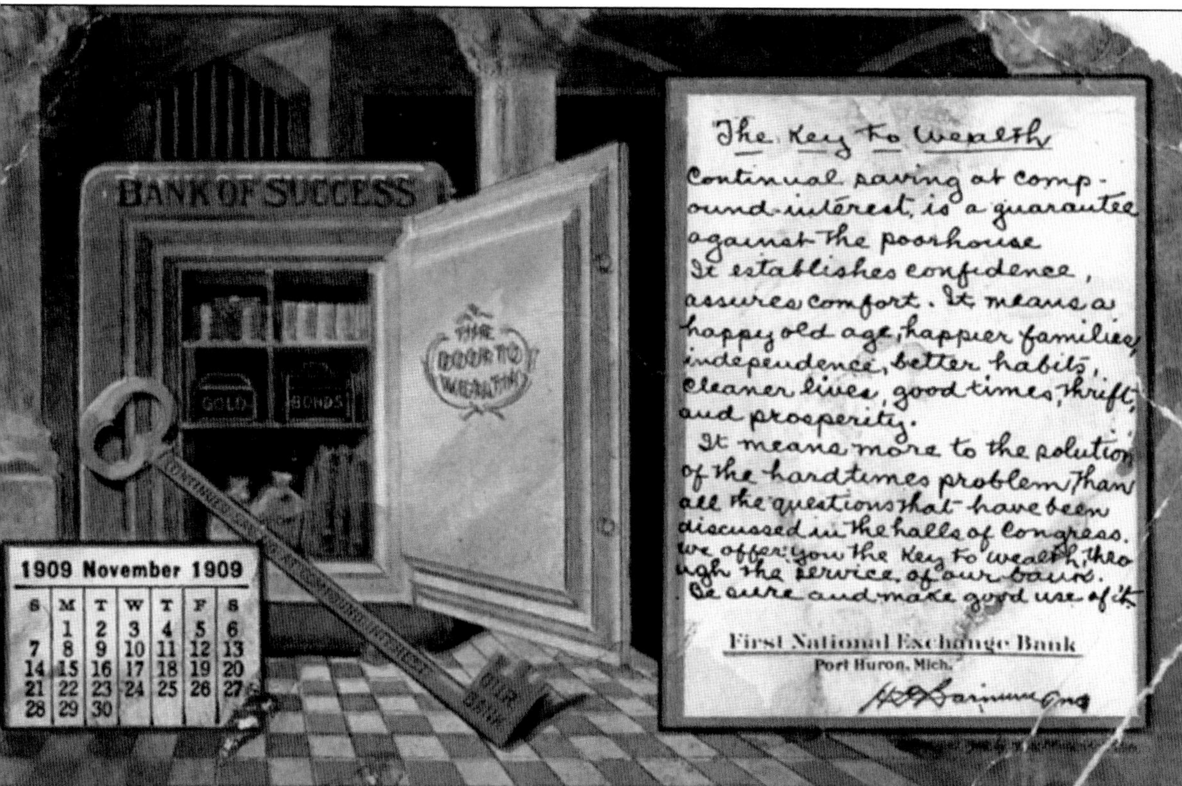


On an advertising card dated November 1909, the First National Exchange Bank is offering the "Key to Wealth" as an incentive for using its services. Postcards were used as much for advertising as they were for cordial greetings, and merchandisers were quick to capitalize on these images.

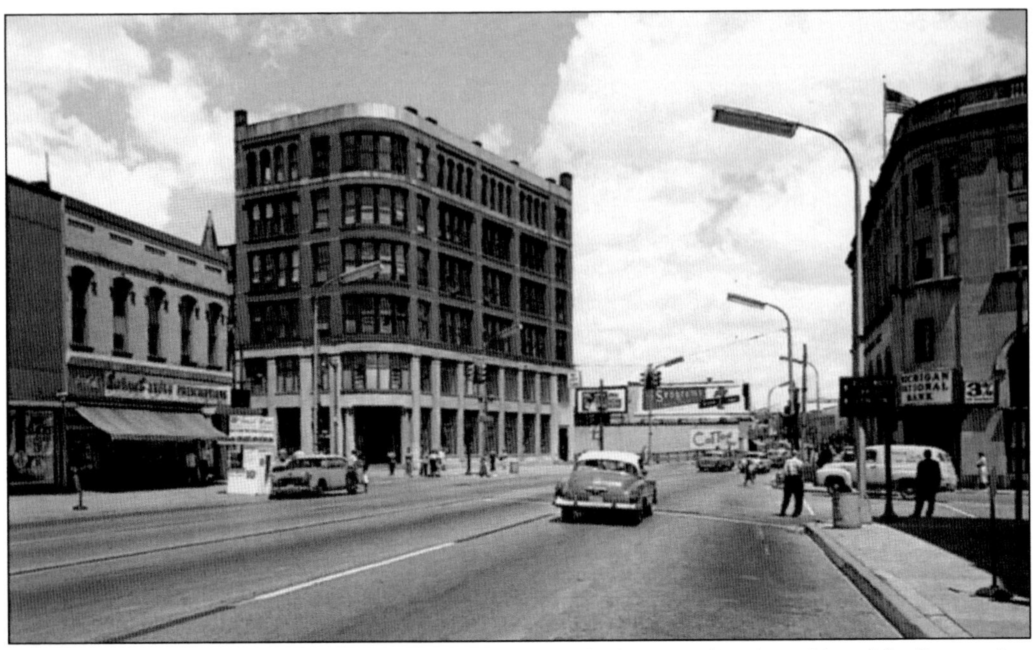

This view shows the original People's Bank Building, which opened in the midst of the Depression after the collapse of many other local banks. It remained at this location for nearly 50 years, until the building was torn down in 1979.

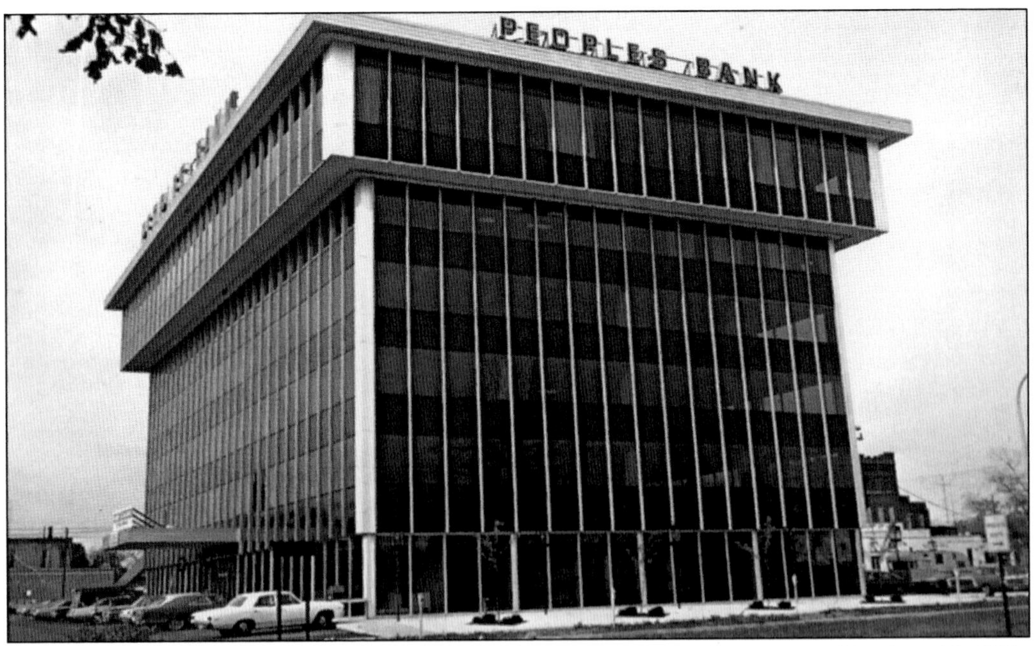


The new People's Bank, the massive glass and steel structure shown here, opened in the mid-1970s to a great deal of fanfare. Located at 511 Fort Street, it boasts the highest dining experience in Port Huron, the Fogcutter, with one of the most panoramic views of the city.

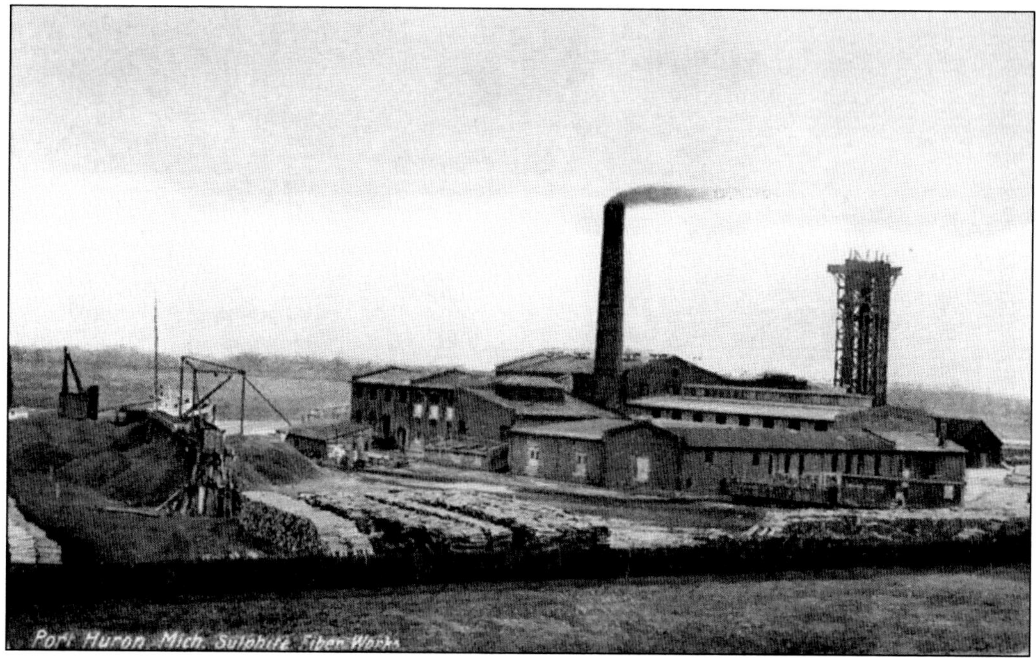


The Michigan Sulphite Fibre Works was opened in 1889 by Dr. Herman Kiefer. Becoming the Port Huron Sulphite and Paper Company, it continued to be run by the Kiefer and Durand families until the 1970s, when it was sold to E. B. Eddy. Now owned by Domtar, the plant remains in operation today.

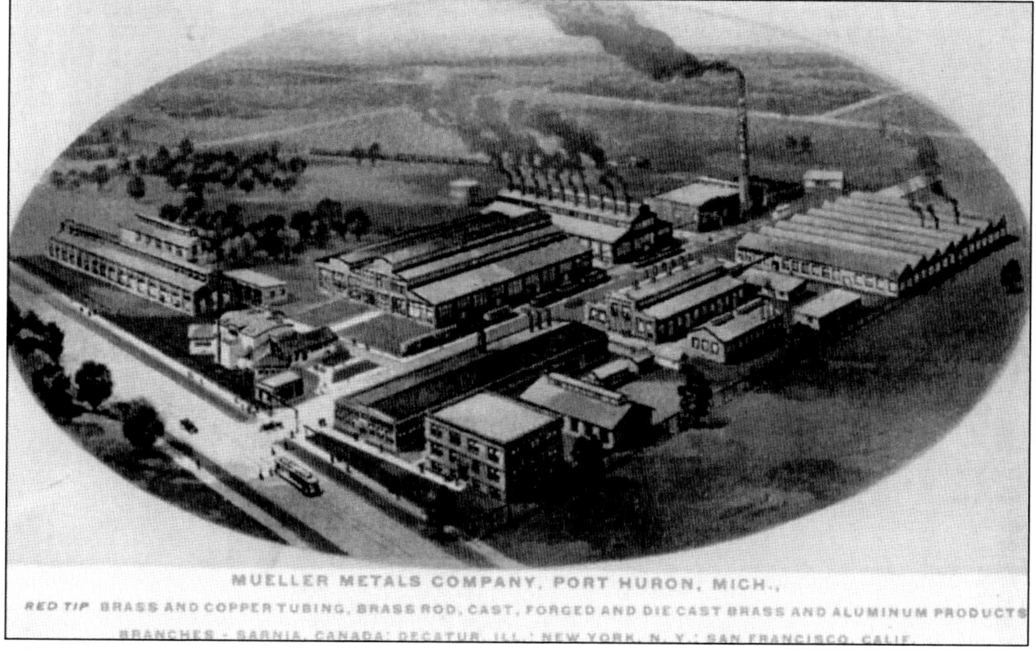


The Mueller Brass and Metals Company plant is shown in this *c.* 1920 view. Founded by Oscar B. Mueller, it once employed nearly 5,000 people and was an important supplier in both the World War I and World War II efforts. Though the plant was downsized in the 1960s and 1970s, Mueller's continues to maintain a presence at the same location.

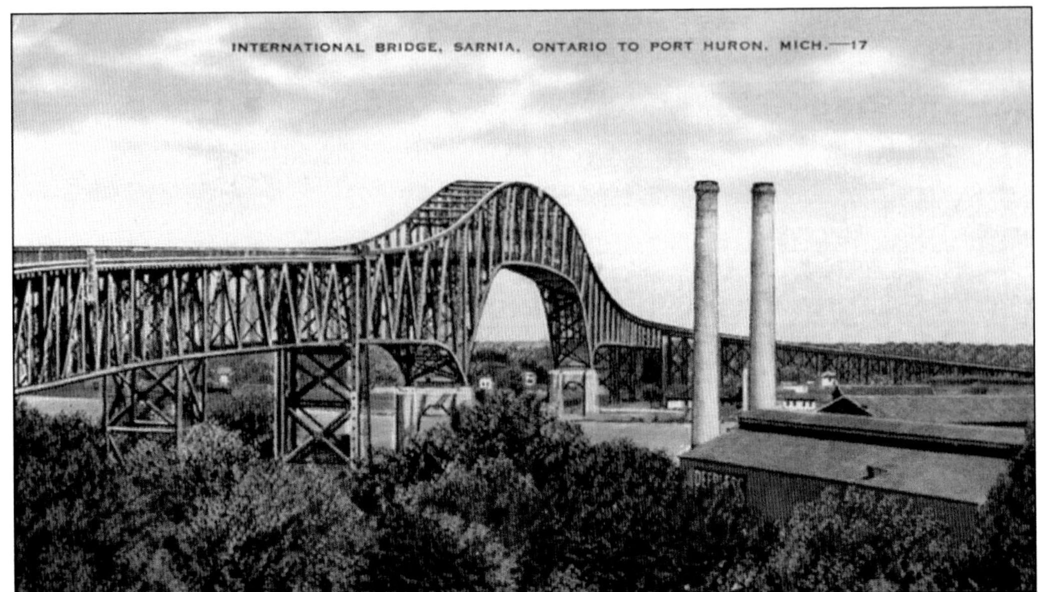


This overhead view, taken around 1939, shows the Peerless Cement Company plant with the first Blue Water Bridge in the background. The Peerless Cement Company purchased the land the plant site in the 1920s from the Grand Trunk Railway, which until 1909 had used the site for its locomotive back shop and maintenance facility. The cement plant closed in the 1970s. The area became one of Port Huron's first brownfield locations, and after clean up, it is home to the Thomas Edison Inn today.

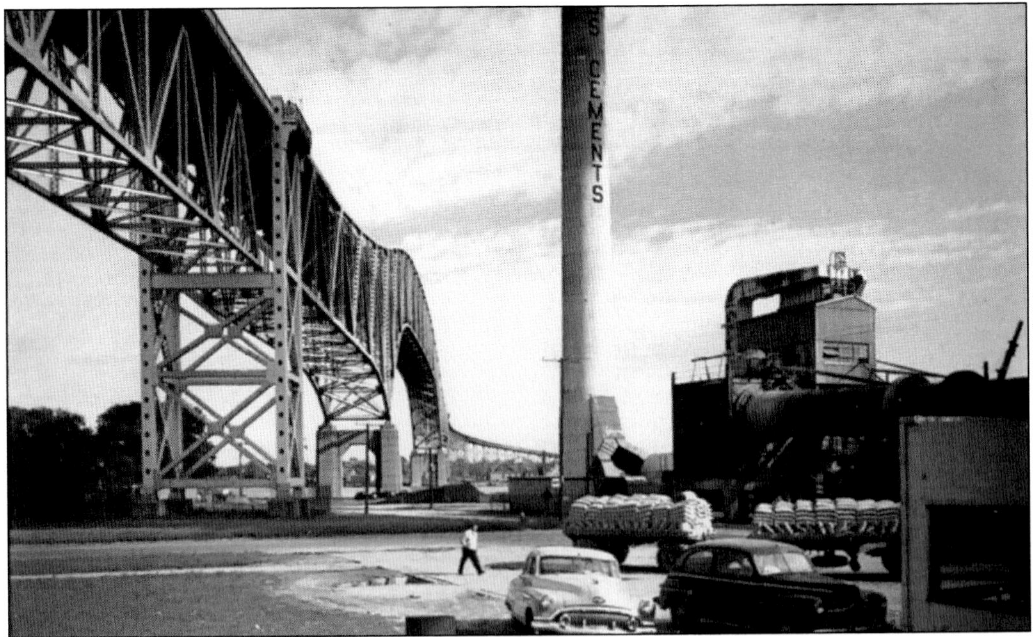


This 1950s-era postcard shows the Peerless Cement plant and its stack, again with the Blue Water Bridge in the background. This area is greatly changed, with the Peerless Cement factory replaced by the Thomas Edison Inn in the 1980s and a second span of the Blue Water Bridge added in 1995.

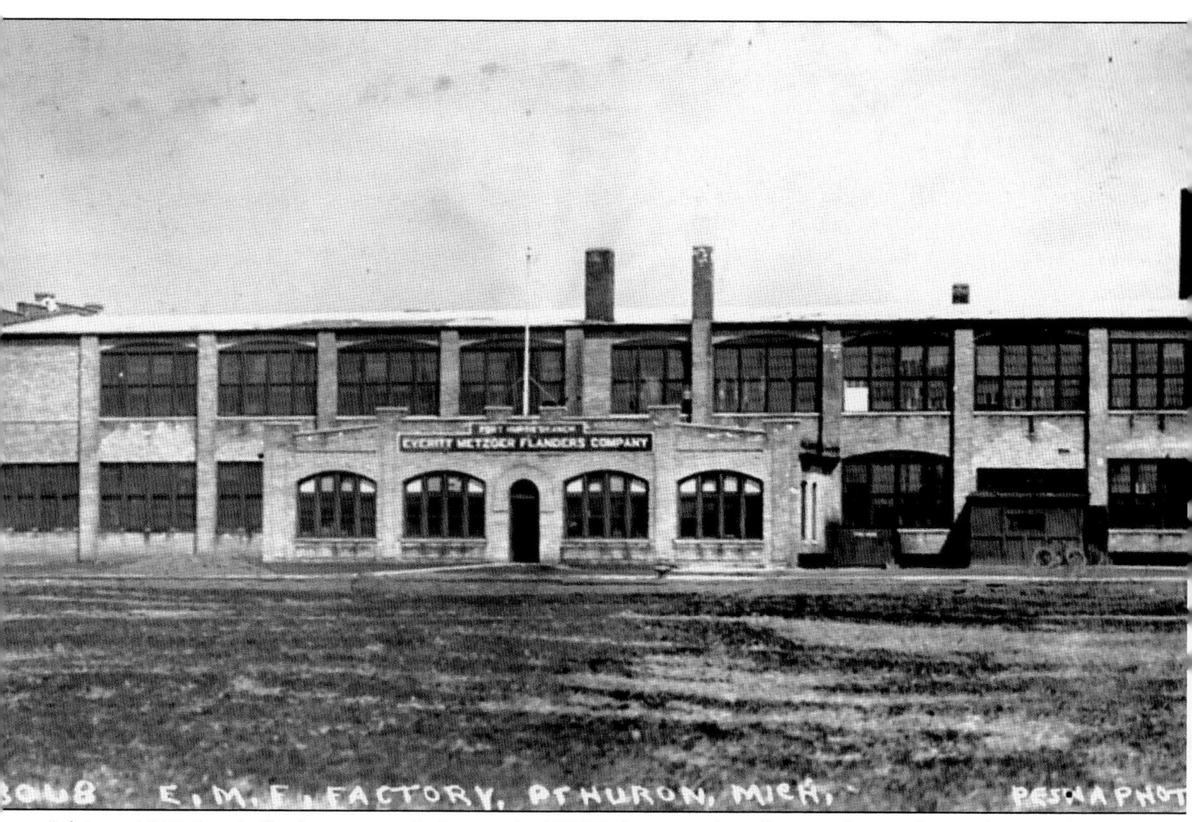


This *c.* 1905 Louis Pesha postcard shows the EMF Automotive factory, located on Elmwood Avenue in Port Huron. Later a division of the Studebaker Company, EMF produced automobiles here from 1905 until 1912. The plant was purchased by the Havers Motor Car Company and subsequently destroyed in a 1914 fire. The site is now occupied by the Can-Am Duty Free shop and the Blue Water Bridge approach from Pine Grove Avenue.

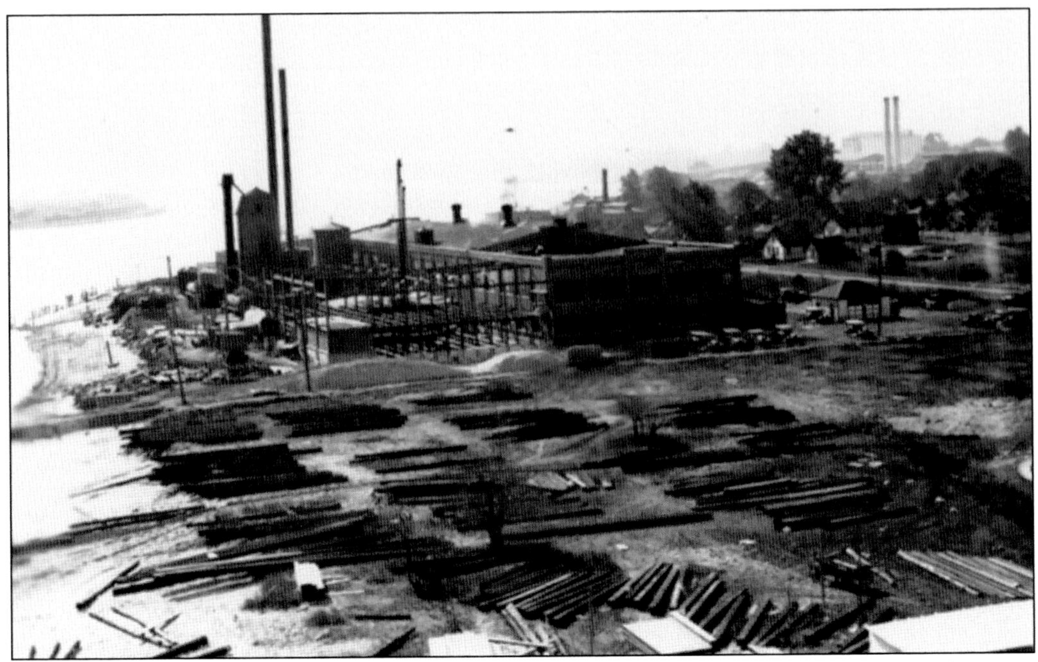

The Dunn Paper Company was constructed around 1924. Founded by Theodore Wiggle Dunn and his son George, the company remained in the family until the 1970s, when it was sold to the Dennison Paper Group. After a series of ownership changes, it became Dunn Paper once again in 2005.

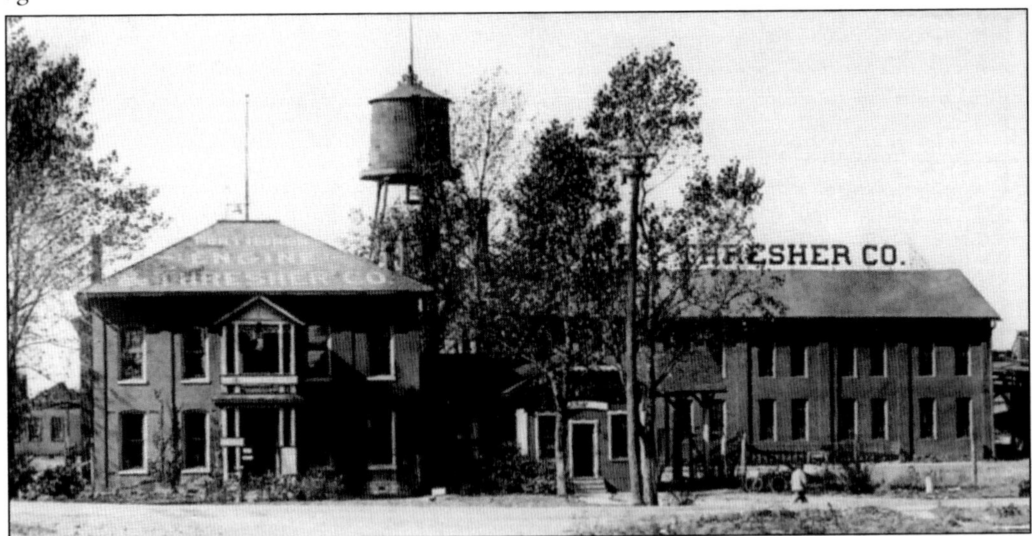


This Louis Pesha postcard view shows the Port Huron Engine and Thresher plant on Twenty-fourth Avenue. The company began producing steam traction engines as the Upton Machine Works, opening first in Battle Creek in the late 1880s. Moving to Port Huron near the start of the 20th century, Upton changed its name and added threshing implements to its line. By the 1910s, the firm was one of the leaders in the industry, able to count Case, Scheidler, and John Deere among its competitors. The gasoline-powered tractor spelled the death of traction steam engines, and although Port Huron Engine and Thresher continued on as a business for many years, its days as a steam engine manufacturer ended in the 1920s.

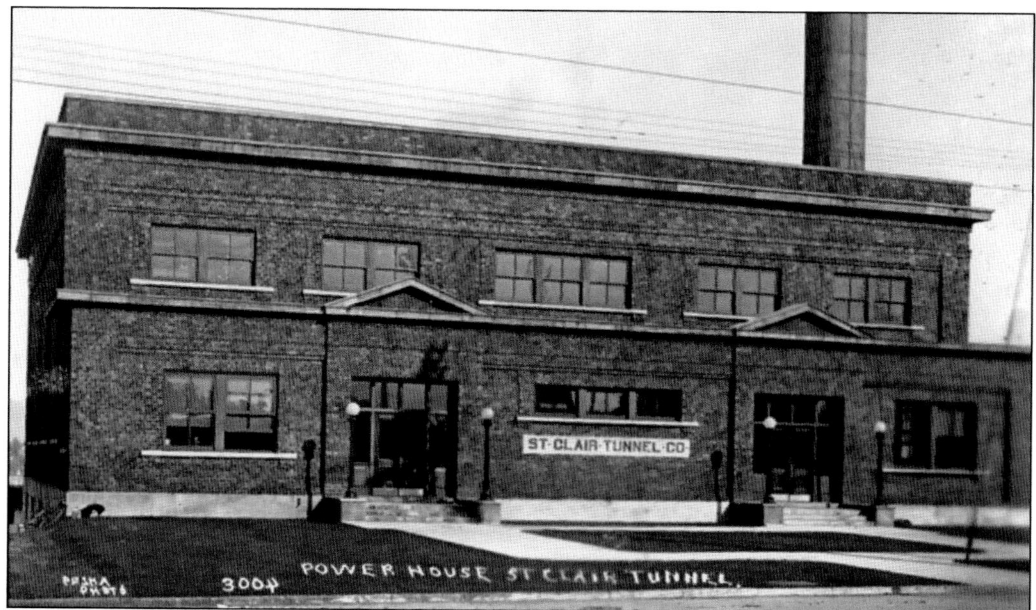


The offices and power plant of the St. Clair Tunnel Company are pictured here in 1908. When electric power was abandoned in favor of diesels for the tunnel in 1958, the site became the offices for the Port Huron Seaway Terminal. Today, the location is owned by Acheson Ventures, which was able to purchase the site through a mandate of city voters of nearly 90 percent. It is home to the ex-USCG cutter *Bramble* and the tall ship *Highlander Sea*.

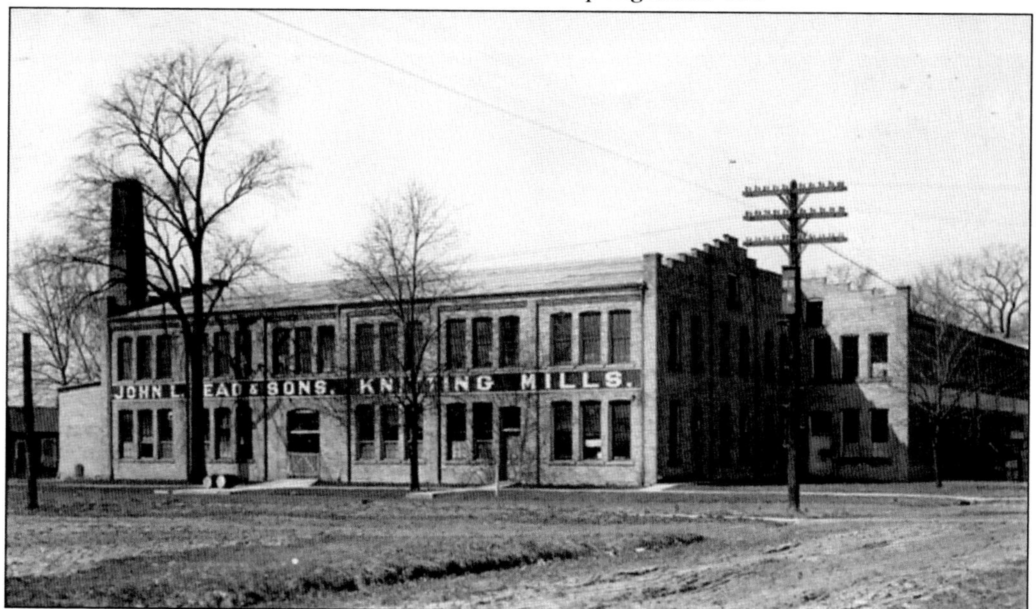

This *c.* 1910 Pesha view shows the John L. Fead and Sons Woolen Mills. Located at the corner of Tenth and Whipple Streets, the company was a major employer in the area just north of Pine Grove Park. The Fead family was instrumental in producing materials for the country's effort in both World Wars I and II, concentrating particularly on the production of socks for the uniforms. Although the knitting mills closed after World War II, the building remains standing, still owned by members of the Fead family.

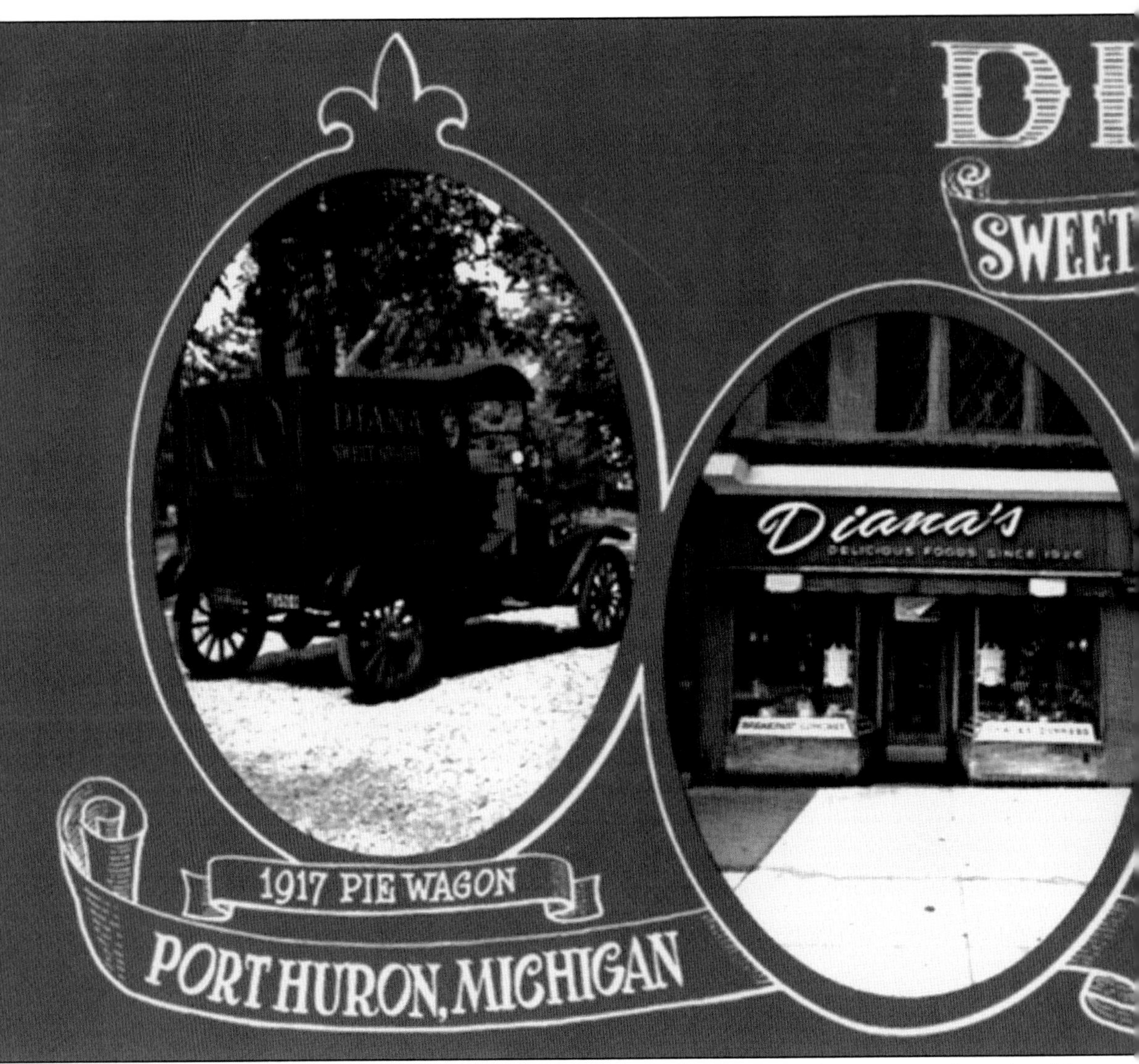


A landmark business in Port Huron, Diana's Sweet Shoppe opened in 1926 and retained its Roaring-Twenties character for nearly 75 years. Although many small towns had candy and sweet shops, most either closed due to the Depression or the advent of the drugstore soda shop. What

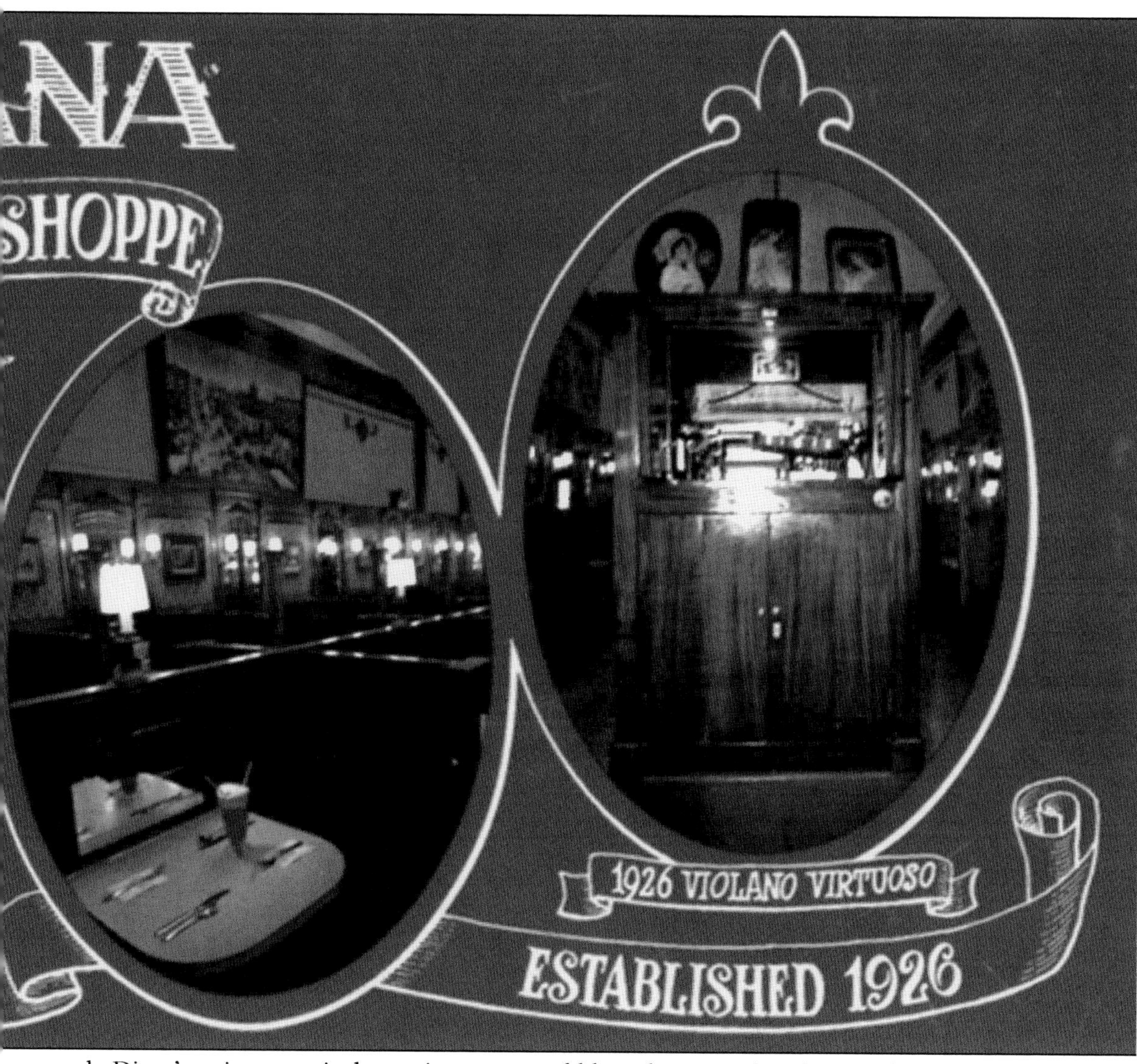


made Diana's unique was its longevity—you could buy the same phosphate in the 1990s that your great-grandfather bought in the 1920s. Sadly, time is a relentless mover, and the business, run by the Deliginas family, closed its doors forever in 2001.

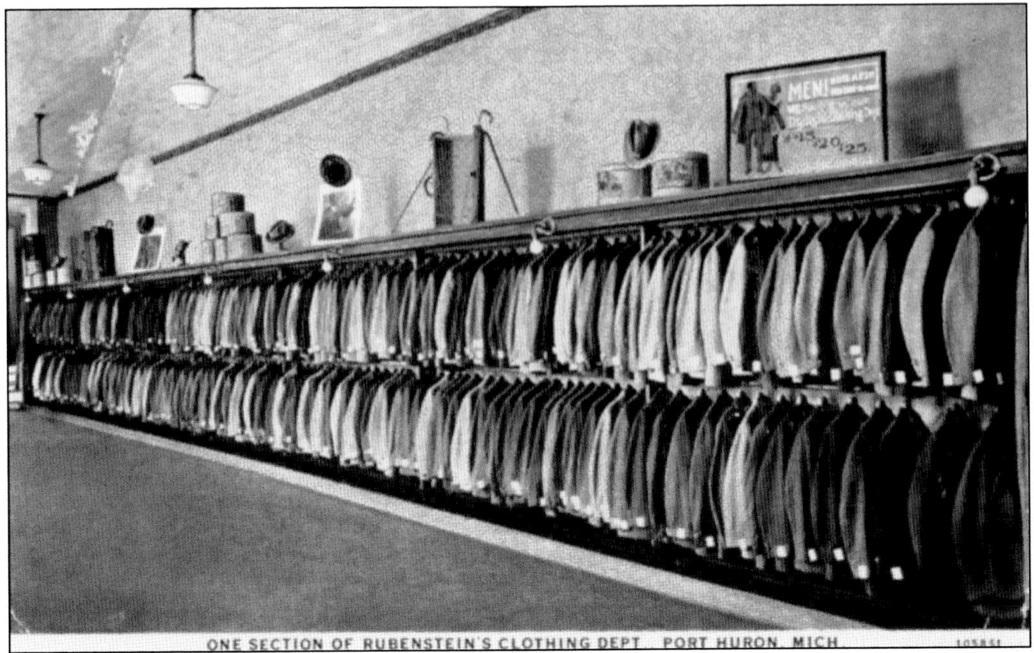


The interior of Rubenstein's Mens Store, located on Huron Avenue, is seen here about 1915. Rubenstein's was one of seven men's stores operating in the downtown area at the time. Changing attitudes in men's fashion in the 1970s doomed the small town men's stores, and not a single one remains in Port Huron today.

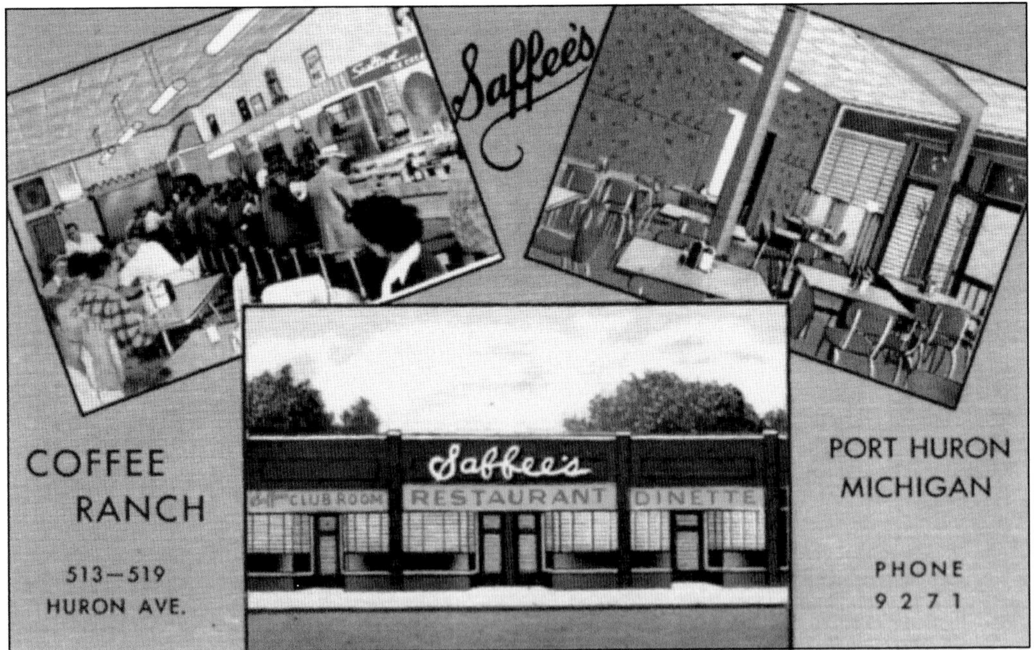


For more than 30 years, Saffee's Coffee Ranch was where many Port Huron residents started their mornings. Saffee's opened in the 500 block of Huron Avenue in the late 1940s, serving "good food" at great prices until closing in 1985. This building is now occupied by BMJ Engineers and Surveyors.

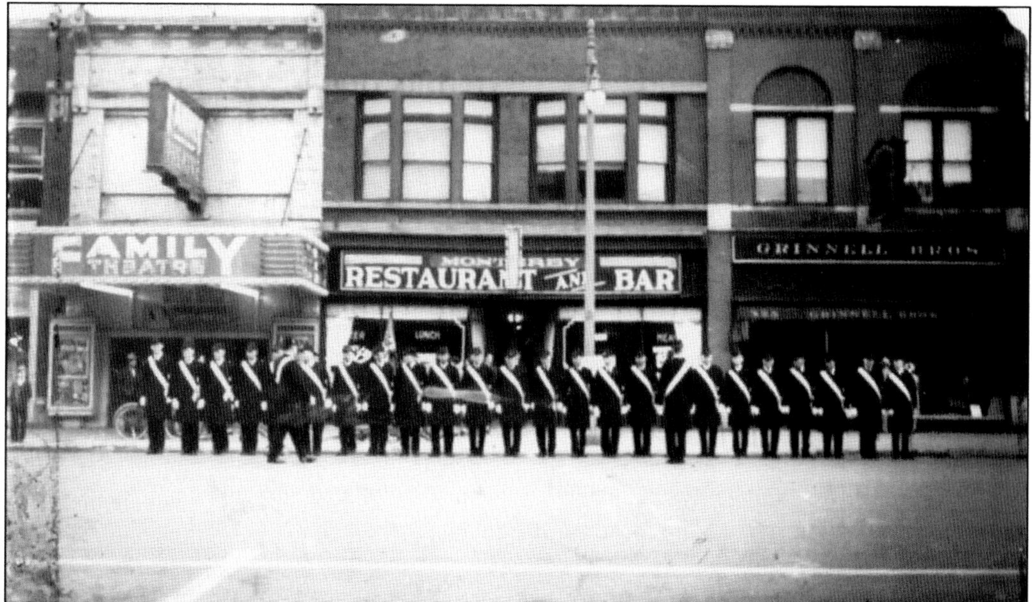


Taken just down Huron Avenue from the above image, this 1940s view shows the Knights of Columbus in front of a string of longtime Port Huron businesses. Seen here from left to right, the Family Theater, the Monterey Restaurant and Bar, and the Grinnell Brothers Music Store all remained here well into the 1950s. In 2006, the Huron Athletic Club occupied the site of the first two businesses; the third was occupied until recently by Blue Water Title.

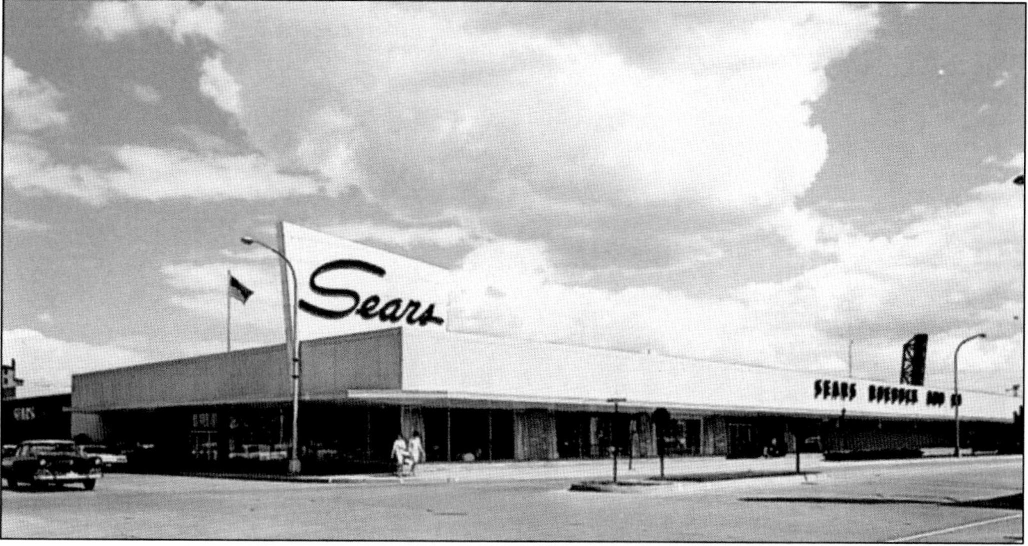


Every medium-sized town in 1950s America had a Sears, and Port Huron was no exception. When the city began to clean up the former First Ward area in the early 1950s, Sears, which had been situated at 905 Military Street for a number of years, decided it was time to relocate. Rather than just move the store, the company built a new facility that encompassed the department store, farm store, and warehouse, which had been at other sites. The new building, opened in 1960, took up nearly an entire city block on Michigan Avenue. Its glowing red neon sign became an icon to a generation of Port Huron children until Sears relocated to Birchwood Mall in Fort Gratiot in the early 1990s.

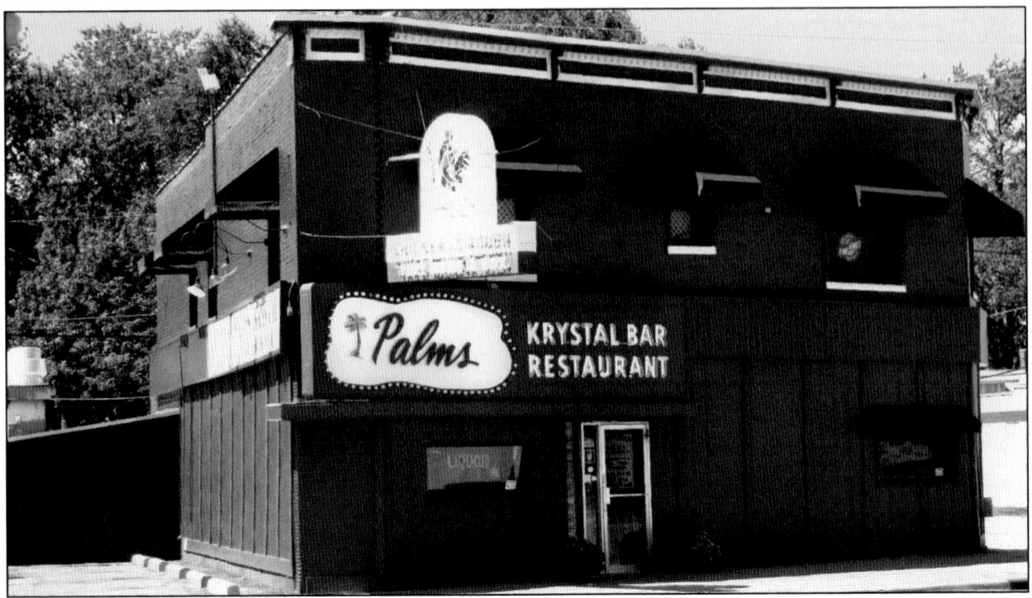


If Port Huron has a heart, it is Palm's Krystal Bar and Chicken-in-the-Rough. Opened in 1936, Palm's has been the gathering spot of all generations for better than 60 years. Its 1940s decor is straight out of a film noir, so much so that you half expect Barabara Stanwyck or Veronica Lake to crawl out of one of its red-and-cream vinyl booths. Palm's is currently owned by Russ and Martha Schulz, who carry on the tradition of good food and great atmosphere.

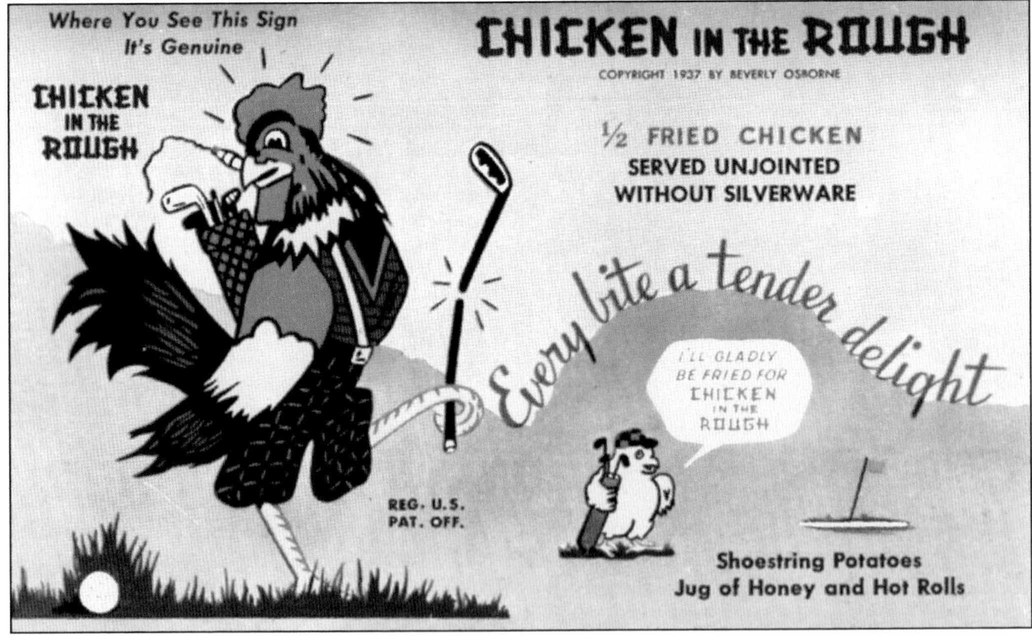


The best fried chicken in the area is served at Palm's. The Chicken-in-the-Rough recipe was first developed by Beverly Osborne in the original restaurant in Oklahoma and was later franchised around the country. This postcard was used as an advertising gimmick to get hungry travelers to stop at as many locations as possible. If a person ate at 25 or more Chicken-in-the-Rough locations in a given year and mailed in this card, he was eligible for a $100 cash prize.

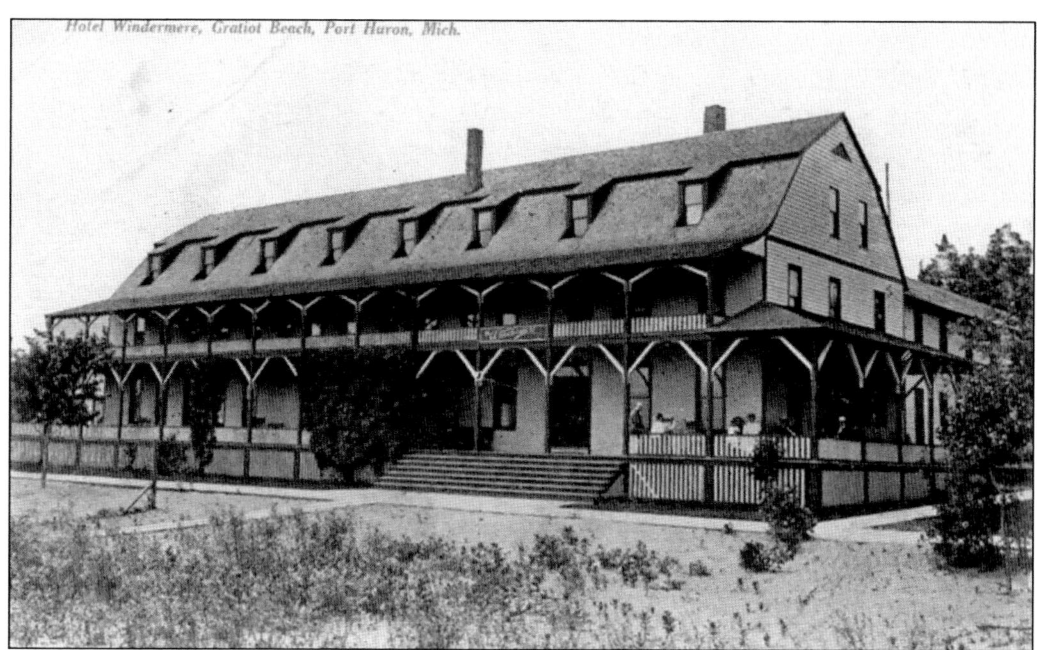


An important early resort hotel in Port Huron is shown in the above *c.* 1890 view. The Hotel Windermere (also spelled Windemere) was located along Gratiot Avenue, near the current intersection with Krafft Road, and was known throughout the area for its good service and beautiful lakeside views. One of its early proprietors was J. B. Sperry, who became better known as the owner of Sperry's Department Store. Another view of the Windermere, taken about 1910, can be seen below. It shows the later addition of Victorian-style towers in its roof line. Like so many wooden structures in the Port Huron area, the Windermere met an untimely end by fire in the early 1920s and was not rebuilt.

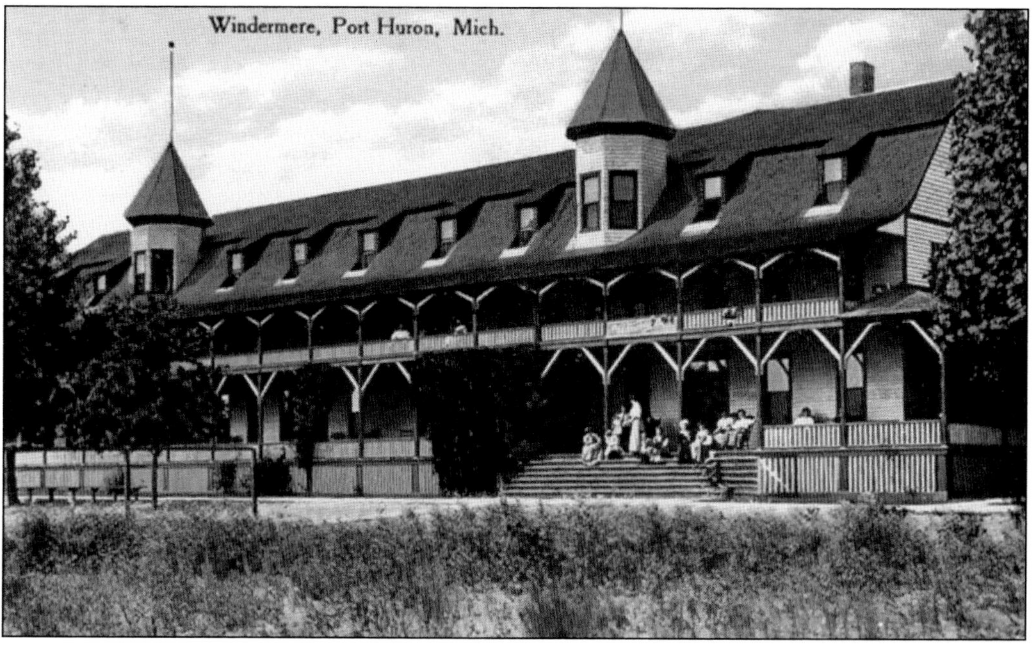

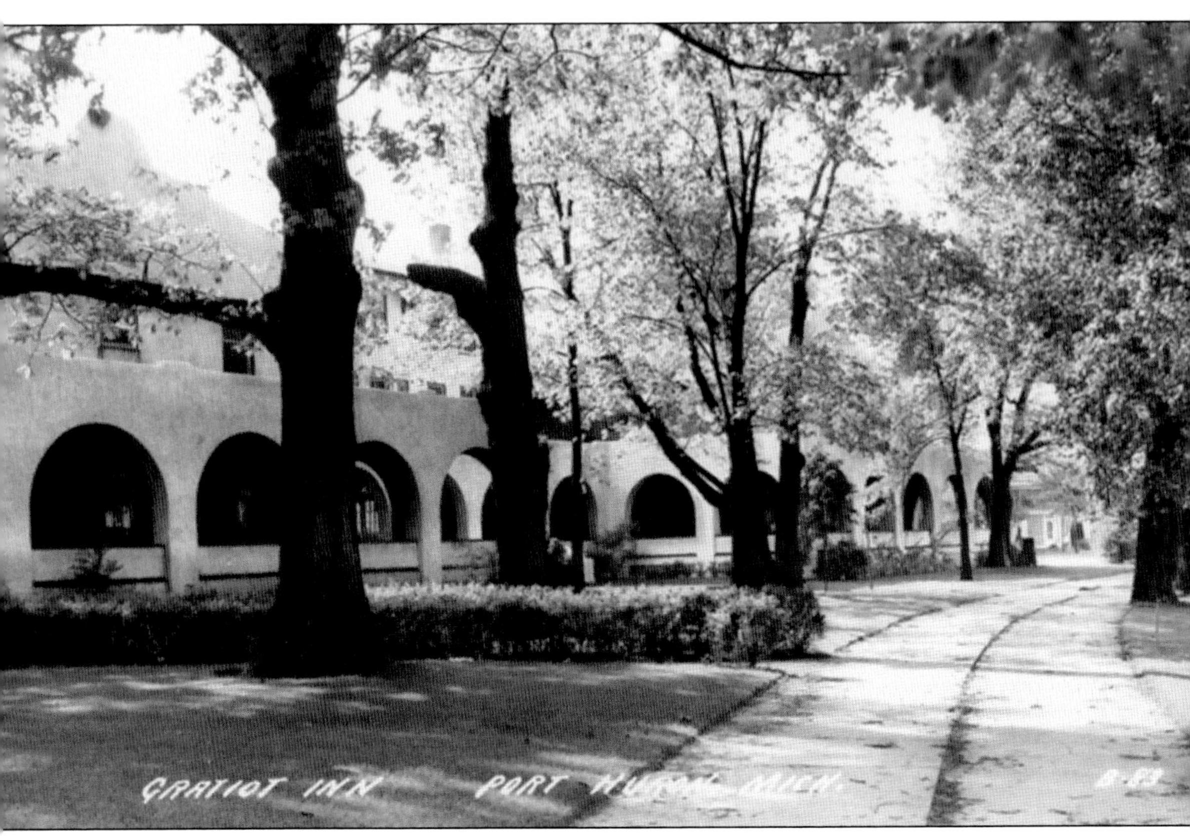


Another longtime resort was the Gratiot Inn, seen here in the 1940s. Like many resort hotels of its time, the Gratiot often had guests from Detroit and other areas who stayed for weeks or sometimes months at a time. By the 1960s, however, travel tastes and the decline of the two-week vacation had changed attitudes toward travel, and it was closed.

# *Four*

# The Maritime Capital

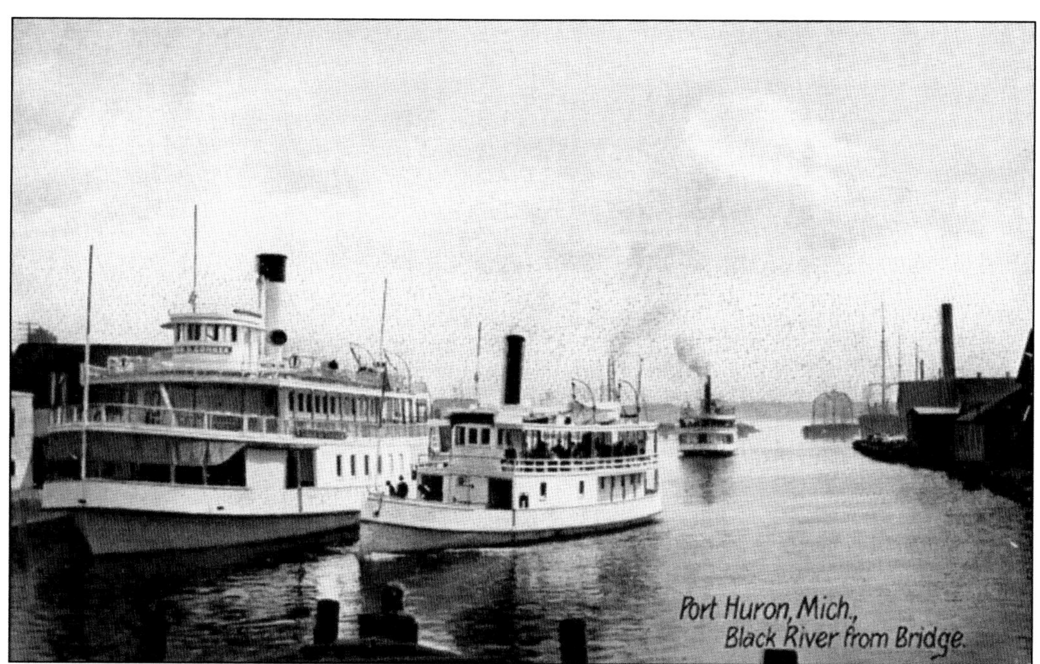


Two Port Huron Sarnia ferries are pictured here around 1910. Built in 1881, the *Omar D. Conger* was named for one of the more important politicians in Port Huron history. Conger was a U.S. representative and senator from Michigan from 1869 to 1887. After the ferry had served the area for nearly 40 years, the *Conger* met a sad fate when on the morning of March 26, 1922, her boiler exploded in the middle of downtown Port Huron, killing four crewmen, injuring several bystanders, and shattering windows for four city blocks. A lifeboat davit crashed through the side of the Peg Tire Company, whose owner used it to hang his sign for the next 20 years.

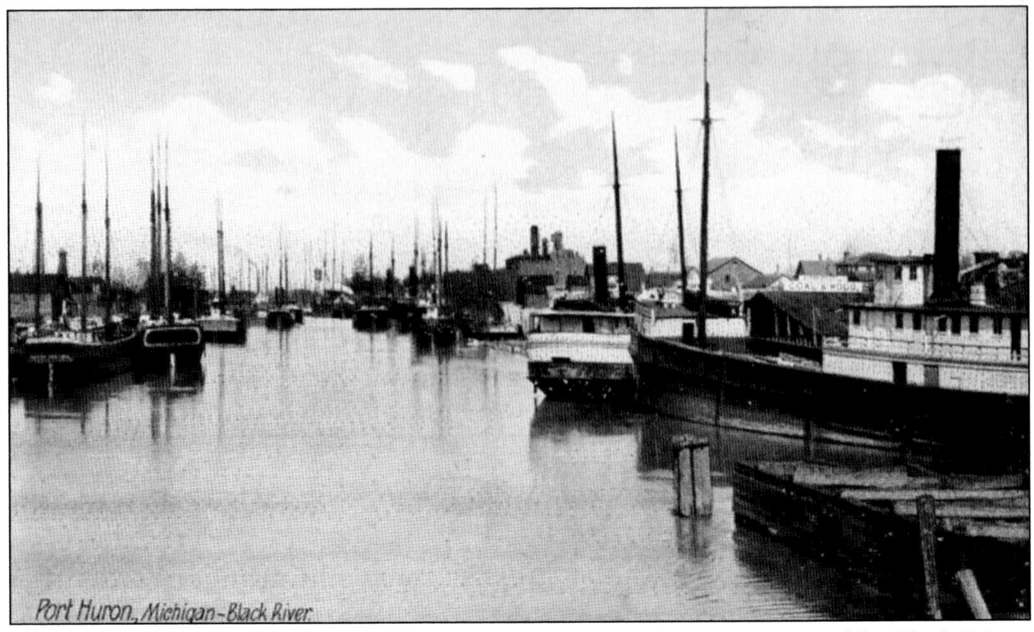

The transition period of sail to steam can clearly be seen in this 1880s view of the Black River, looking west from Seventh Street. This image would look strange to pleasure boaters of today, but not because of the many ships; the Tenth Street Bridge, a Port Huron fixture, would not be constructed until 1890.

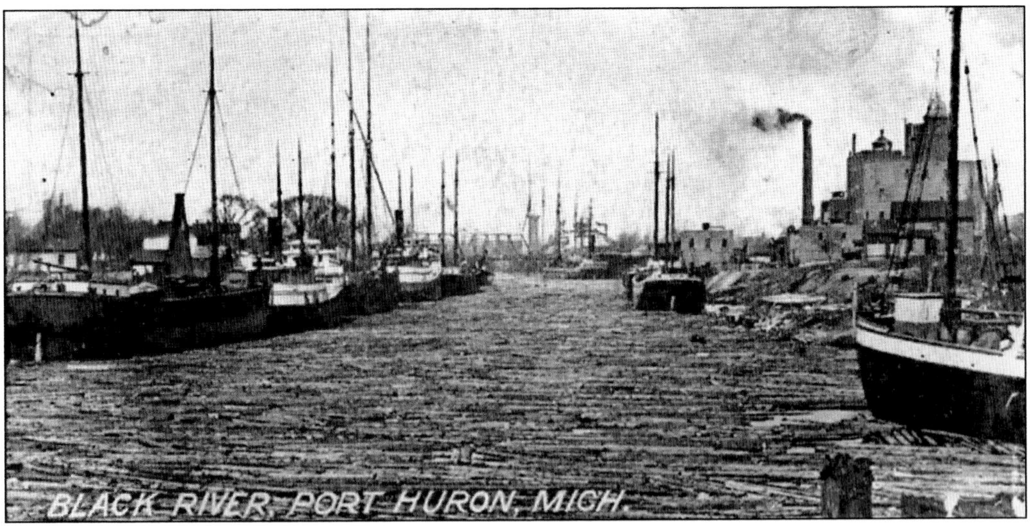

A similar view of the Black River is shown about 10 years later, with the aforementioned Tenth Street Bridge in the background. The most intriguing element of this image is the river itself. It is filled from bank to bank with logs, headed for the sawmill and then for delivery to other Great Lakes ports. The Black River Steam Mill, one of Michigan's first steam-operated mills when it opened in the 1830s, remained in operation just to the west of the Seventh Street Bridge until the 1890s.

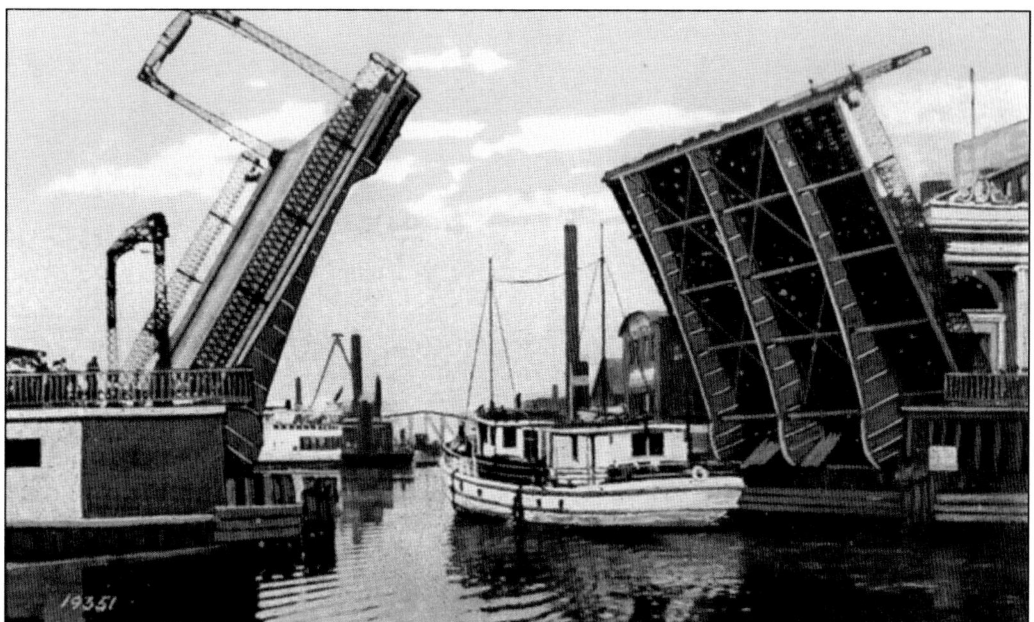


The leaves of the newly-opened Military Street drawbridge have opened to allow a small ship to pass beneath around 1915. It was not uncommon to see small freighters, known as canallers due to their ability to pass through the Welland Canal and other small rivers, travel up the Black River to the Port Huron Paper Company to unload pulpwood, a practice that lasted well into the 1950s.

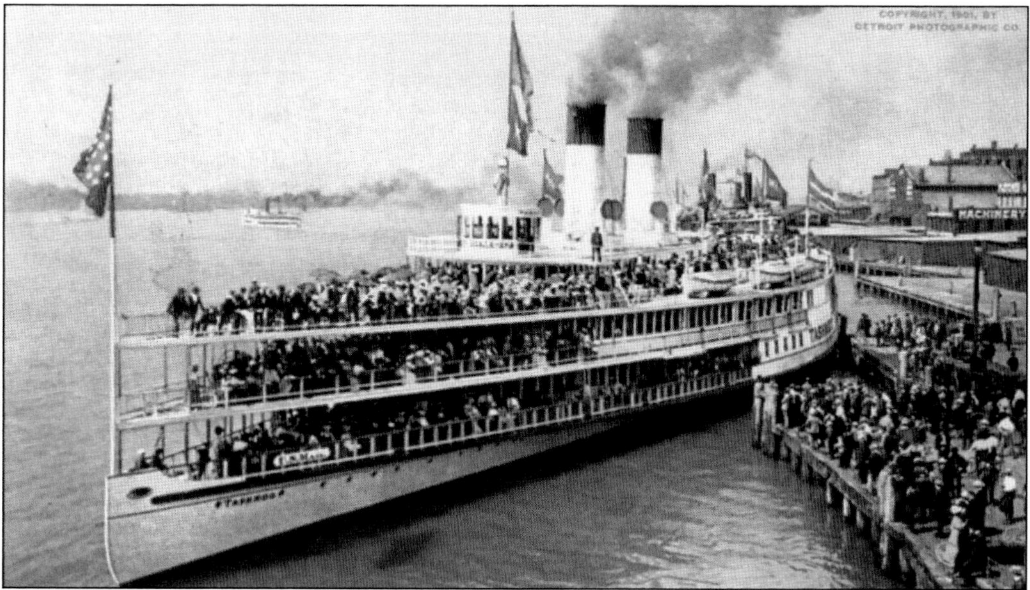

The undisputed queen of the Detroit–Port Huron passenger run, the *Tashmoo* prepares to leave the Detroit dock for Port Huron about 1910. Built in 1900, she became a much-beloved way of travel for many, and her dim lights and soft music could be seen and heard by many in the area on warm summer nights for close to 30 years. Her lengthy career came to an end when, in 1936, she hit a rock near Amherstburg, Ontario. Although she made it to shore and seemed to be salvageable, her back was broken when overzealous salvagers tried to raise her too quickly.

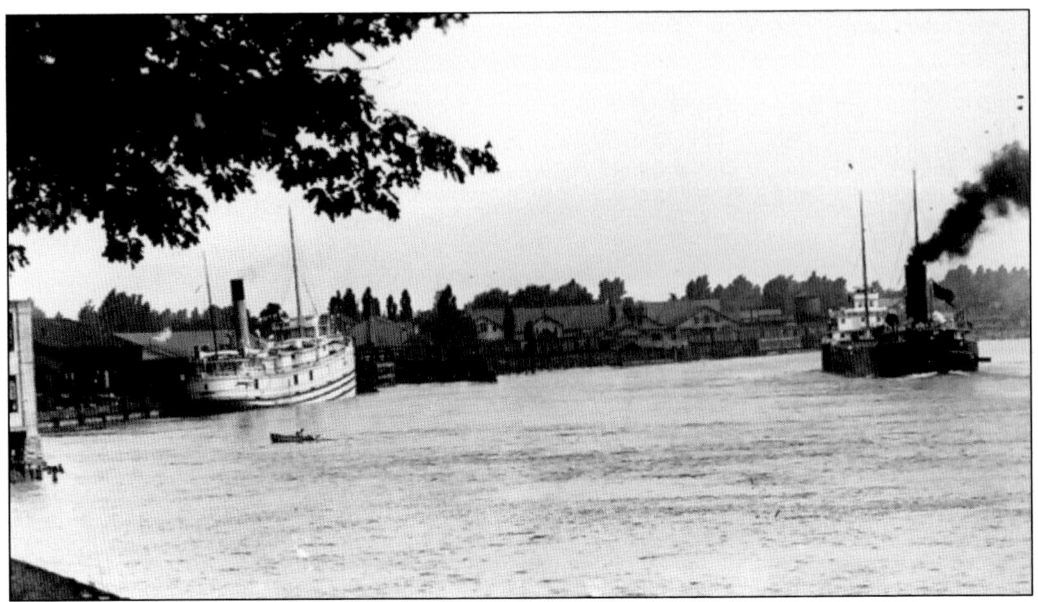

In this *c.* 1905 Louis Pesha postcard view, the Port Huron and Duluth Steamship Company's package freighter *Lakeland* sits at the company's docks just north of Pine Grove Park. The Grand Trunk Railway's locomotive maintenance shops can be seen in the background, as well as their extensive freight yard. Like so many others, the *Lakeland* would meet a sad fate when on December 3, 1924, she sank mysteriously to the bottom of Lake Michigan off Sturgeon Bay, Wisconsin, with a load of new automobiles.

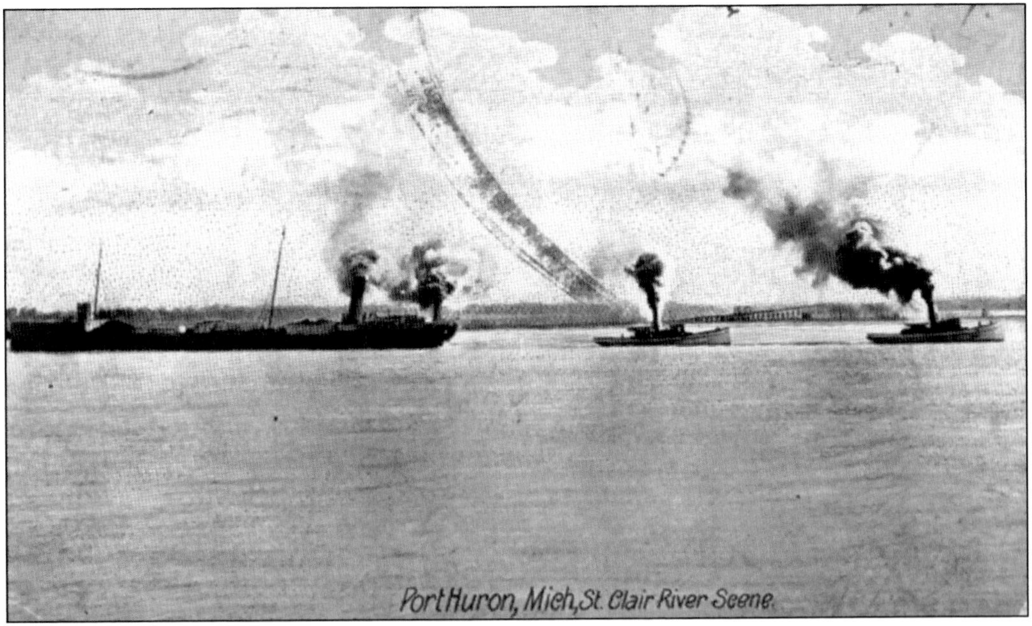


A pair of steam-powered tugs tries to help a freighter that has run aground in this early 1900s view. These tugs were most likely those of the Reid Wrecking Company, an operation opened by Port Huron's Capt. J. T. Reid, who became famous throughout the Great Lakes for his ability to save wrecks that seemed unsalvageable by others. His exploits were detailed in the 1960 book *The Salvager* by Mary Francis Donor.

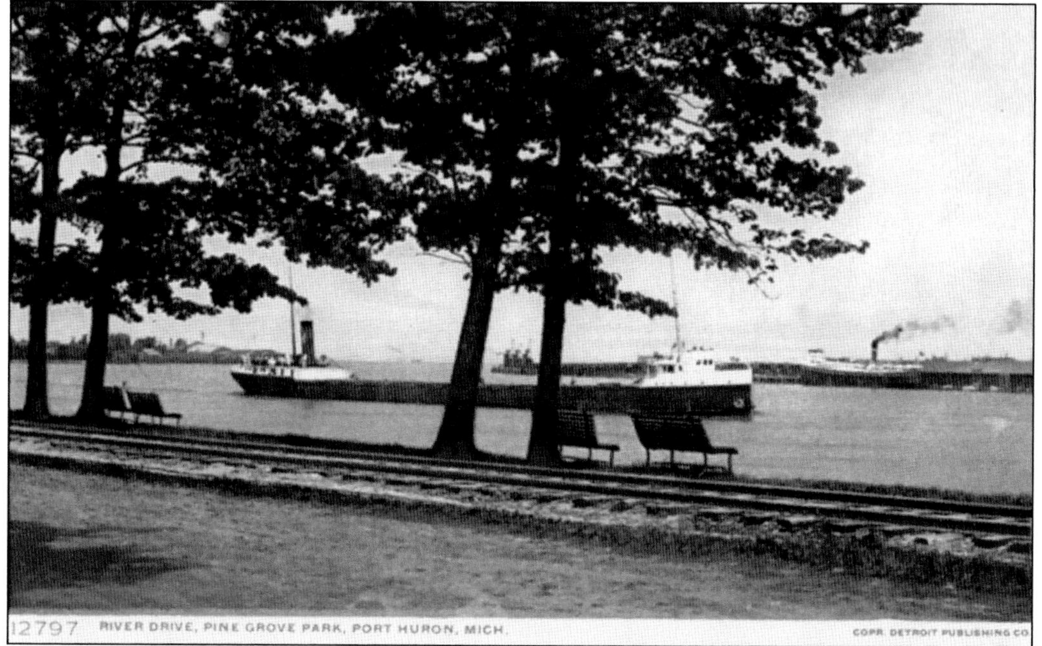


An early steel freighter, probably 500 to 600 feet in length, is visible in this view, taken from Pine Grove in the early 1900s. The track of the Pere Marquette Railway line to Croswell and points north can be seen in the foreground.

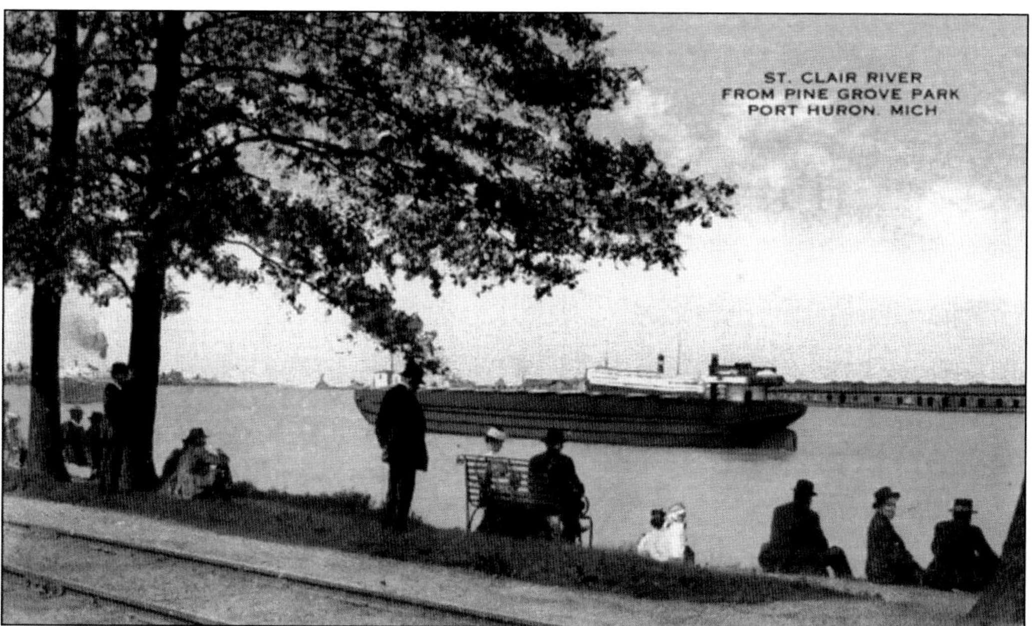


Although similar to the above postcard, this view shows a whaleback, or "pig-boat," designed by marine architect Alexander McDougall. Shaping hulls similar to a cigar, McDougall intended to create a ship where waves rolled over it rather than slammed into it. Although believed by many on the Great Lakes to be a new phenomena, this image shows that freighter watching has been a popular pastime in Port Huron form many years.

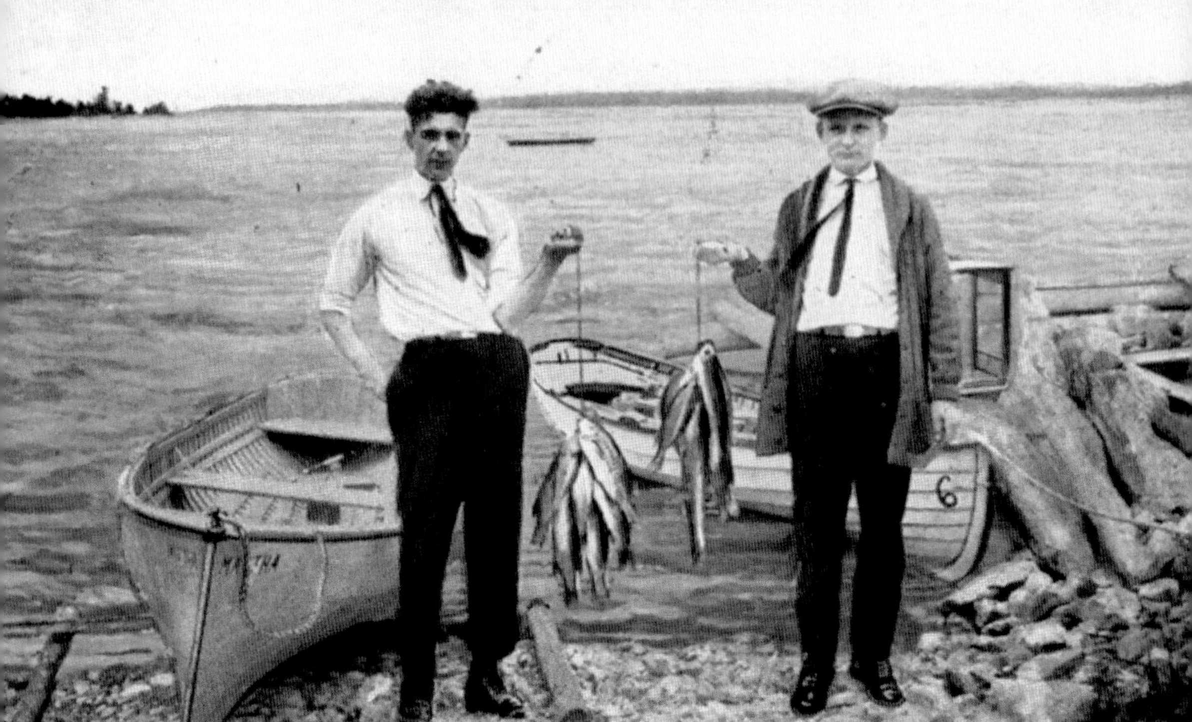


These sport fisherman have quite the catch in this *c.* 1920 view. Catches of this sort were unheard of for many years, as bad environmental and fishing practices decreased the quality of fishing on the St. Clair River. Recent strides for cleaner water and better habitats seem to have borne fruit, however, and fisherman can once again be seen lining the banks of the river on summer nights.

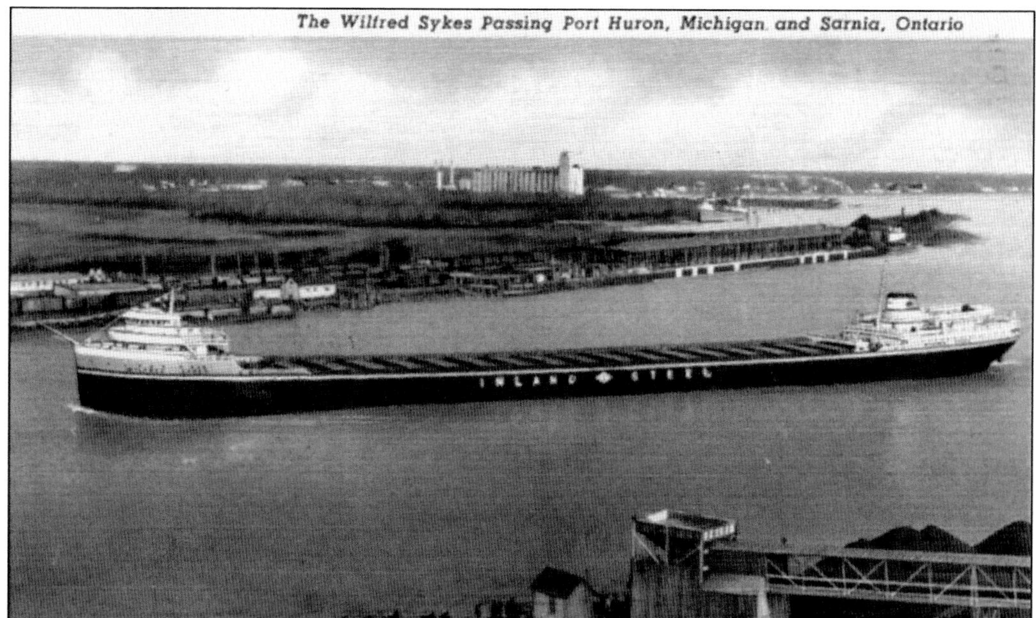


Taken by local photographer Russell E. Sawyer, this *c.* 1950 view shows the nearly new *Wilfred Sykes* passing the Peerless Cement plant in Port Huron and the Canadian Steamship Lines dock in Sarnia, Ontario. Built in 1949 by the American Shipbuilding Company of Lorain, Ohio, for the Inland Steel Company, the *Sykes* was the first new Great Lakes freighter to be completed after World War II. She still carries cargos to this day, nearly 60 years after her construction.

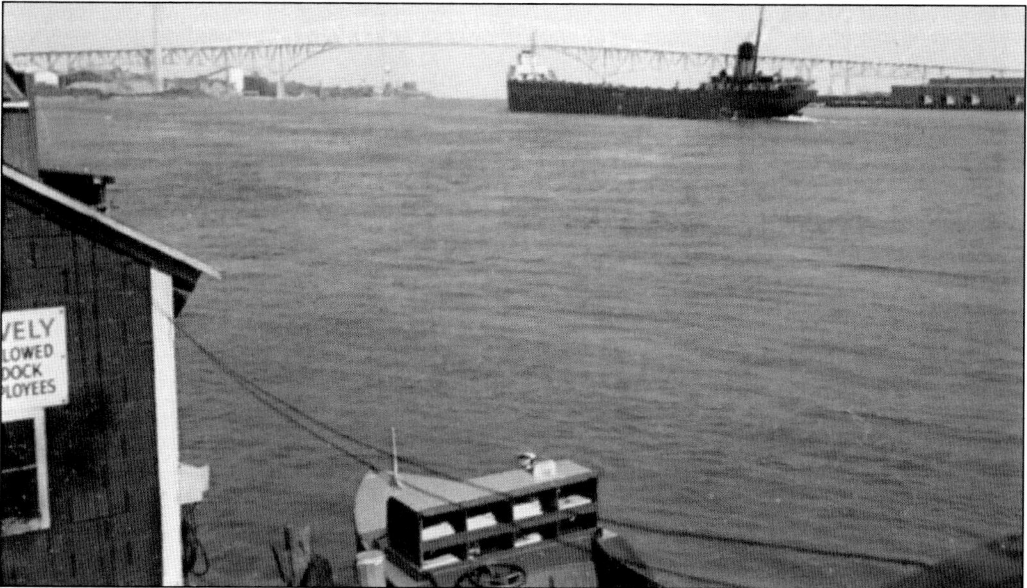

The *Daniel J. Morrell* readies to enter Lake Huron in this 1950s view taken from the J. W. Wescott Company's mail boat dock. Although better known for its Detroit operation, the James T. Lynn Marine Service (later the J. W. Wescott Company) also delivered mail to waiting seaman from a location in Port Huron for well over 100 years. The *Morrell* continued to sail until November 1966, when it broke in half in Lake Huron near Pointe Aux Barques. Only one of her 29-man crew, Dennis Hale, survived to tell the tale of her sinking.

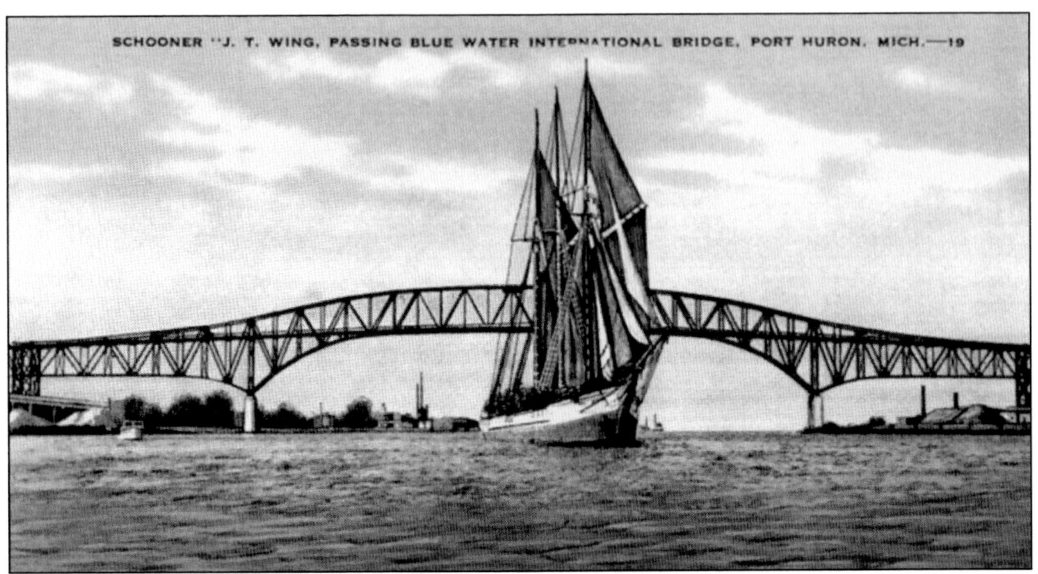


This 1939 image of the schooner *J. T. Wing* passing beneath the first Blue Water Bridge has become one of the most iconic in Port Huron tourism. Taken by Fred Askar, it shows the last commercial schooner on the Great Lakes on one of her final commercial voyages. Although she survived to be turned into the first Dossin Marine Museum on Belle Isle in Detroit, the *Wing*'s reprieve would be short, as her elderly condition was such that she needed a great deal of repair. After just a few short years as a museum ship, she was stripped of all her salvageable assets and set afire in 1959.

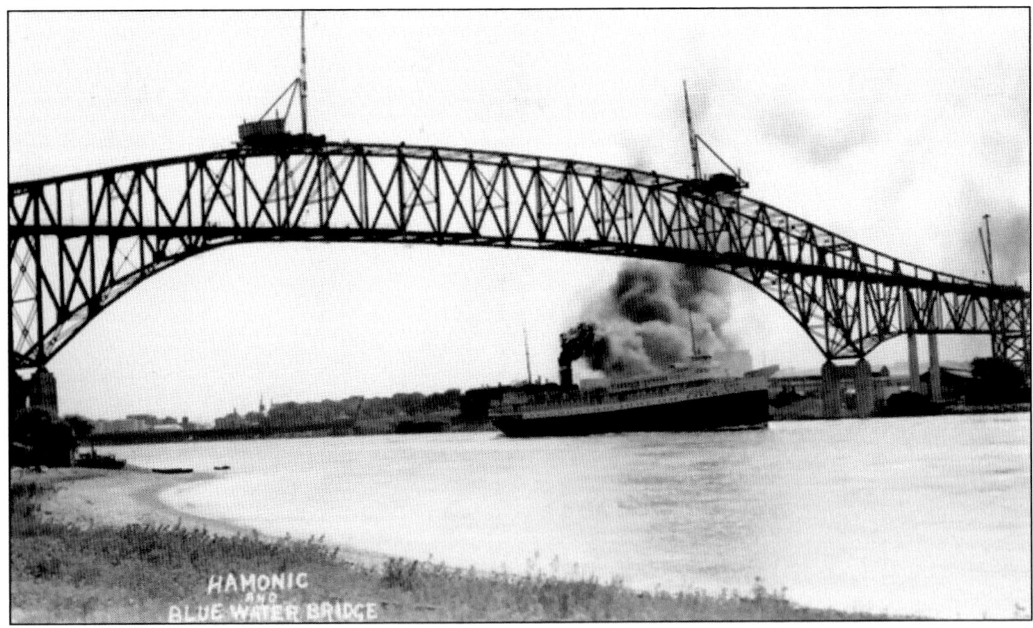


The passenger steamer *Hamonic* travels beneath the nearly completed first Blue Water Bridge about 1938. Built in 1908, the *Hamonic*, along with her CSL sisters *Noronic* and *Huronic*, was one of the most popular Great Lakes passenger ships. On July 17, 1945, the *Hamonic* caught fire at her dock in Pointe Edward, Ontario. Through the heroic actions of the U.S. Coast Guard and others, all but three of her passengers and crew were saved.

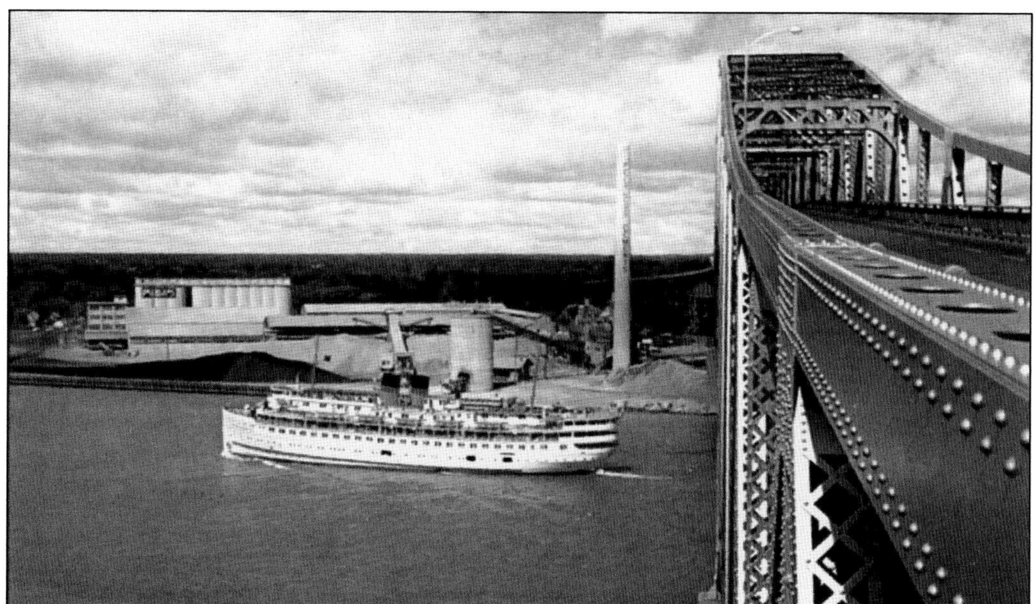

One of the last Great Lakes passenger steamers, the Georgian Bay Lines *North American* passes the Peerless Cement Company and beneath the first Blue Water Bridge in the early 1960s. Built in 1913, the *North American* and her sister ship, the *South American*, plied the Great Lakes for 50 years. In 1963, the *North American* was sold to Canadian interests and sank in September 1967 while under tow 25 miles from the *Cape Hatteras* lightship, where she lies today.

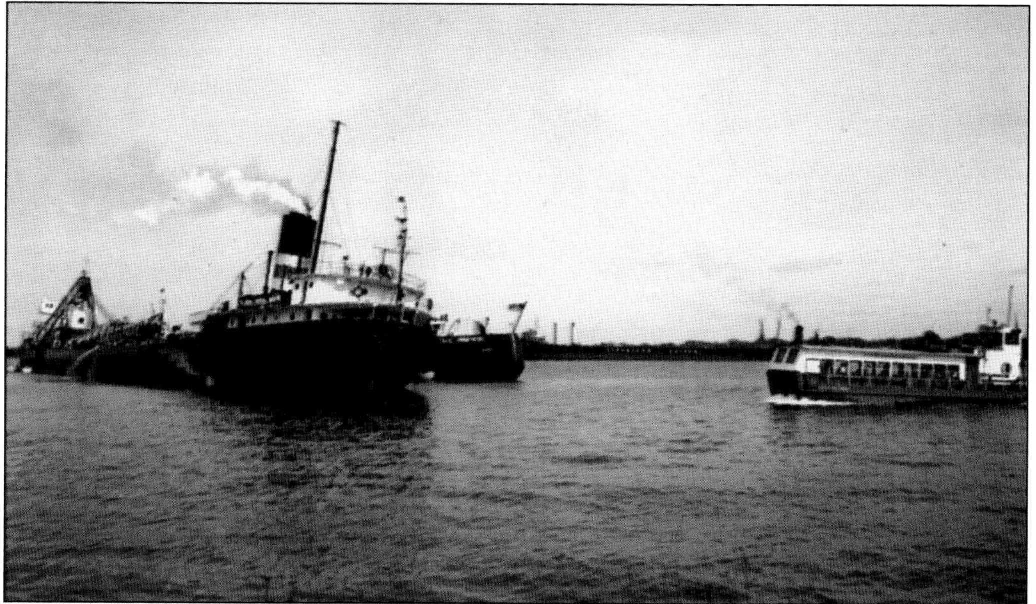

The passenger ferry *City of Port Huron*, made from a World War II troop carrier, travels past the disabled Great Lakes freighter *George F. Rand* on her daily trip to Sarnia, Ontario. The St. Clair River has always been a busy and dangerous waterway to navigate, as evidenced by the collision of the downbound *George F. Rand* with the upbound *Harvey H. Brown* on October 18, 1951. The *Rand* was refloated and repaired, renamed the *Avondale*, and went on to sail for another 30 years before being sent to Spain for scrapping in the early 1980s.

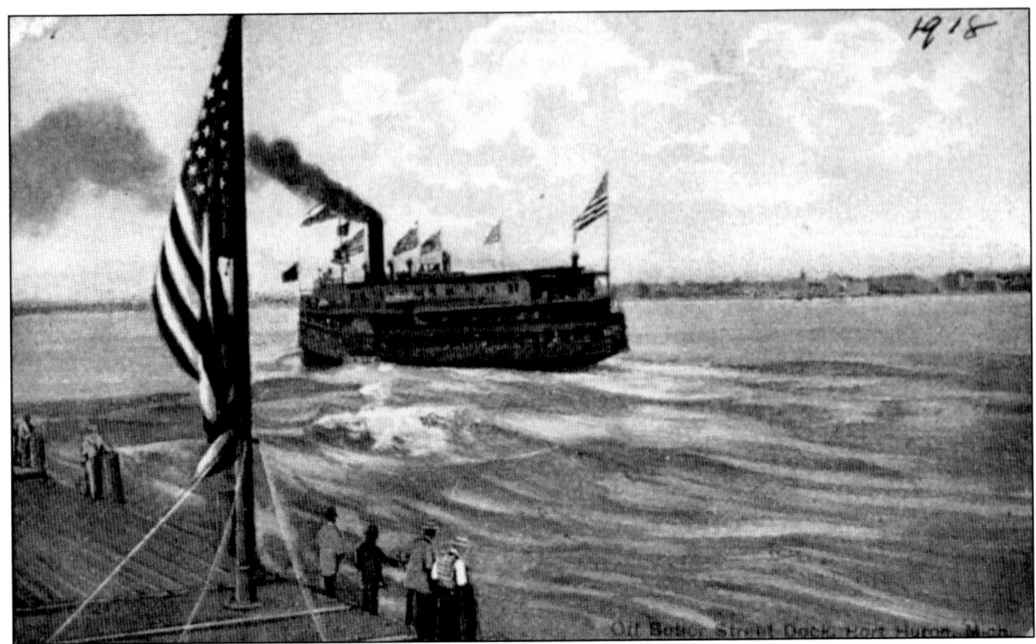


In this *c.* 1918 view, spectators watch a passenger boat leave the Butler Street dock. Although the image is stylized, one can make out that it is most likely a Detroit and Cleveland boat, quite possibly the *City of Alpena* or *City of Mackinac*, both of which plied the route from Detroit to Mackinac Island for many years.

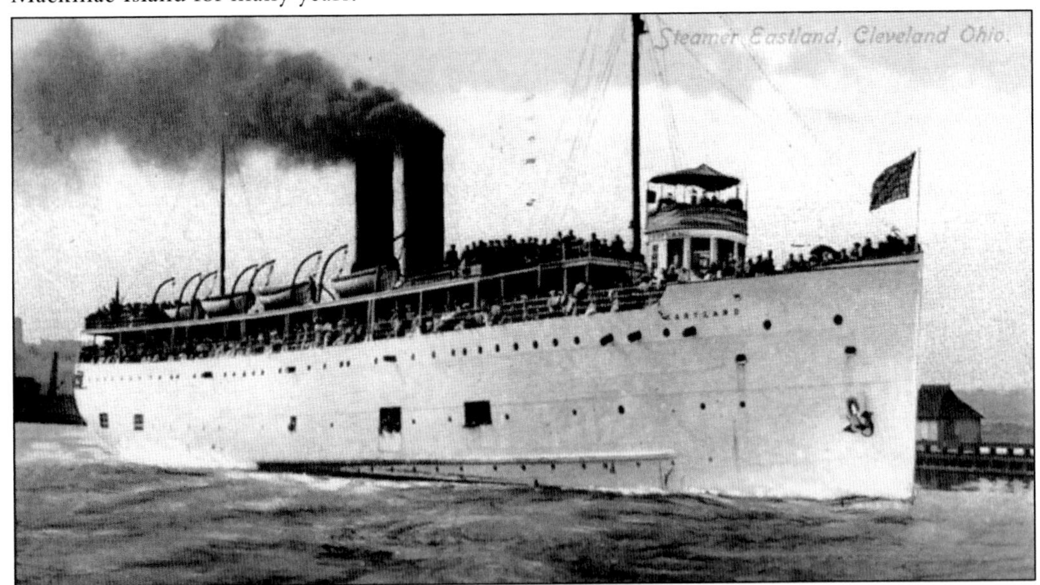


The passenger steamer *Eastland* was built by the Jenks Shipbuilding Company of Port Huron in 1903. Although a popular boat in her day, she had a reputation for being unstable in heavy weather. This reputation proved true when on July 24, 1915, the *Eastland* rolled over in the middle of downtown Chicago while loading passengers for a Western Union company picnic. The mass confusion, mixed with the many languages of the new immigrants crowding her decks and cabins, led to a death toll of 835 people, making it the worst disaster in terms of lives lost in Great Lakes history.

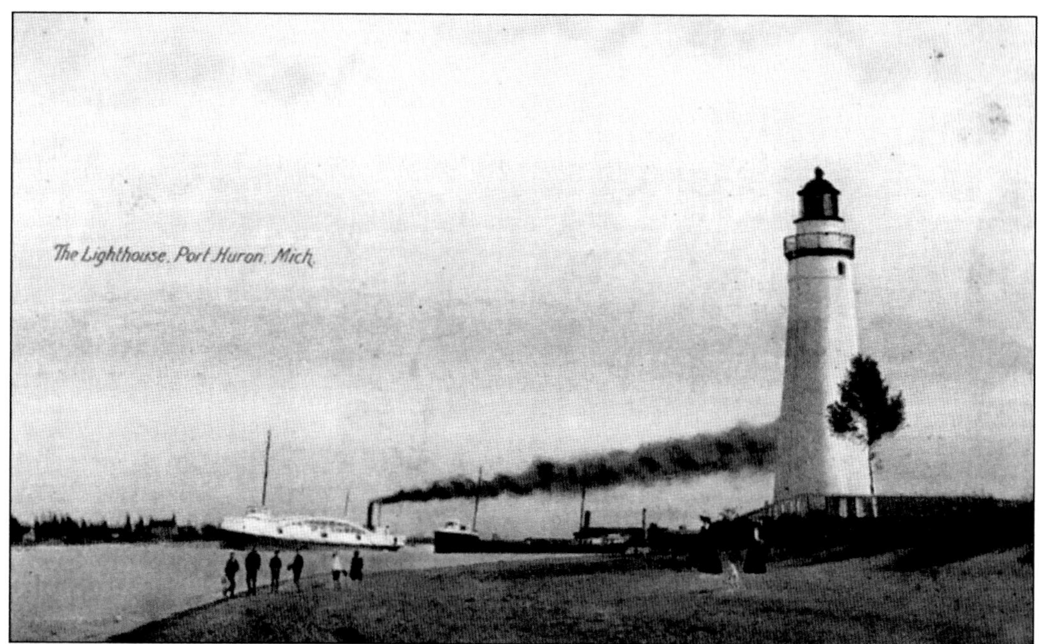


This early-1880s image of the Fort Gratiot Lighthouse was taken from what is now Lighthouse Park in Port Huron. Built in 1829, the Fort Gratiot Lighthouse is Michigan's oldest and the second oldest on the Great Lakes. Only Marblehead's lighthouse, built in 1825, is older than the Fort Gratiot.

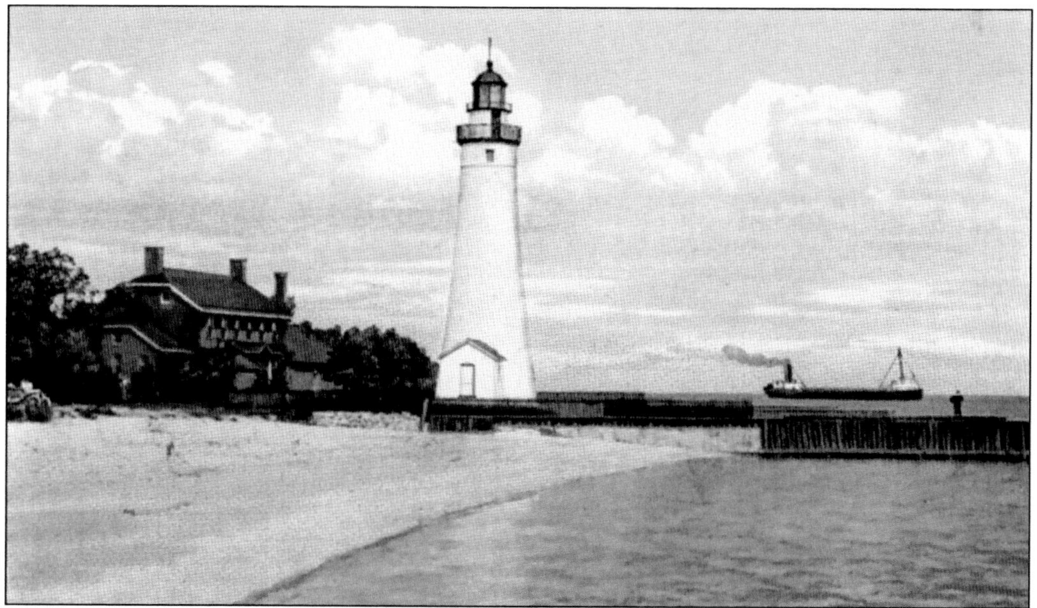

Pictured here in the 1920s, the original dock and lighthouse keeper's duplex was built in 1874. It replaced the first keeper's home, which had burned due to the negligent keeper putting candles on his Christmas tree, a rule violation of the United States Lighthouse Service. Still standing today, the duplex currently houses U.S. Coast Guard personnel, but will soon be restored under the auspices of the Port Huron Museum.

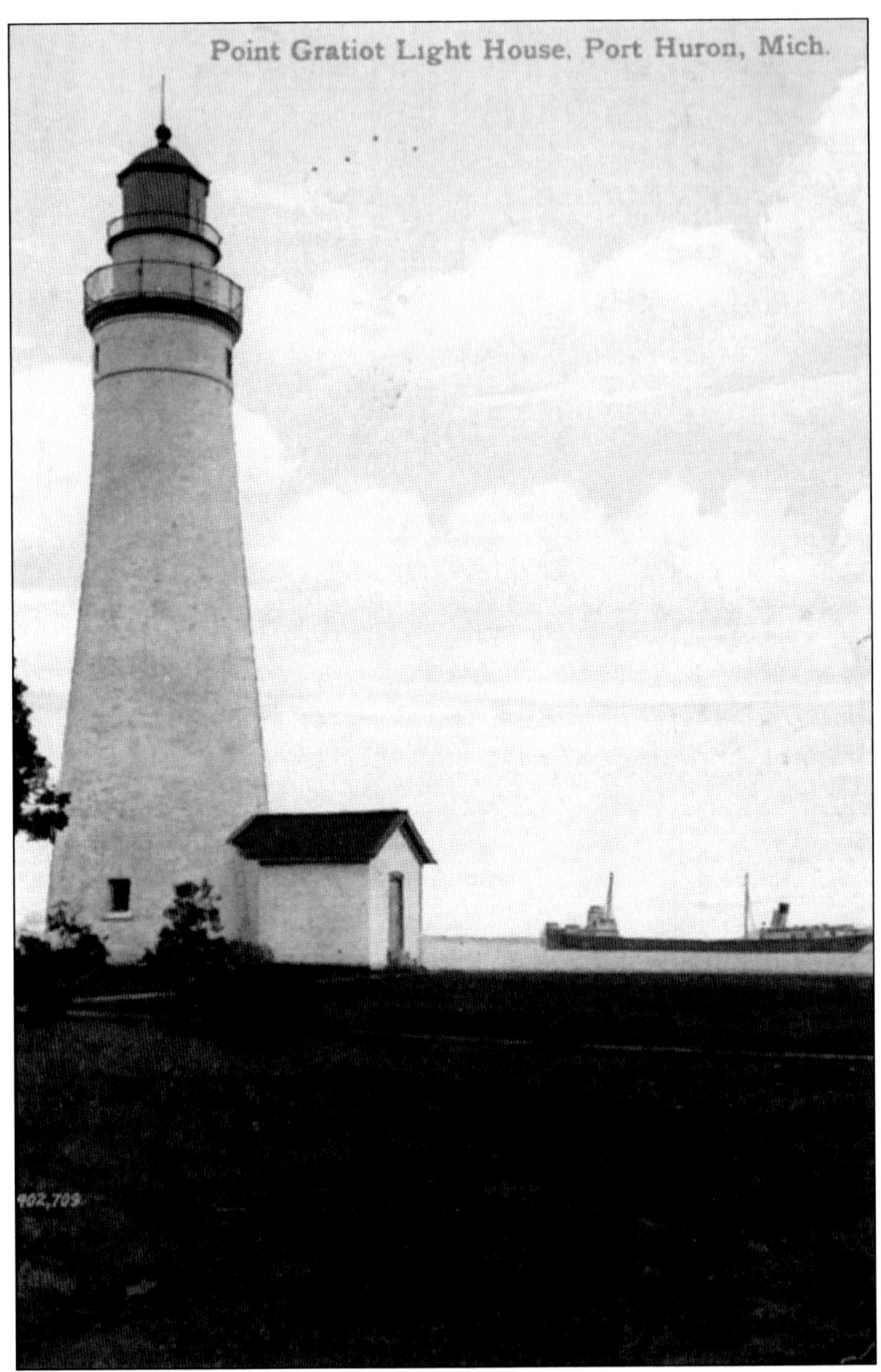


One of the few photographs giving an indication of the Fort Gratiot Lighthouse's full 86-foot height, this image was taken by the photographer Henry Denkleberg prior to 1913. It can be partially dated because the savage storm of November 1913 so damaged the tower and its foundation that a retaining wall was built the next year to prevent further wave destruction.

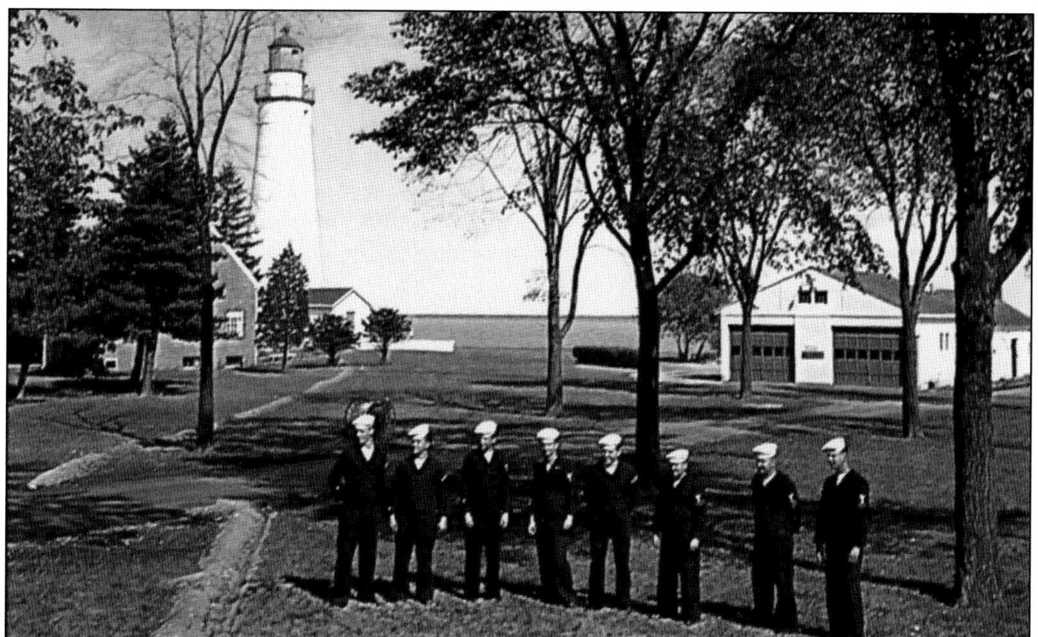

Seen in the 1950s is the eight-man United States Coast Guard crew posted at the Port Huron Station. A series of Dutch Elm trees, destroyed in the 1960s by Dutch Elm disease, is visible, along with the 1932-built maintenance garage and head of the station home. Much of the right-hand corner of this view is occupied by the new Port Huron Station, built and opened in 2003.

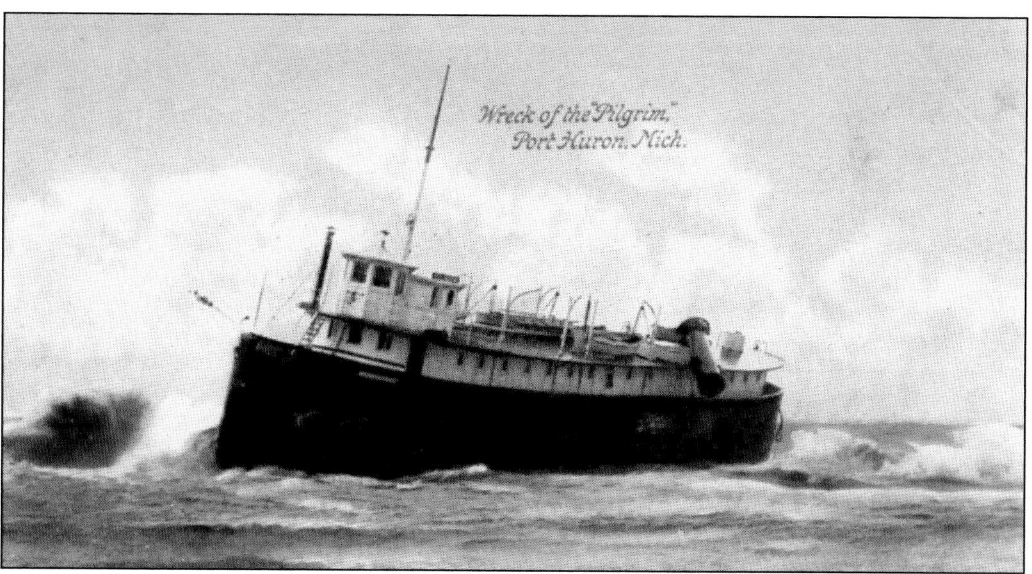


Scenes such as this required the constant vigilance of the U.S. Coast Guard's predecessor organization, the United States Life Saving Service. Built at Saugatuk in 1888, the passenger steamer *Pilgrim* plied the Lake Huron route from Port Hope to Port Huron for many years, transporting passengers and freight between the small coastal communities. On April 29, 1907, she struck an ice floe in an early-season run, and her captain beached her near what is now Lakeside Beach in order to save her. Although attempts were made to salvage her, she was driven too far up on the beach to recover and became a total loss.

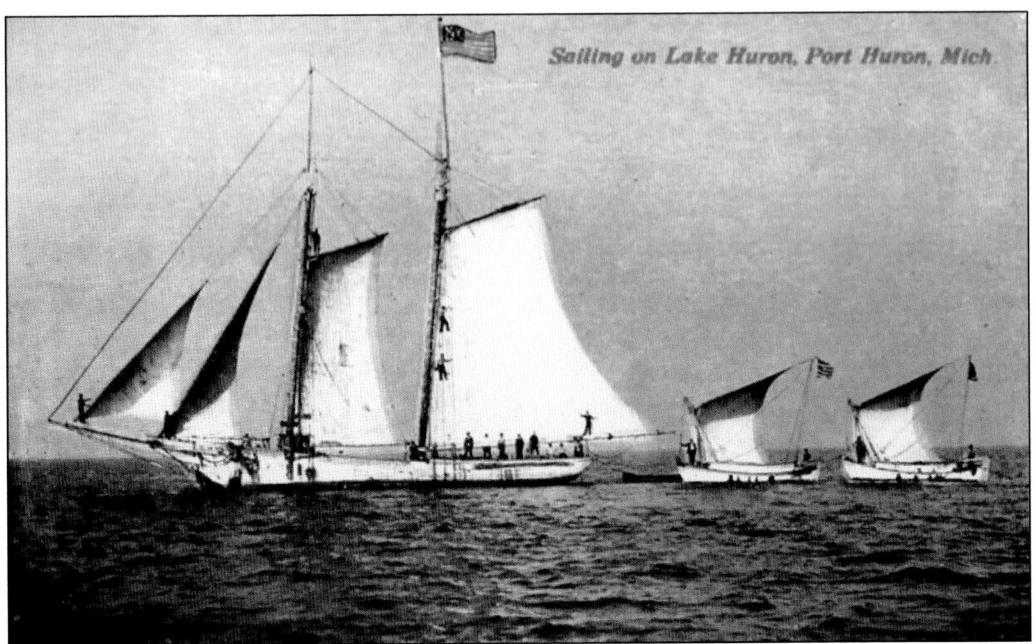


This *c.* 1900 view shows a typical schooner of the age on the Great Lakes. Although this image is a bit staged for the photographer (note the two dinghies and the men posing on various places on the schooner), it gives a sense of what the average citizen in Port Huron would have seen prior to the age of steam.

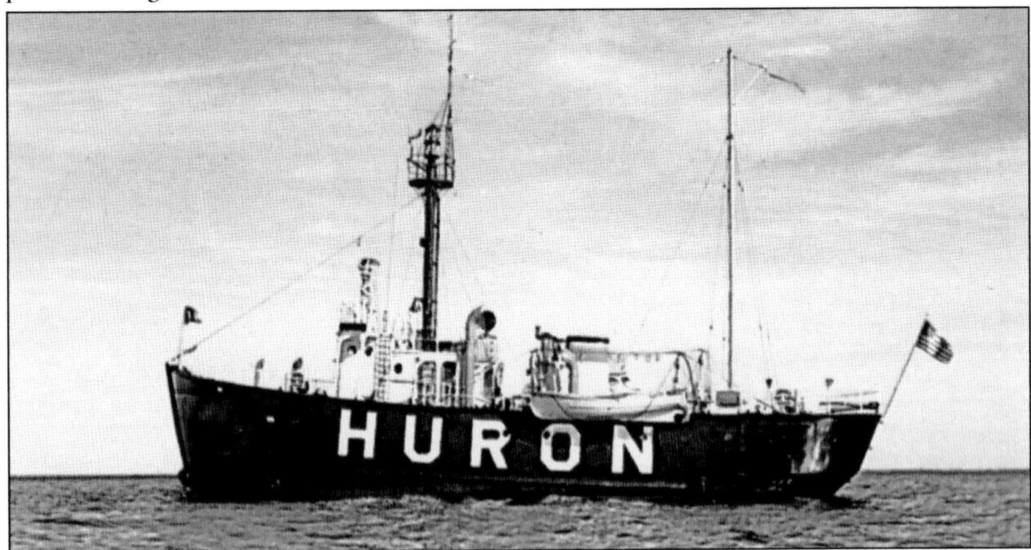


The *Huron* lightship is stationed in Lake Huron in the 1950s. Built in 1920, LV-103 was also based at Manitou and served for a time as the relief lightship. In 1935, she was moved to Corsica Shoals near Port Huron, where she marked the freighter channel and warned freighters of the treacherous sand bars in the area. Nicknamed "Old B-O" due to the sound of her foghorn, she remained on station until her decommissioning in 1970 as the last lightship on the Great Lakes. She was presented to the City of Port Huron and permanently landlocked at Pine Grove Park in 1972. Lovingly restored in the late 1980s and early 1990s, she became the first satellite site of the Port Huron Museum in 1990 and can be toured during the summer months.

# *Five*

# Serving the Community

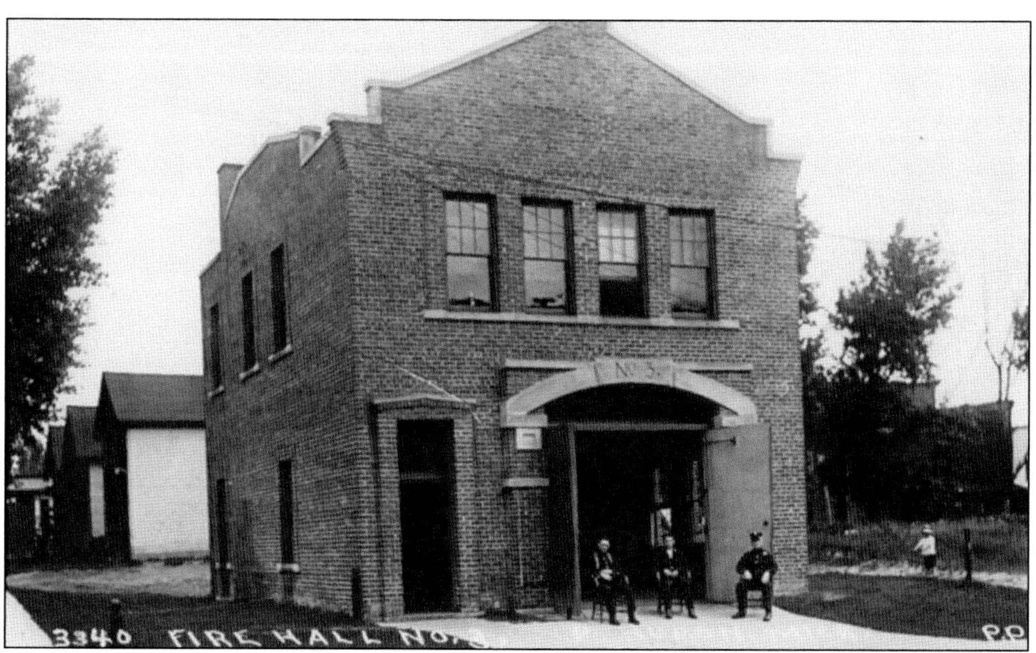


It seems to be a relaxing day at the No. 3 Fire Hall in this *c.* 1905 Louis Pesha view. At the time of its construction, sometime around 1900, No. 3 was one of the newest fire stations in the state. Constructed of brick, it broke with the tradition of its predecessor stations, which had been primarily wood. It included sleeping quarters for the men on duty and room enough for a single truck.

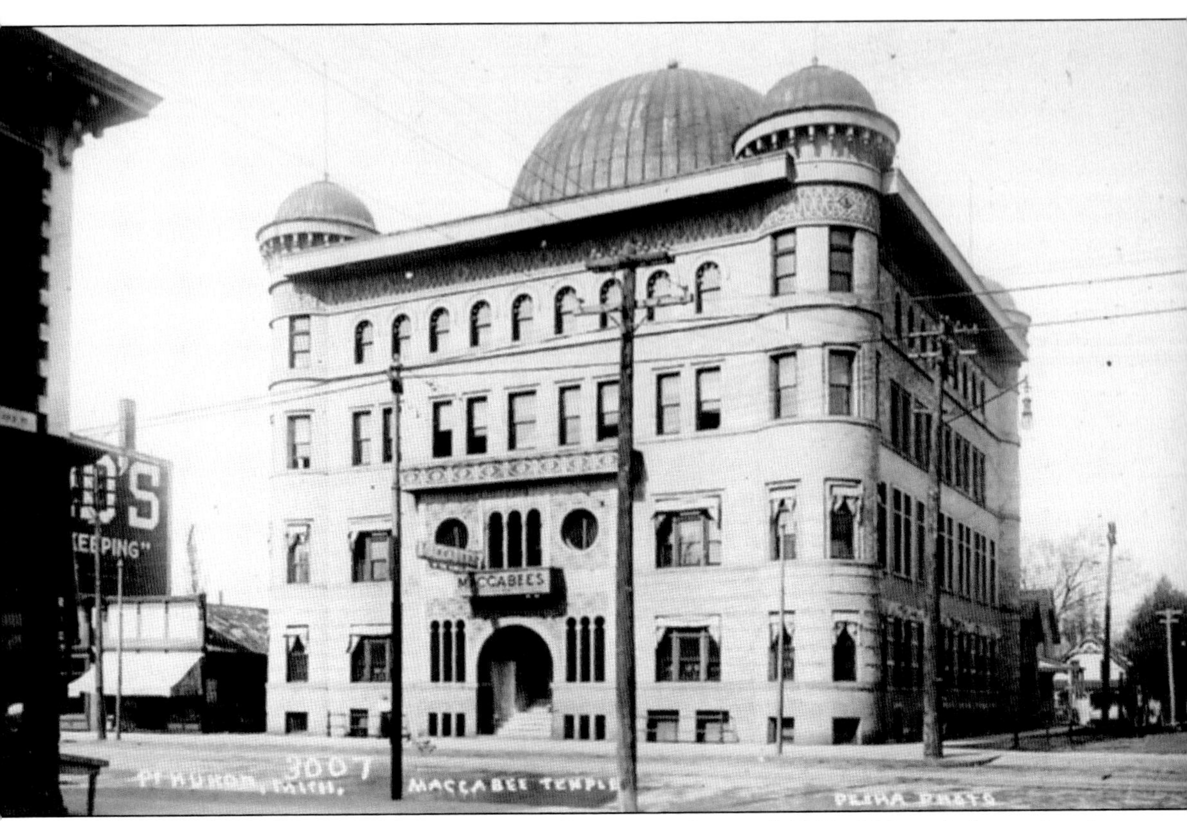


The Fraternal Order of the Maccabees hall is pictured around 1900. Although shown in a later image in chapter one, the hall did once bear a central copper dome, as evidenced here, as well as the three smaller domes over its towers. One of the only Port Huron buildings known to have a Moorish influence, it remained the headquarters of the Maccabees until 1904, when a new building was constructed at the point where Huron and Pine Grove Avenues converged.

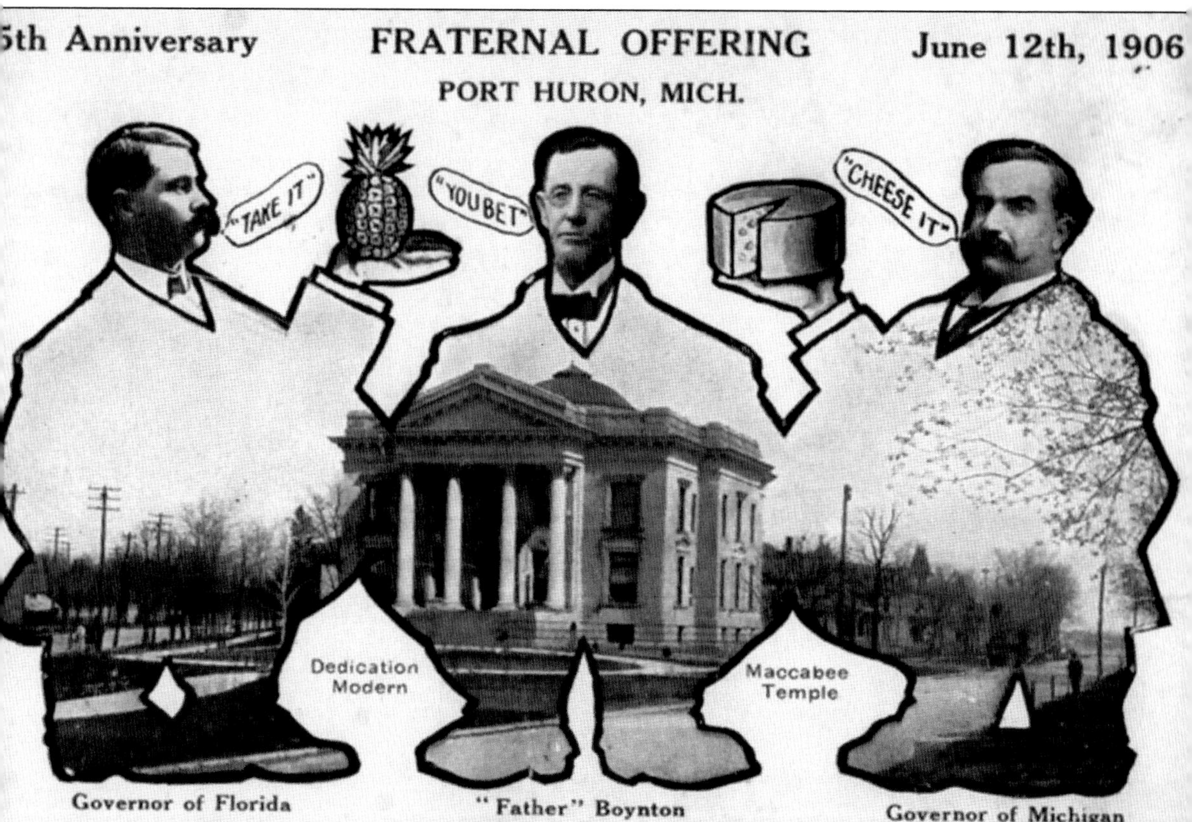


This cartoon-like card was created for the 25th anniversary of the founding of the Fraternal Order of the Maccabees in 1906. It shows the governors of Florida and Michigan flanking Nathan Boynton, the supreme commander and father of the order. Boynton had direct connections with both states; he not only founded the Maccabee order here, but helped create the community of Boynton Beach, Florida, which was named for him.

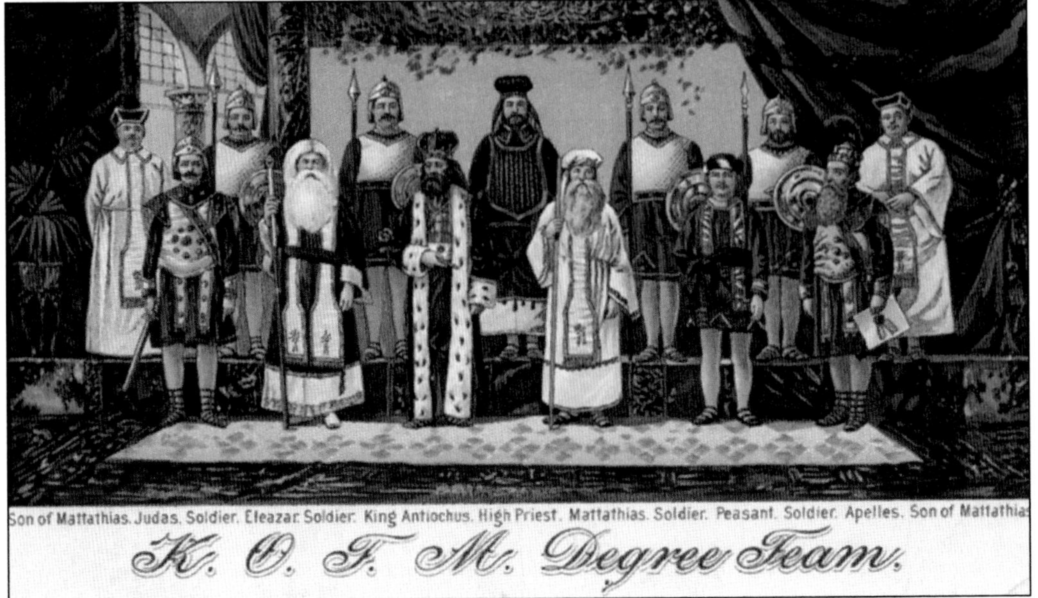


This very rare postcard shows the complete degree team of the Maccabee fraternal order about 1898. Founded in 1871 by Nathan S. Boynton, the organization had grown to a membership of over 90,000 by 1900. Originally designed as a beneficiary order, it eventually became an insurance firm, consolidating its offices in Detroit after Boynton's death.

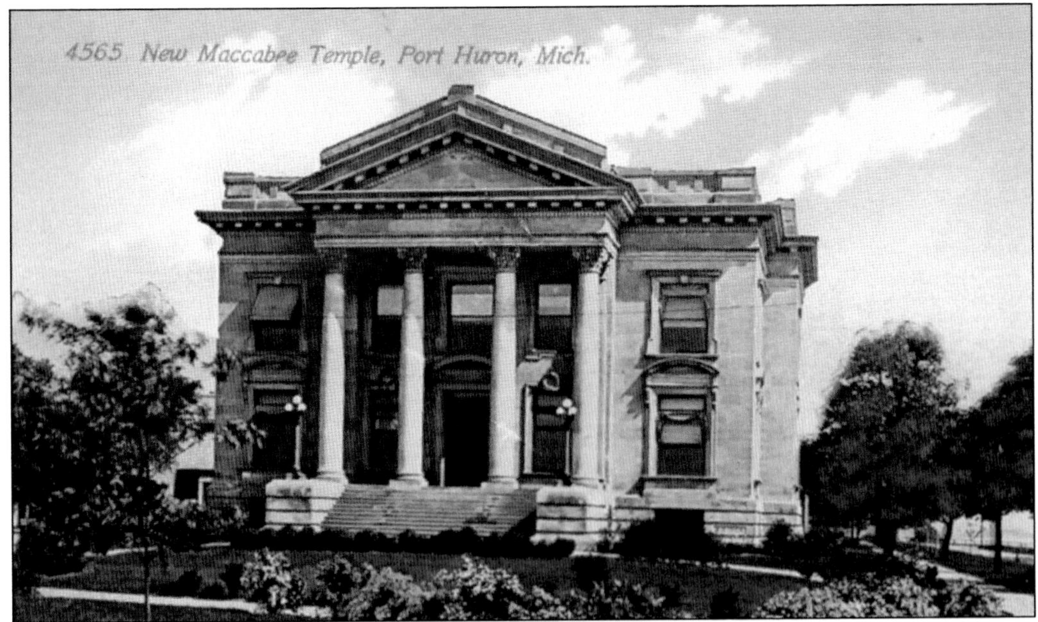


The final home of the Maccabees while in Port Huron, this Beaux Arts structure began being constructed in 1904, but was not completed until 1906. After the order moved to Detroit in the 1920s, the building became home to the Port Huron Junior College. Still standing on its 100th birthday, it now houses the law offices of Hill and Devendorf, among others.

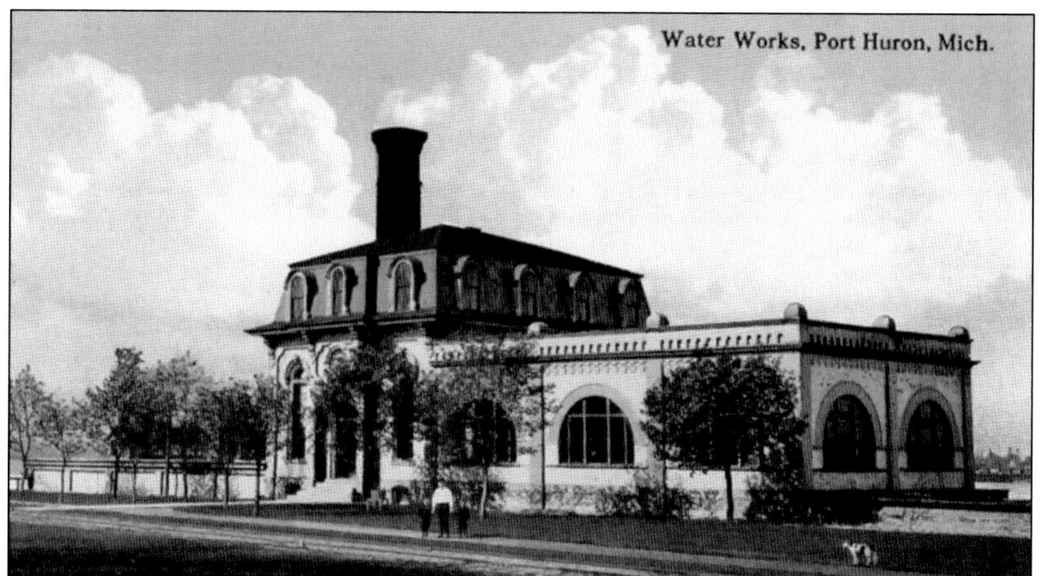


In a scene very changed from today, a man, his two boys, and a young dog stand in front of Port Huron's first waterworks building. Constructed in the 1870s, the first water and sewage treatment center greatly enhanced the health of the community, reducing the number of cases of dysentery, cholera, and other water-born diseases by nearly 75 percent within two years. All but the lower half of the building was torn down and replaced in the early 1950s, with the upper half used today as an observation deck.

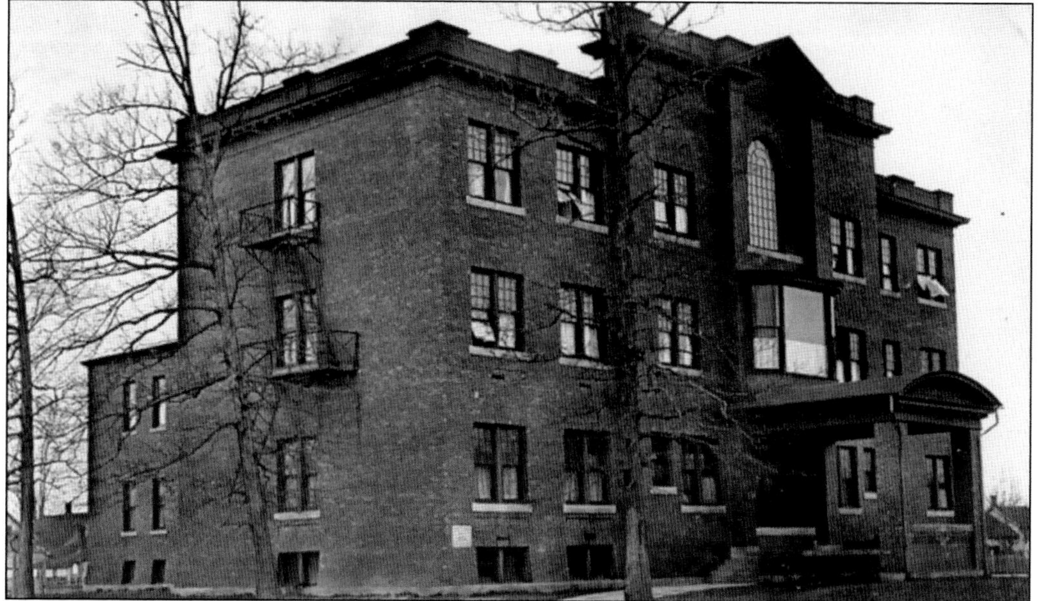

The second Port Huron Hospital building, pictured around 1910, is located at the corner of Stone and Richardson Streets. A somewhat unusual feature of the rather mundane space is the operating room, situated on the second floor. Originally founded in a converted home on White Street in 1882, the Port Huron Hospital built this structure as a response to the northward growth of the city limits. Several additions built, Port Huron Hospital has grown into one of the premiere health care centers in southeast Michigan.

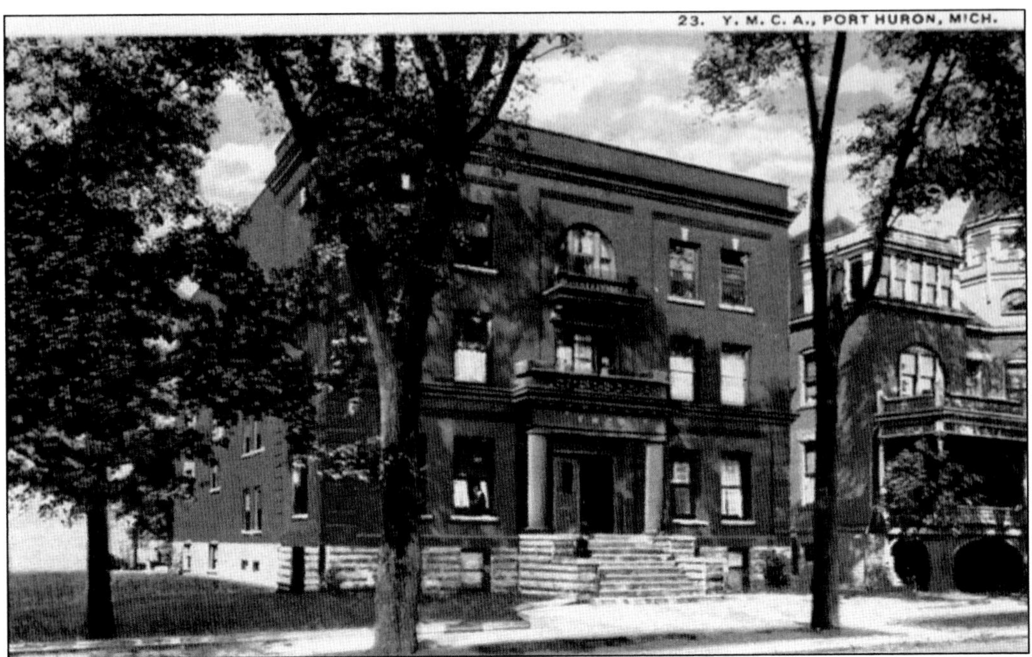


The YMCA building at 937 Sixth Street is shown in this *c.* 1925 view. Founded in 1886, the local chapter of the YMCA remained in this structure until the mid-1950s, when it moved to a location at the corner of Glenwood Avenue and Fort Streets in Port Huron.

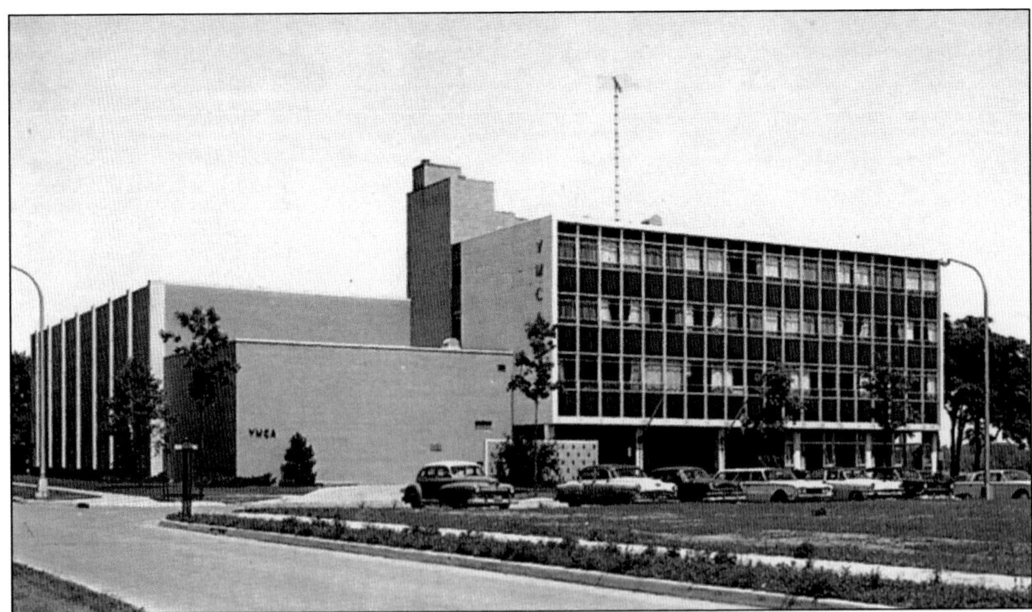


The new YMCA opened at 700 Fort Street in 1959. Constructed by the firm of Collins and Caitlin, this thoroughly modern structure greatly enhanced the organization's ability to serve its membership in the community, as well as those young men traveling to our area. Now nearly 50 years old, this building, too, has outlived its usefulness, and a multi-million-dollar campaign over the past five years has led to the groundbreaking of a new structure to be located at the corner of Fourth and Griswold Streets as part of the Acheson Ventures revitalization project.

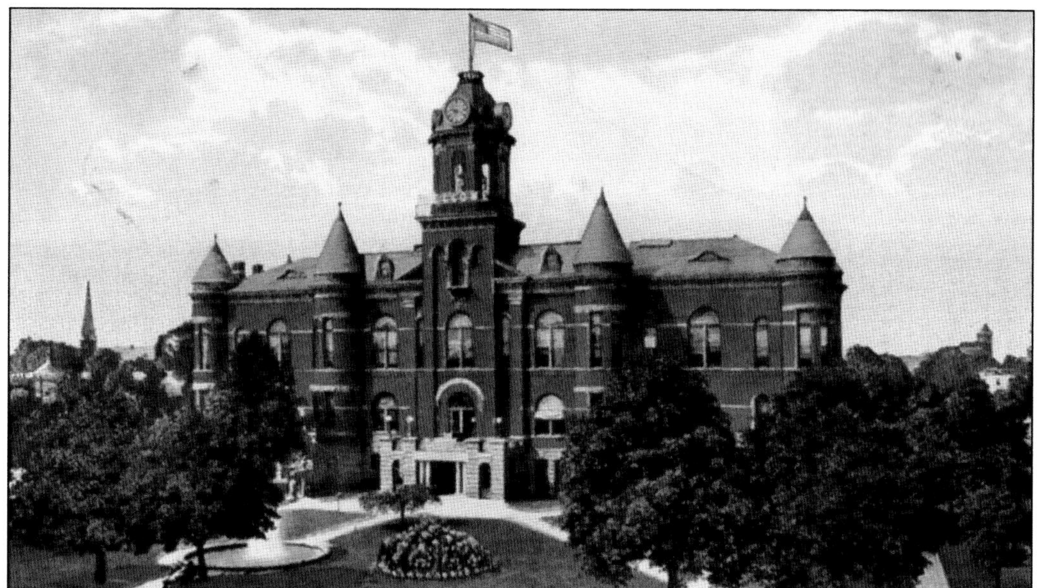

First constructed in the late 1860s, the Port Huron City Hall was added onto in 1886, creating the building in this 1920s view. One of the most recognized structures in its day, it housed the Port Huron city offices, the Port Huron Police Department, and the county clerk, as well as several other city and county offices. This magnificent building burned in 1949, but its bell, which fell three flights to the basement during the fire, was removed and restored and now rests on the lawn of the St. Clair County Court House on McMorran Boulevard.

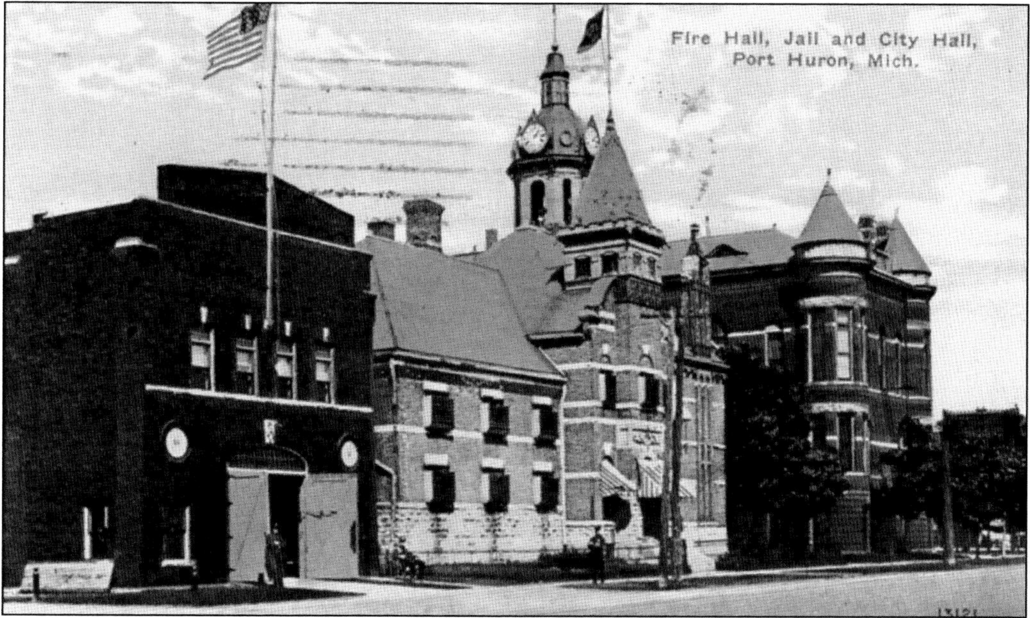


This 1920s view shows, from left to right, the Port Huron No. 2 Fire Hall, the city/county jail, and the backside of the Port Huron City Hall on Butler Street. Built between the 1860s and the 1890s, all three of these structures remained relatively unchanged for nearly 50 years. With the burning of city hall in 1949, things began to change, and by 1955 none were standing. Broad Street was even renamed McMorran Boulevard.

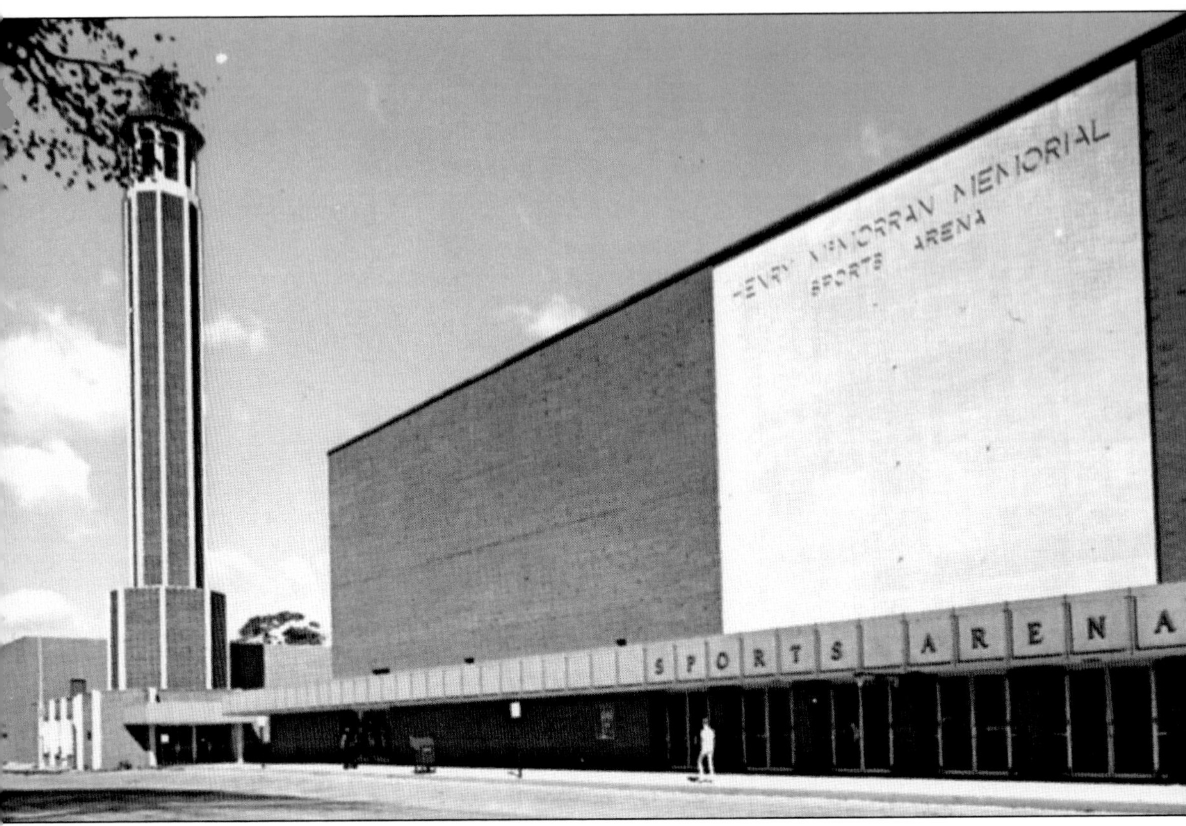


What a difference a decade can make in the face of a city. Although this is a similar view to the previous, all similarities stop there. The Henry McMorran Auditorium and Sports Arena was designed by the famous Midland-based architect Alden Dow, a student of Frank Lloyd Wright. The money to construct the arena was donated by Andrew Murphy and his wife, Emma McMorran Murphy, in memory of Henry Gordon McMorran, Emma's father. Between 1953 and 1966, the McMorran Sports Complex grew to become the center of entertainment in downtown Port Huron. Now almost 50 years old, it remains the home of the Port Huron Flags minor-league hockey team, as well as that of the first Great Lakes Football League champion, the Port Huron Pirates. Since 1961, it has hosted the finals of the International Silver Stick Hockey Tournament, whose Pee Wee and Bantam finals bring players from all over the United States and Canada each January.

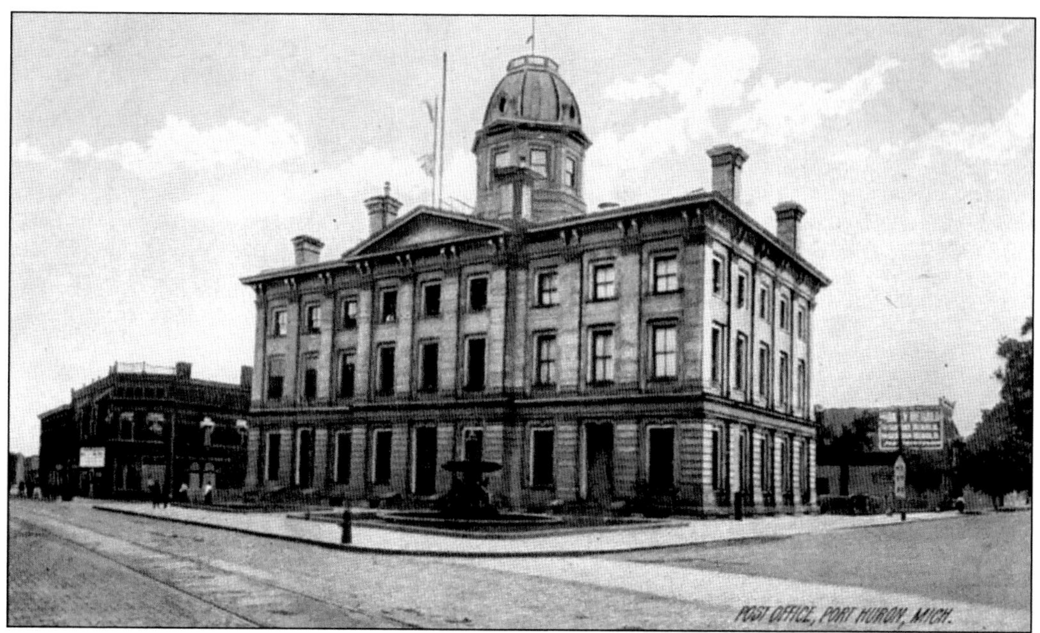


The Port Huron Customs House and Post Office is pictured here around 1910. This building has served the community for over 120 years. The location, however, has changed greatly in the 90 years since this photograph was taken. The Citizens First Savings Bank drive-through and the *Port Huron Times Herald/USA Today* building now take up most of the surrounding area.

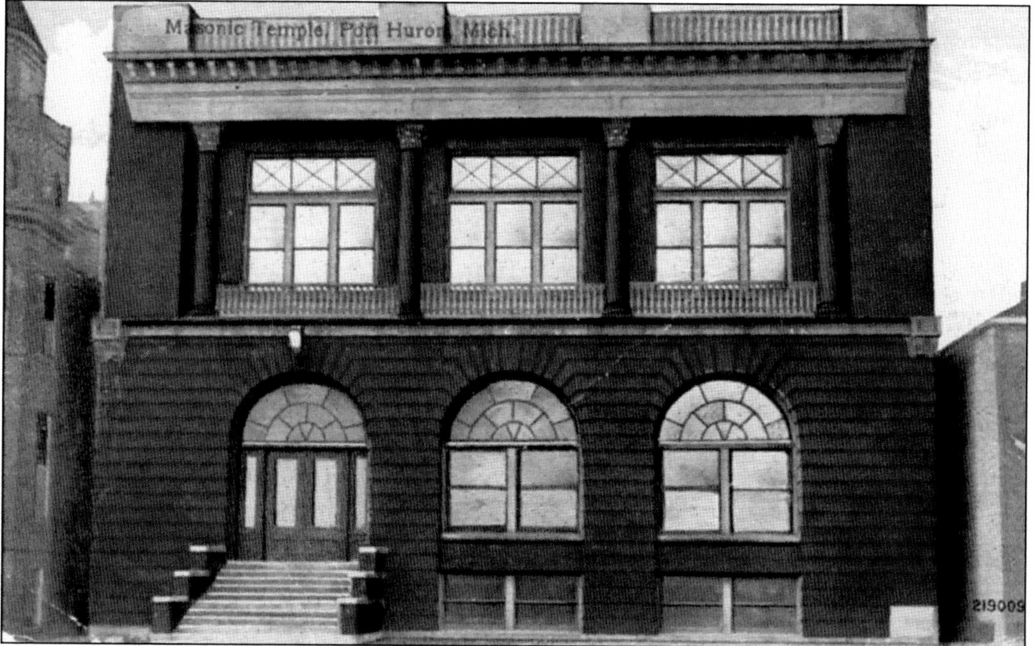


The Port Huron Masonic Temple, built in 1902, has remained an important part of the fraternal community in Port Huron for over 100 years. Nearly destroyed by fire in the 1980s, the Mason center at 927 Sixth Street has seen dramatic changes to its interior. It remains almost original on the exterior, with only a small addition for an elevator in the late 1980s interrupting the original facade.

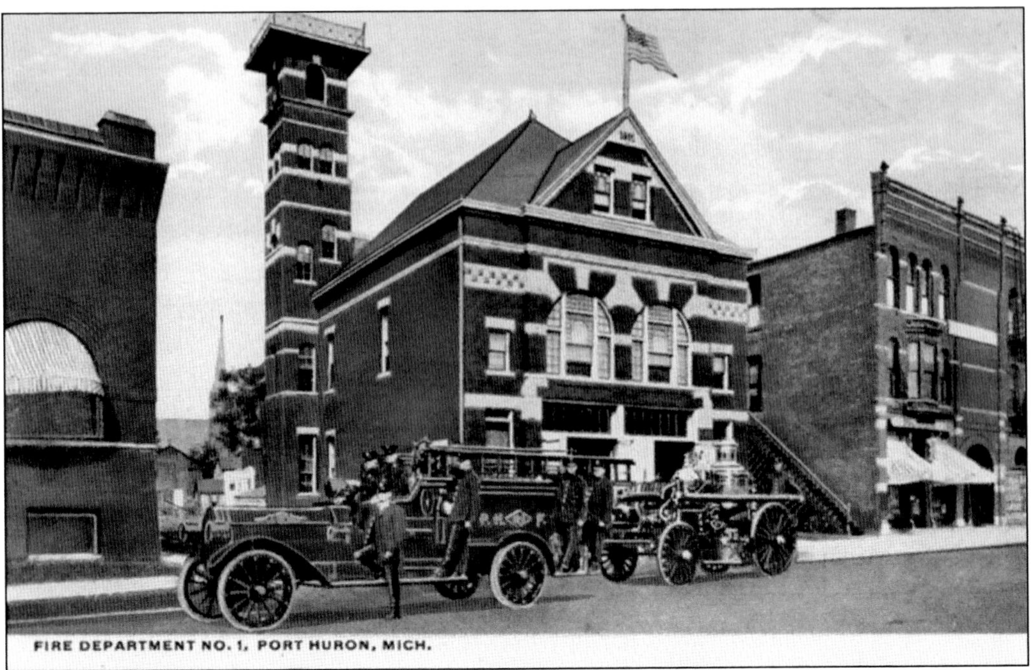


The men of Ladder Company No. 1 pose with their old and new equipment in this *c.* 1915 view. Built in 1891 at 813 Seventh Street, the Port Huron Engine Company No. 1 replaced an older wooden structure located elsewhere which dated to the 1860s. To the left is the original Michigan Bell Telephone Exchange building, and to the right is the Mills Drug Store.

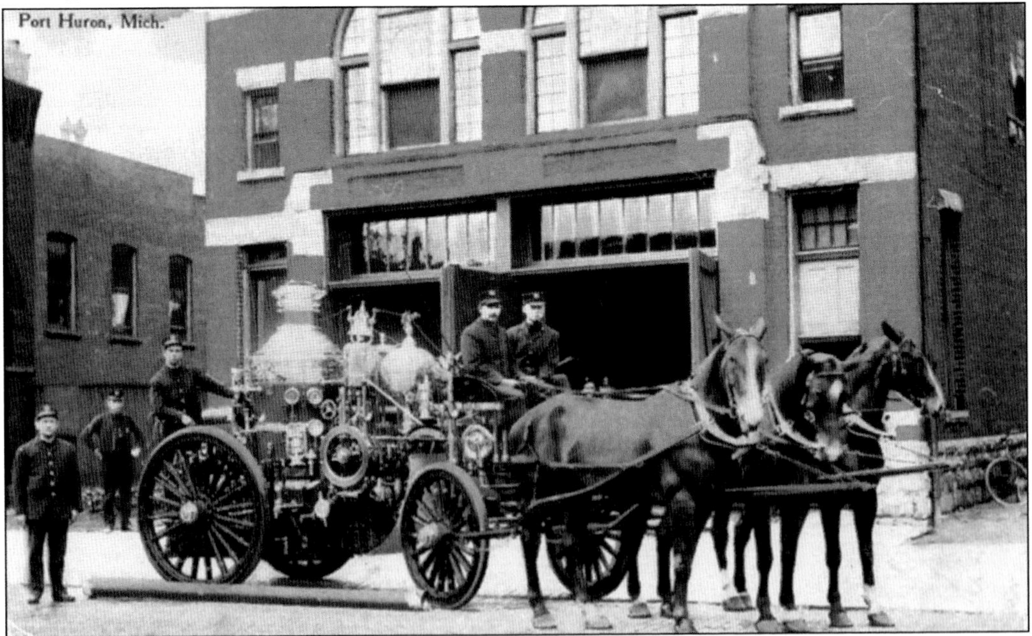


This early-1900s view gives a closeup of the horse-drawn steam pumper and the facade of Engine House No. 1. Sadly, this building was demolished in the early 1960s. Of the buildings shown in this and the prior view, only the former Michigan Bell Telephone building still stands today, now home to the Blue Water Clubhouse and the St. Clair County Council on Aging.

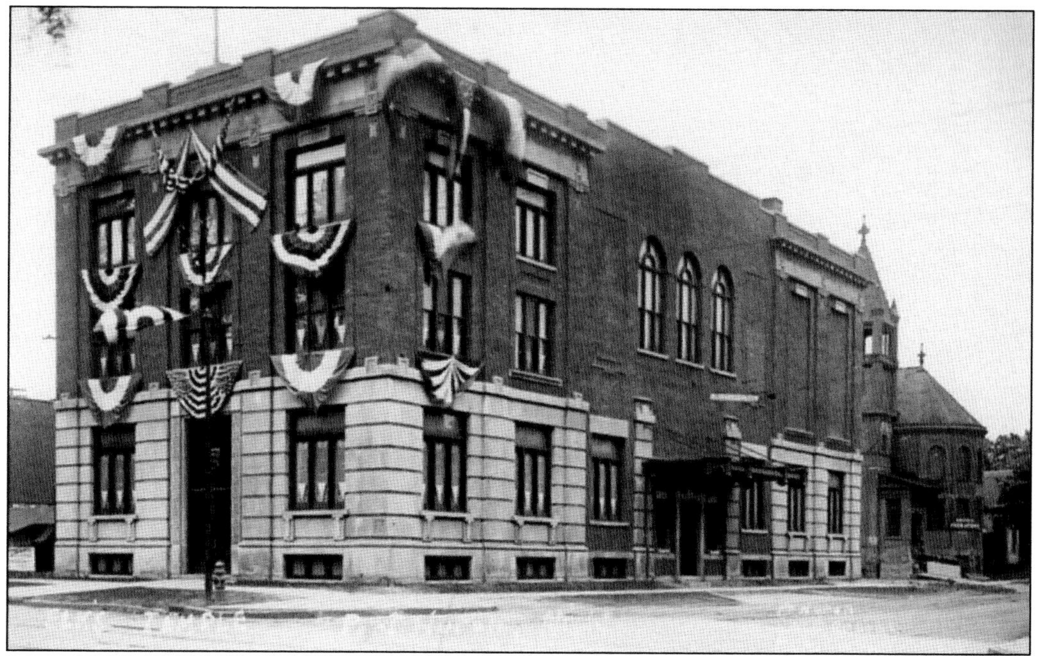

The Benevolent Order of Elks Lodge No. 343 was originally established in 1895 at 935 Military Street. In 1912, the group moved to this structure at 1001 Military Street, where it would remain for over 70 years. In addition to the lodge, the well-loved restaurant Boardwalk and Park Place was located on the ground floor for a number of years.

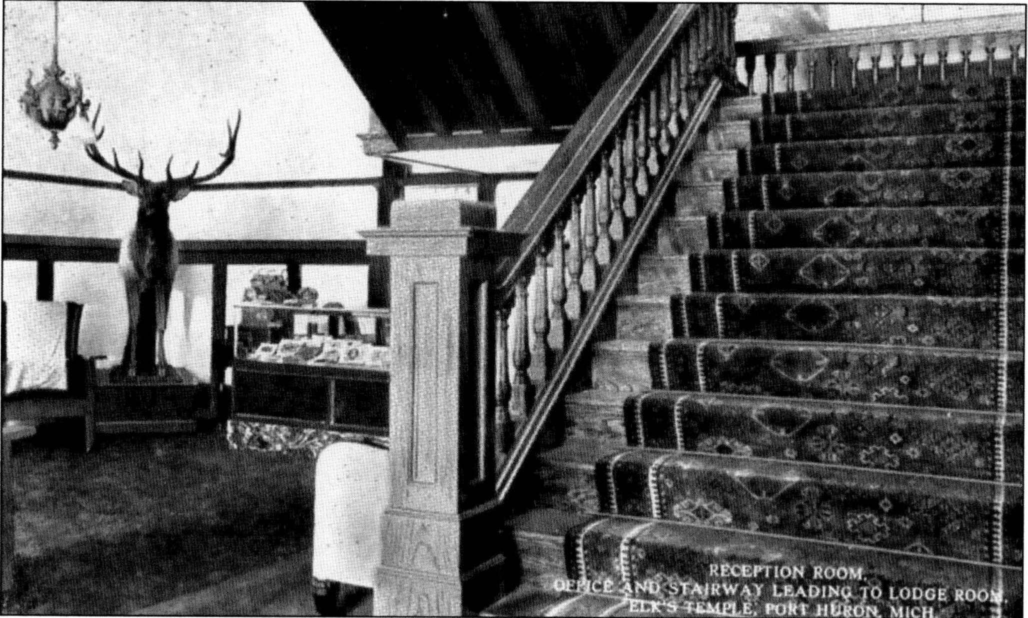


The reception room and front staircase of the above structure is shown about 1915. Note the stuffed elk on display, as well as the ornate oriental rug runner on the stairway. This entire interior was destroyed in a November 1983 fire, leaving only this image to show its one-time grandeur. The remains were remodeled into a one-story structure that now houses the Center for Human Resources.

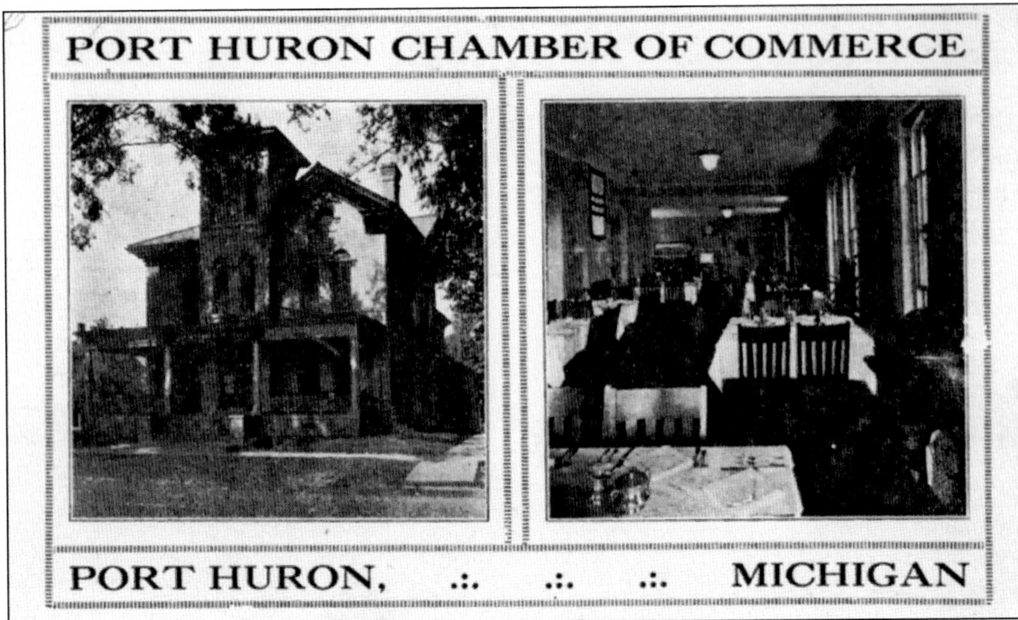


Today, very few people would recognize this building located at 1101 Military Street. Now housing the Blue Water Pregnancy Center, it was home to the Red Cross Canteen and the chamber of commerce in 1918. In the 1950s, the Moore and Wright Insurance firm inhabited the space. During this period, the building was extensively modified with a change to the roof line and the addition of a tower dome.

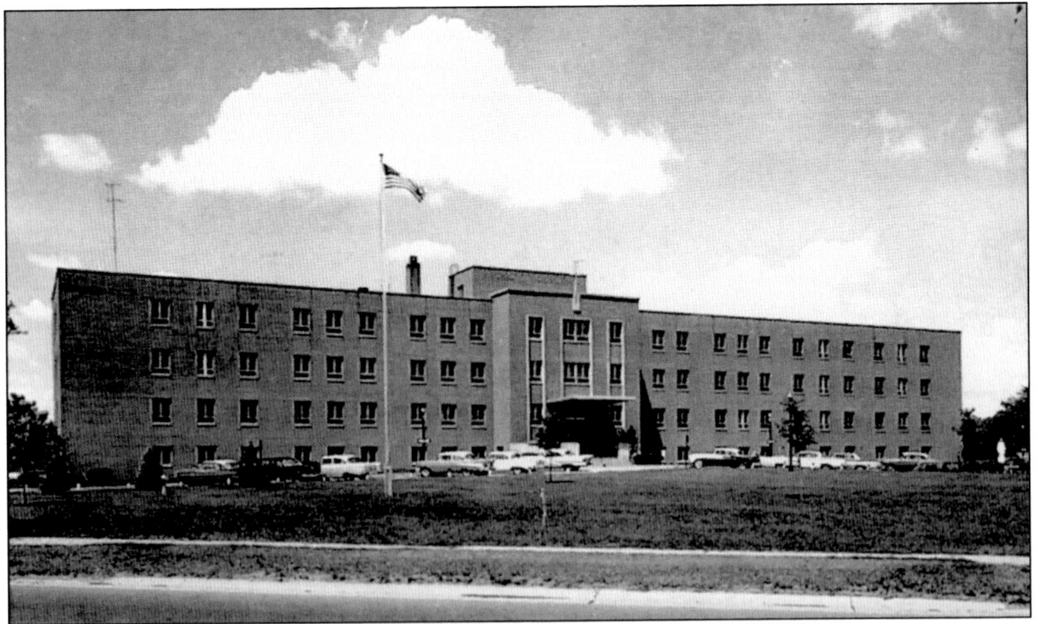

Mercy Hospital, situated at the intersection of Electric Avenue and Tenth Street, is pictured in this *c.* 1960 view. Built by the Sisters of Mercy on land given by the McMorran-Murphy families, it was originally designed to serve the large Catholic population in this portion of southeast Michigan, but has since grown into a multi-cultural facility for the entire community of St. Clair County.

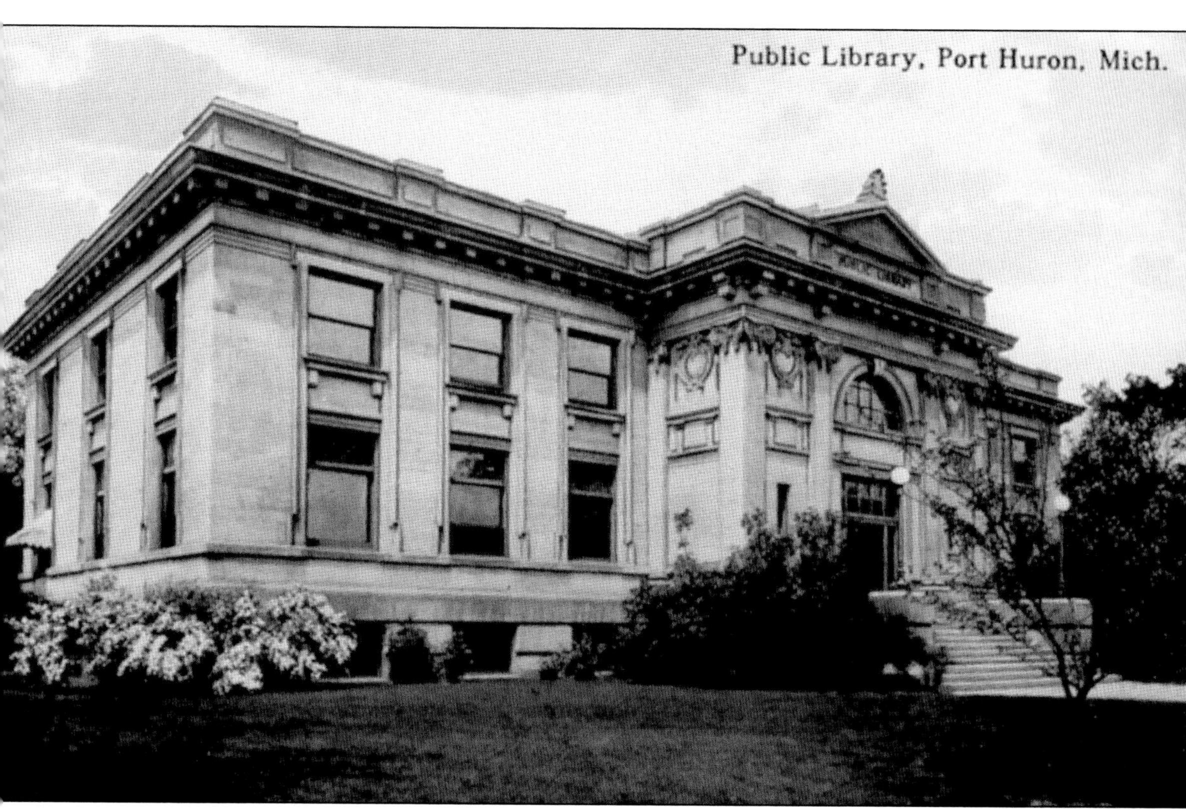


Opened in 1904, the Port Huron Public Library building was one of hundreds constructed through the benevolence of philanthropist Andrew Carnegie at the start of the 20th century. Like so many other communities, the contract originally called for a $40,000 structure, but as the building neared completion, local citizens had to request an additional $5,000 to finish the job. The structure opened to great fanfare on May 26, 1904, with New York State librarian Melvil Dewey, known best for the cataloguing system that bears his name, giving the dedication. The building remained the Port Huron Public Library until 1967, when a new structure was built on McMorran Boulevard. The old space, threatened with demolition, was saved the following year and became the Museum of Arts and History. Now known as the Port Huron Museum–Carnegie Center, it survived an October 1987 fire and remains one of the most active buildings in the community more than 102 years after its construction.

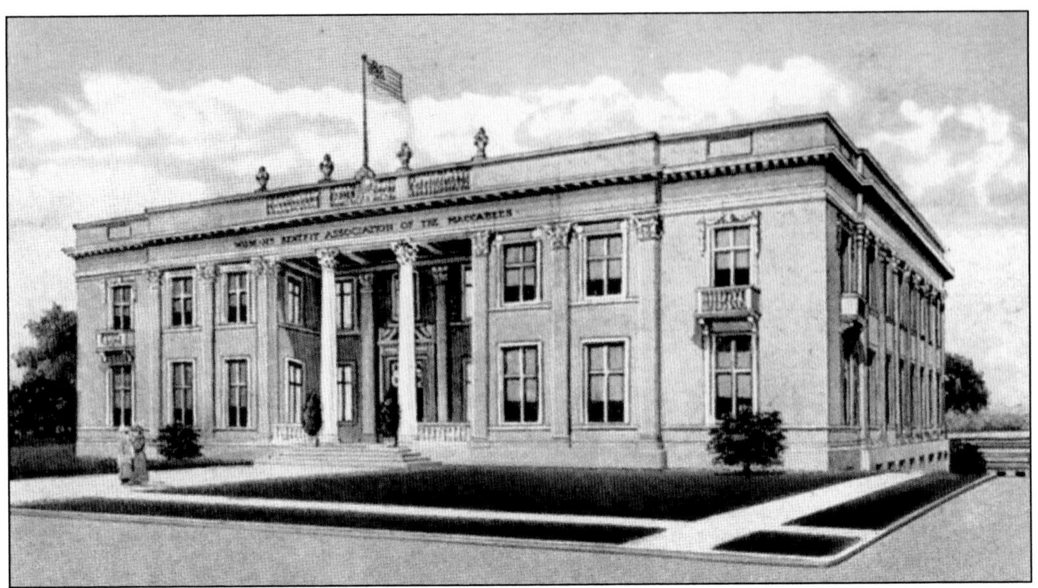

The Ladies of the Maccabees was formed as a fraternal society in 1892. Founded by Bina Mae West-Miller, a former schoolteacher from Capac, it operated out of the original Maccabee temple on Huron Avenue, later known as the Algonquin Hotel. Within 10 years, the Ladies of the Maccabees had grown into one of the largest "widow and orphan" insurance firms in the country. In 1918, the group moved into this newly built structure at 1338 Military Street, designed by local architect Walter Wyeth. Known over the years as the Woman's Benefit Association and NABA, the organization remains strong today as the Women's Life Insurance Society.

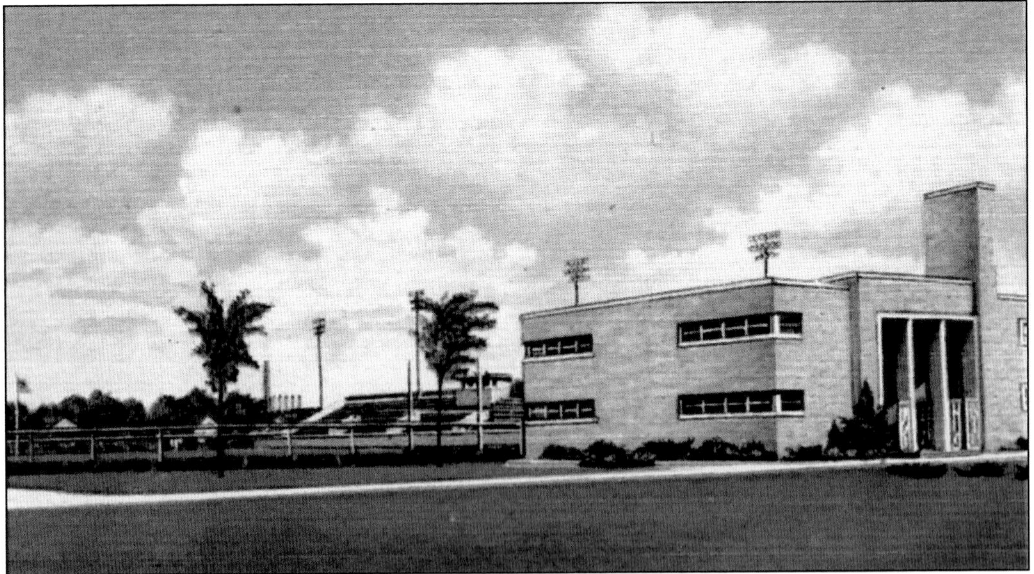

Memorial Stadium is a post–World War II complex including a football and baseball stadium built in remembrance of former players who had served in the armed forces. Also designed by local architect Walter Wyeth, it was noted as one of the finer high school football stadiums in the state and remains among the top facilities. Originally built for the sports teams of Port Huron High School, Memorial Stadium has also hosted the varsity football teams of Port Huron Northern and, until 1981, Port Huron Central High School.

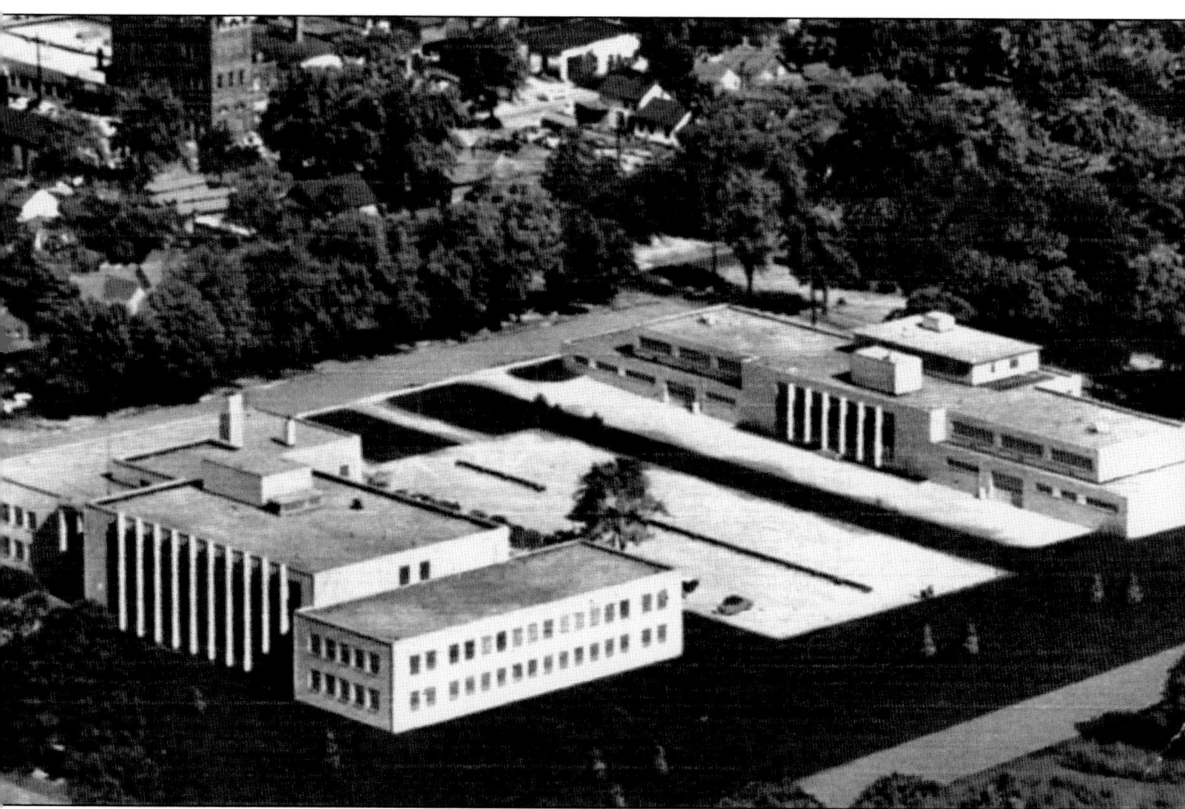

This view shows the county-city building with the new county-city jail upon completion in 1953. Constructed through funds secured during urban renewal, it replaced a series of small homes and business that had been part of Port Huron's traditional First Ward. Many of the buildings seen in the upper left corner of this image would soon be leveled as well, replaced by a variety of other more modern structures. With the construction of this building, the traditional First Ward ceased to exist as a residential neighborhood. The fact that Port Huron won its first All-American City Award was due in large part to the "clean up" of this area. During the period from 2000 to 2004, a new county jail was constructed in Port Huron Township, and much discussion has taken place on what to do with this site. County offices still occupy the county-city building; however, city offices were relocated to the municipal office center in the late 1970s.

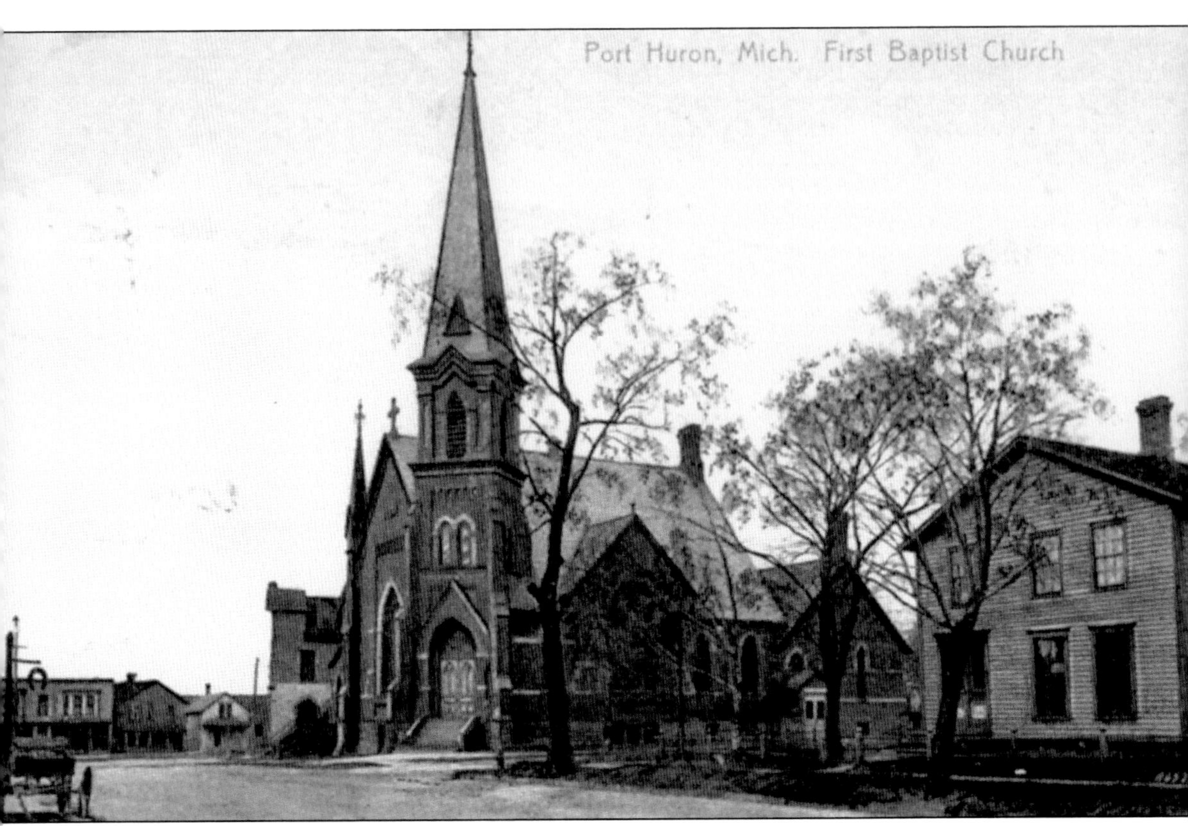


For many years, the spire of the First Baptist Church was a cornerstone of the area known as Erie Square. Built in 1880 on Broad Street at the eastern side of the square, it boasted an interior of ornate stained-glass windows and wonderful ornamental woodwork. Even as the urban renewal movement began to remove its neighboring historic structures, the First Baptist Church remained. Several local citizens fought to save the structure, and for a brief time, it looked as if their efforts might be successful. The money available for urban renewal was more than that for historic preservation, however, and in 1971 the wrecking ball finally struck. The stately old church was no more, to be replaced by the parking lot for McMorran Auditorium. The stained-glass window over the front doors is now on display at the Port Huron Museum.

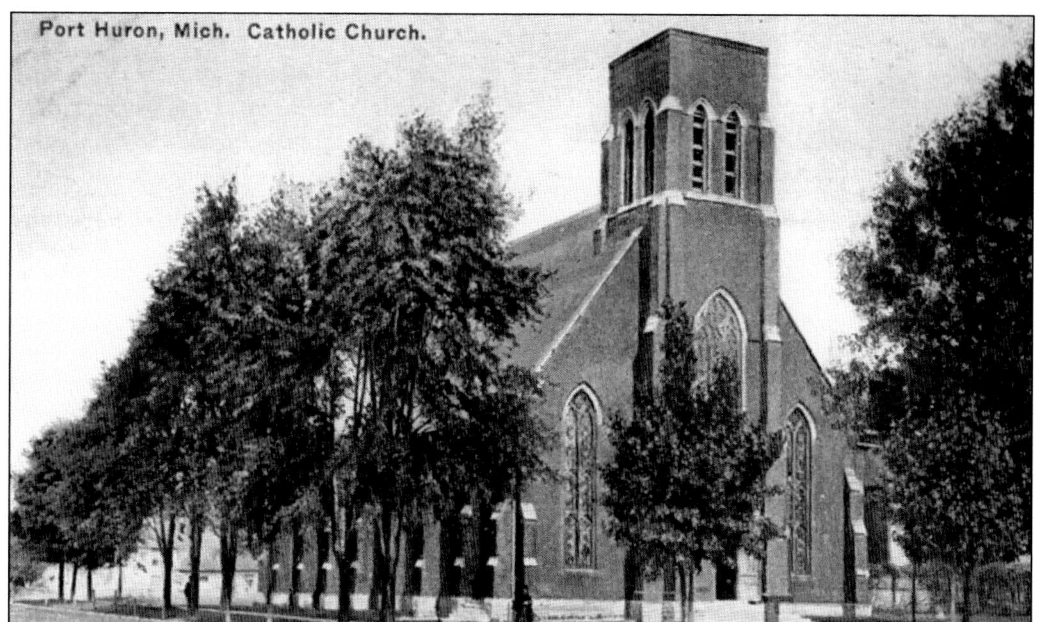


First opened in 1865, St. Stephen's Catholic Church was one of the centers of Catholic worship in the Port Huron community. The image above shows the building in its earlier years, about 1880; the photograph below shows the church around 1910. Home to a rectory and a school, it was a core area of Christian education as well. During the 1960s, the Archdiocese of Detroit began to review its education centers based on population changes and other criteria, and decided that the St. Stephen Catholic School was no longer needed. It was closed in 1964, and its building was sold to the expanding St. Clair County Community College, which had occupied the former Port Huron High School since 1957. With the sale of the school, the church decided to relocate to the western edge of the city, and the original church was torn down.

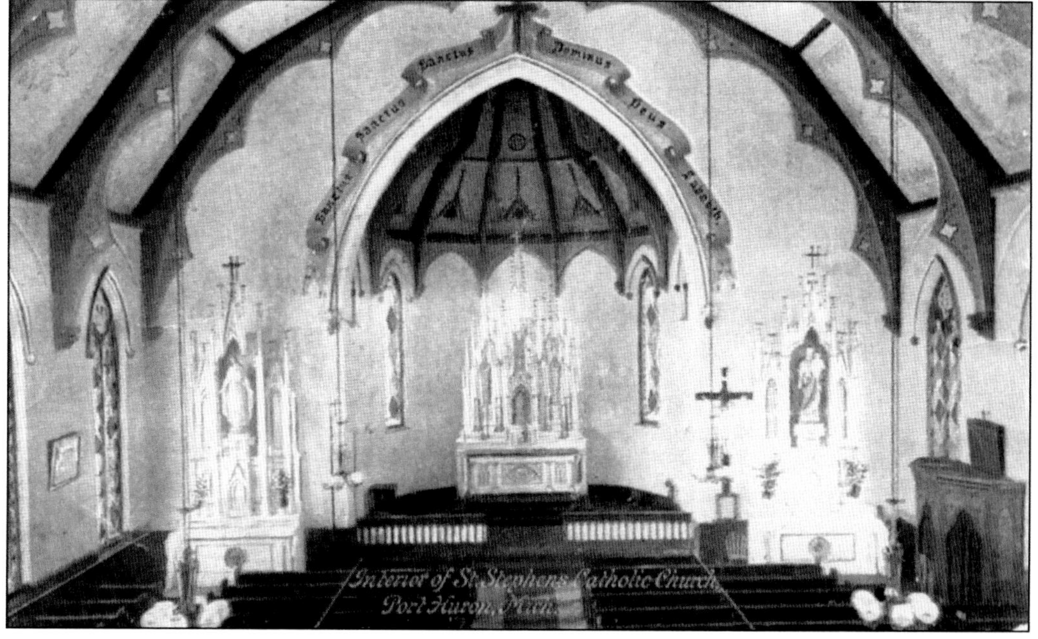

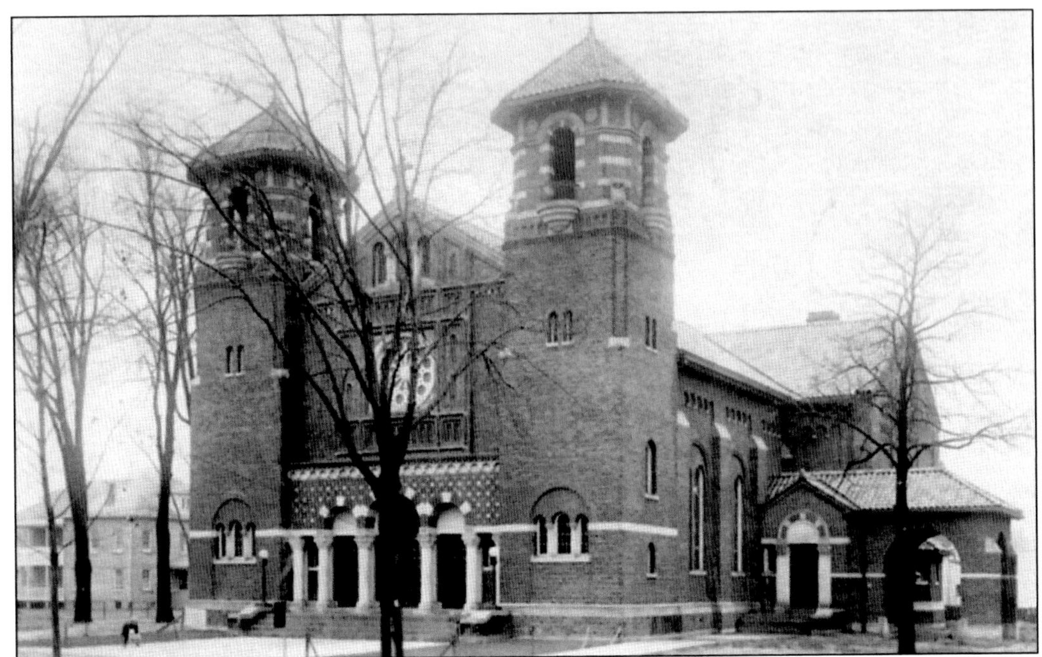

St. Joseph's Catholic Church has a rich history in the religious community of Port Huron. Like its fellow parish on the other side of Black River, "St. Joe's" has had a loyal following that has grown from its surrounding neighborhood. Originally constructed in the 1880s as St. Joseph's German Catholic Church, it, like so many churches throughout the nation during World War I, dropped the "German" from its name due to the anti-German sentiment. Its school, founded a few years later, remained open as a facility serving kindergarten through fifth grade until recently, when the Archdiocese of Detroit realigned its students to remaining schools at St. Mary's in Port Huron and Holy Cross in Marine City.

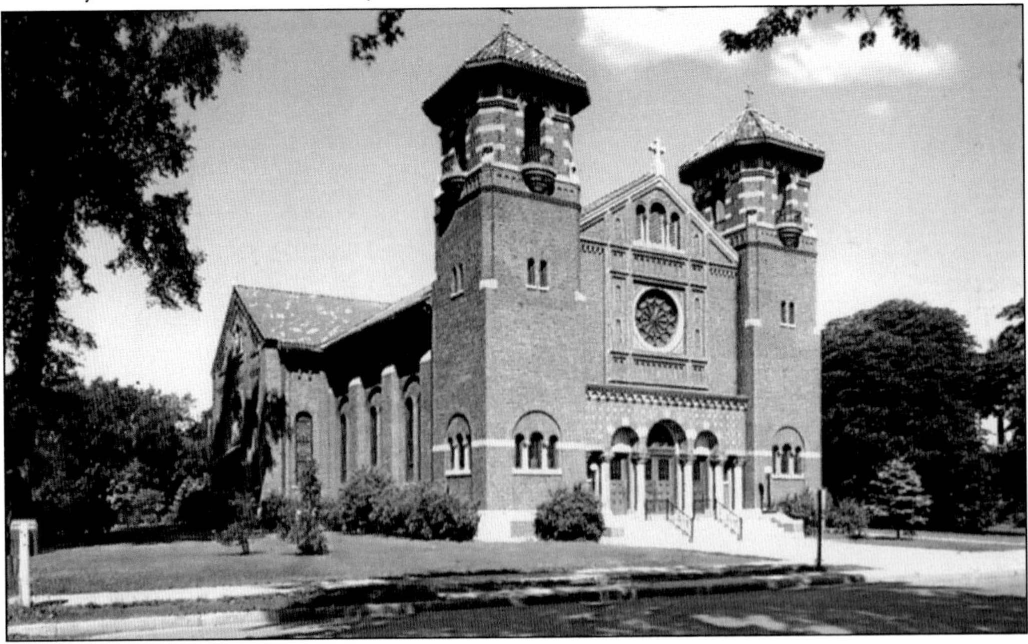

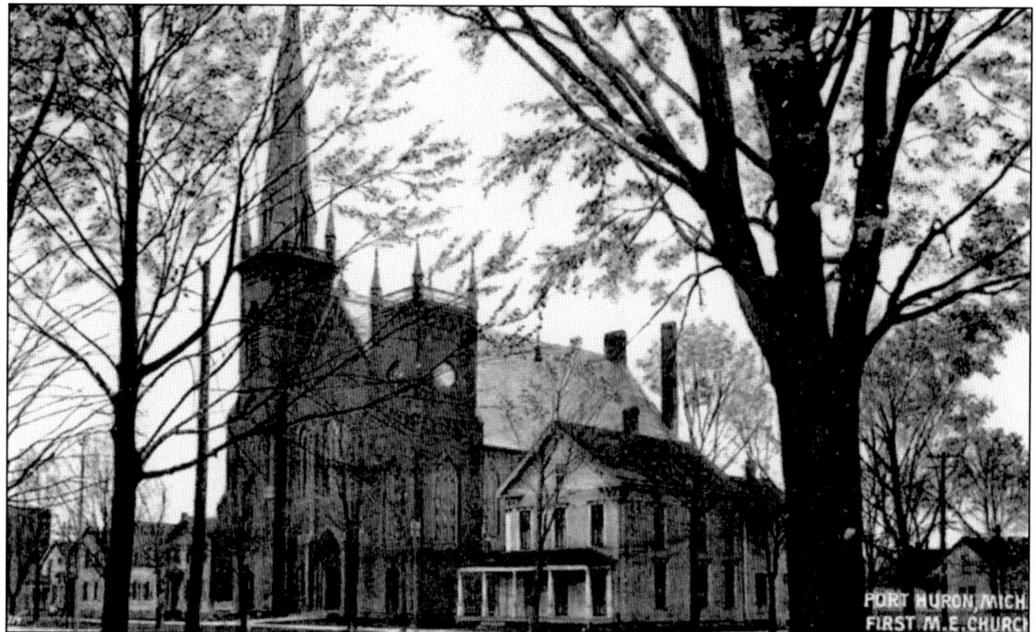


First organized in the 1860s, the First Methodist Church of Port Huron was one of the first houses of worship in the city that greeted travelers coming from villages between Port Huron and Flint and points west. Located at 828 Lapeer Avenue, the church and rectory were some of the highest structures in the neighborhood, with the steeple being one of the tallest in the city. The interior of the church matched the exterior, with fine woods and a raised choir area in front of a large and imposing organ and its pipes, as can be seen in the Louis Pesha image below. The congregation experienced significant growth after World War II, and funds began to be raised at that time for the building's replacement. By the mid-1960s, enough funds had been secured to build a new structure, and the old church was leveled. The new church bears little resemblance to its predecessor, with sleeker, modern lines that echo its 1960s construction.

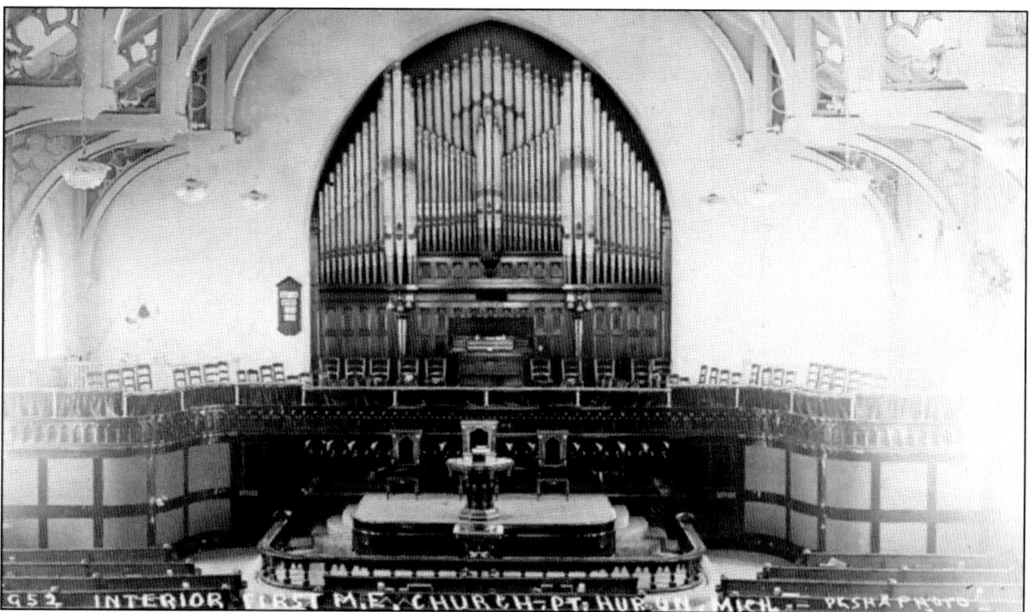

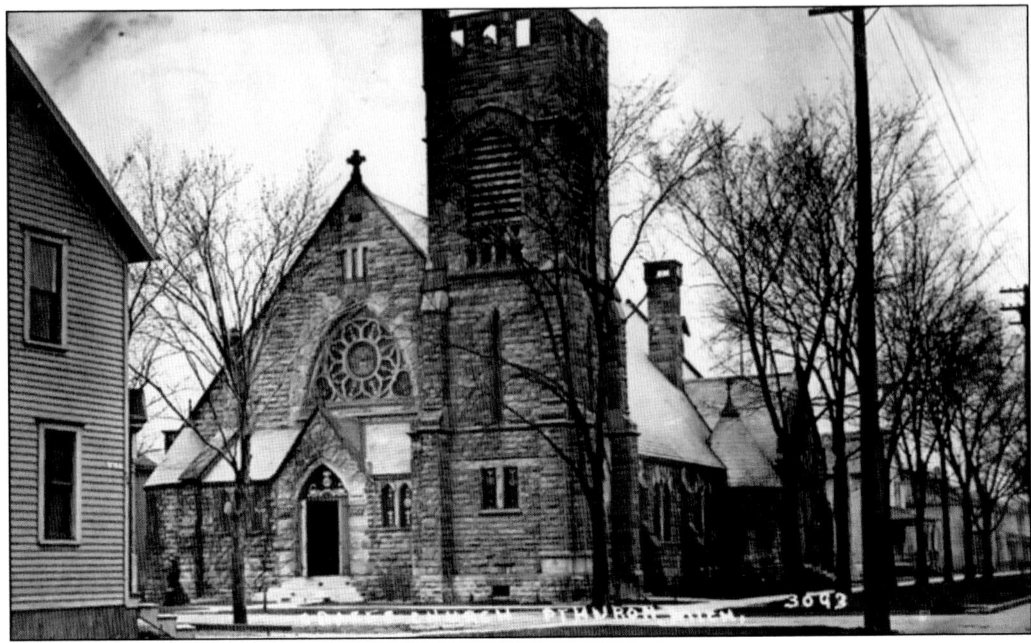


The above Louis Pesha photograph depicts Grace Episcopal Church, whose congregation was first founded in the 1830s. Located at the corner of Sixth and Court Streets, the current building, seen here, has stood for over 100 years and remains one of the cornerstone churches of the area now known as the Olde Towne Historic District. Shown below are rector Rev. A E. Duplan and his assistant, D. R. Lees, dating this postcard to sometime in the early 1950s.

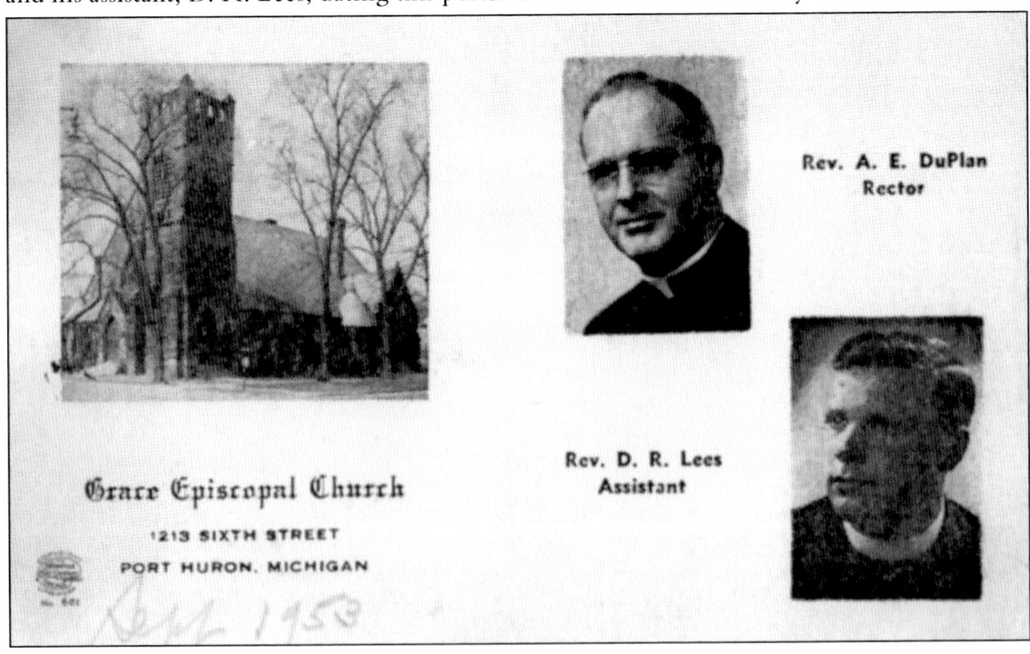

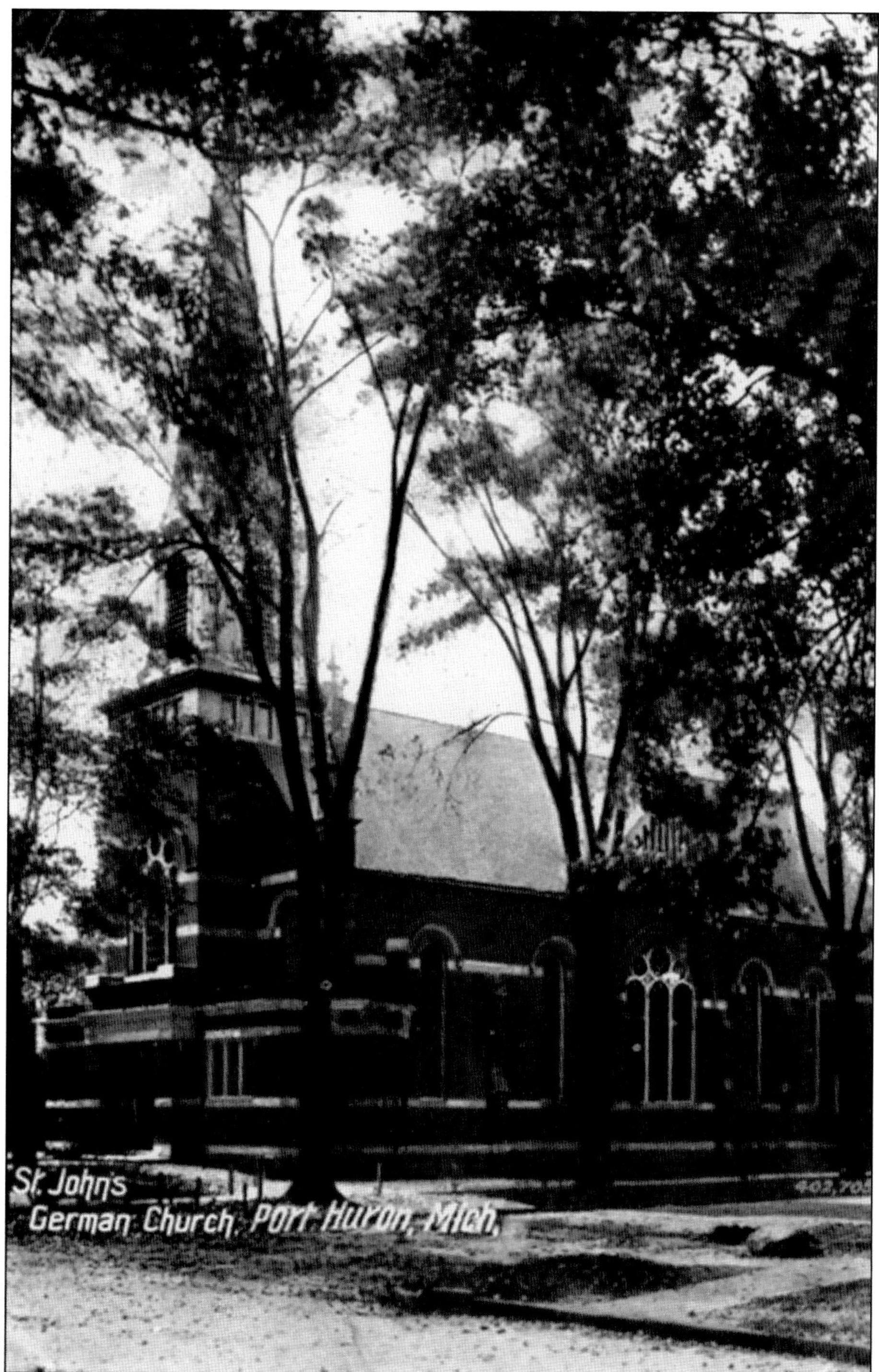


St. John's German Lutheran Church was one of the last in the area to remain completely true to its ethnic heritage, conducting its services entirely in German into the 1970s. During the infamous worldwide influenza epidemic of 1918–1919, the church was the center of local support, furnishing blankets, beds, and its own members to help those in need.

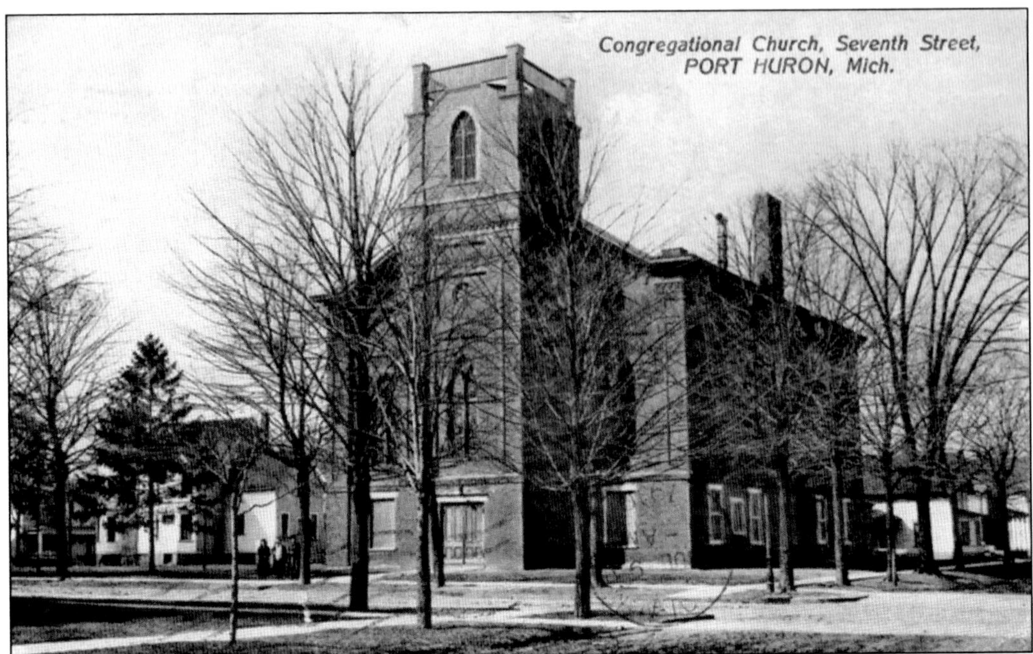


Although listed as simply "the Congregational Church" in these images, the First Congregational Church has a storied past. Long associated with anti-slavery and abolitionism, Congregational churches in Michigan were heavily involved in the Underground Railroad movement prior to the Civil War, and the local congregation was no exception. With the likes of Oren Thompson, a self-proclaimed anti-slavery supporter, as its first pastor, the church reportedly included members who coordinated the movement and supplied many of the safe houses in the Port Huron area. Still one of the most active of Port Huron congregations, this building was torn down in the 1960s and replaced by a structure designed by noted architect Alden Dow.

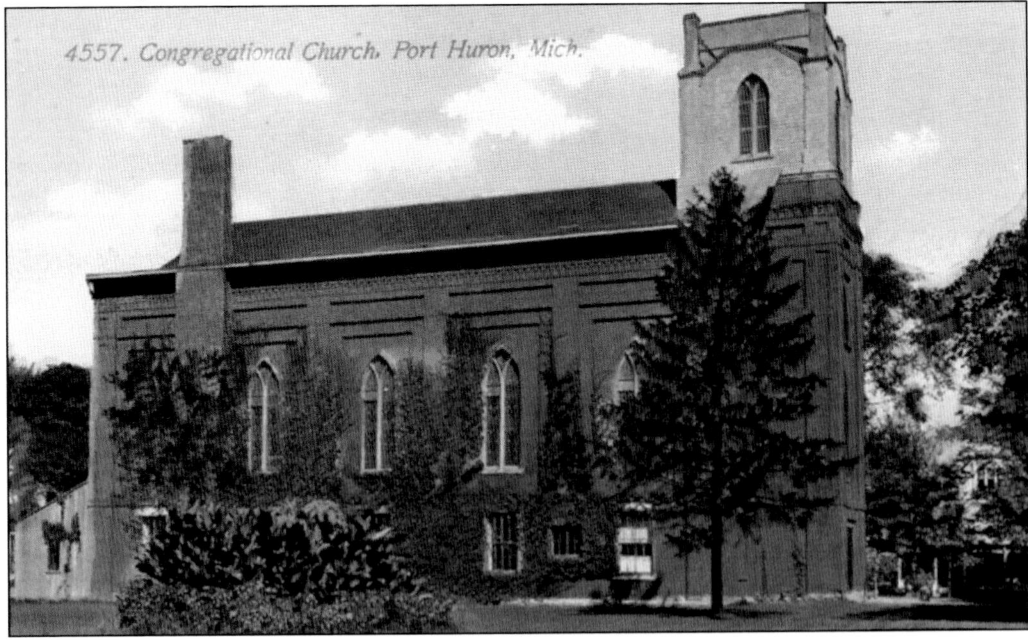

POST CARD

One Cent
Stamp Here

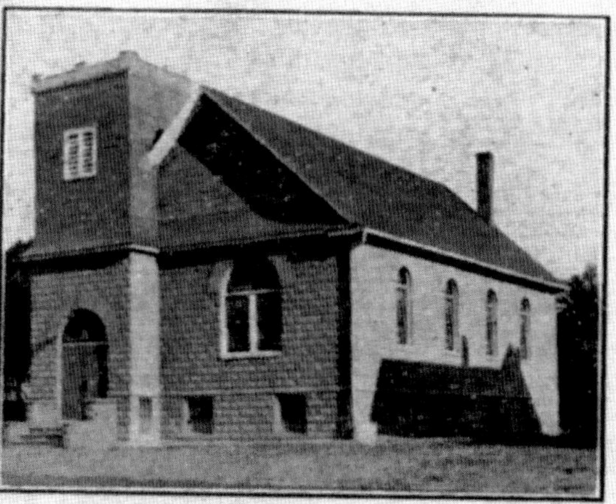

EDIFICE

Of Reorganized Church of Jesus Christ of Latter Day Saints, Tenth and Water Sts., Port Huron, Mich. Erected, A. D. 1913. Original cost $6,250. A monument of labor, sacrifice and self-denial.

By their fruit, ye shall know them.

ADDRESS

The first known location of the local chapter of the Church of Jesus Christ of Latter Day Saints was at the corner of Tenth and Water Streets. This particular building, constructed in 1913, remained standing through the 1950s, when the church relocated to a newly built structure. A particularly interesting postcard, it not only denotes the location and date of construction, but also the original cost of the structure: a whopping $6,250. Of particular interest is the acknowledgment that this church was "a monument of labor, sacrifice and self-denial."

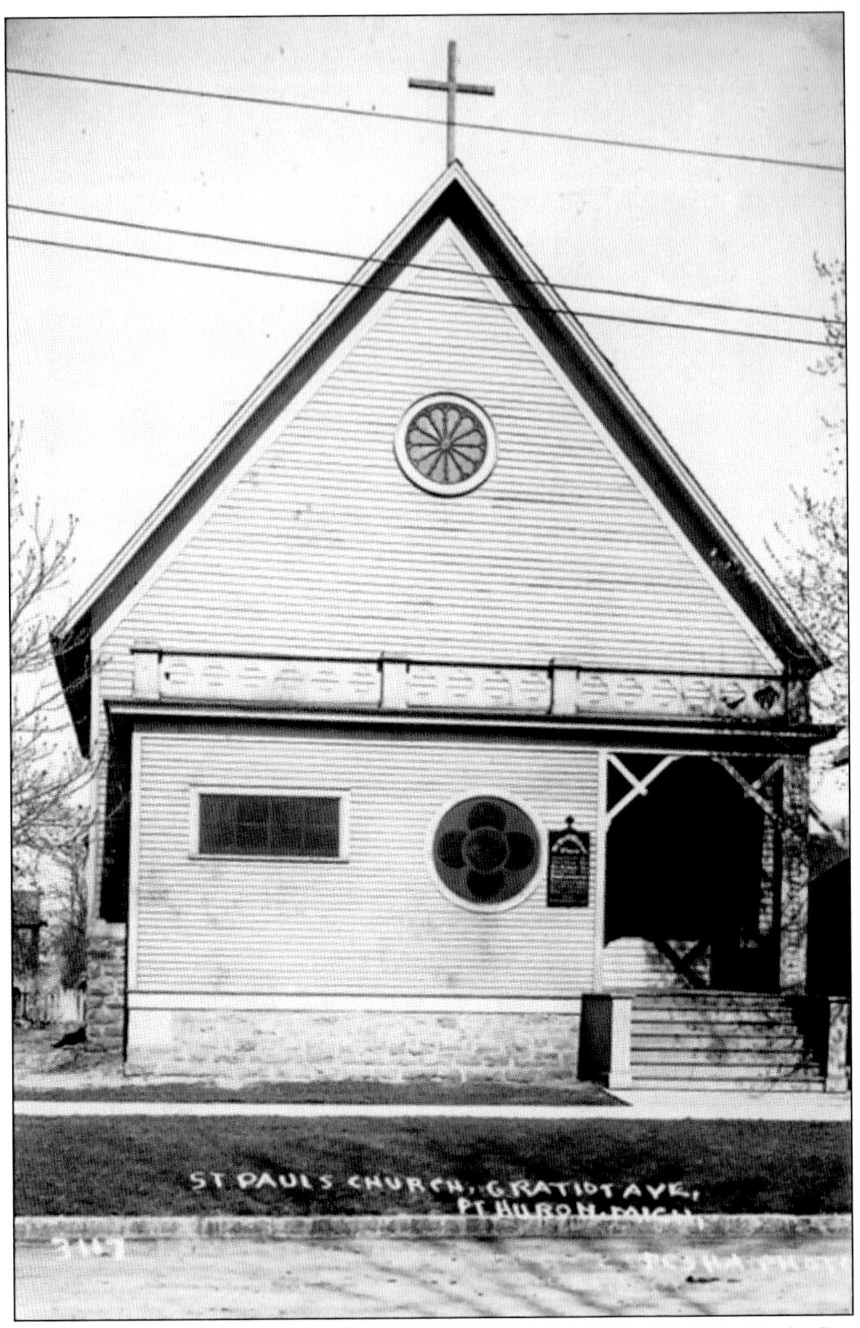


This Louis Pesha image shows St. Paul's Episcopal Church on Gratiot Avenue in Port Huron soon after its 1903 renovations. This congregation, formed in 1876, originally met in the store of Thomas Alva Edison's uncle, located in what was then the village of Fort Gratiot. Not to be confused with the current township of Fort Gratiot a mile or so distant, this village was incorporated in 1882 and remained a separate entity until it was merged into the city of Port Huron in 1893. The congregation continued to use this church into the late 1950s, when its growing congregation necessitated the construction of a larger church. Unlike so many others, however, this building was saved and continues to serve in its original capacity.

## *Six*

# Living in Port Huron

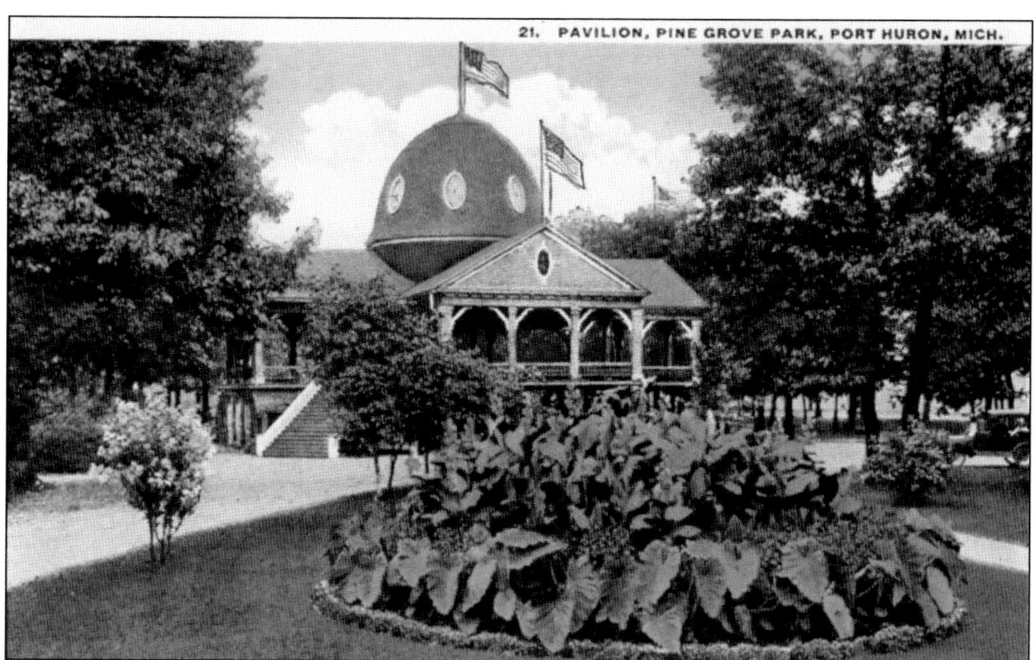


The Pine Grove Park Pavilion was the cornerstone of entertainment in the community for over 50 years. Unlike the small, single-level structures of many small towns, this behemoth of a band shell rose to nearly a three-story height, with a full dance floor and band area completely covered by an amazing half-oval roof structure.

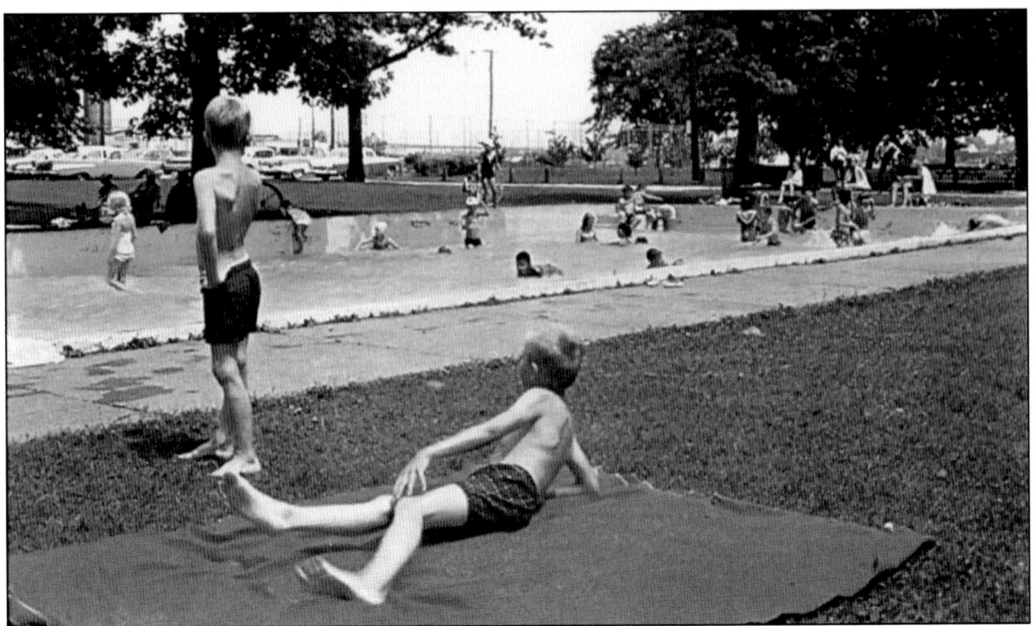

Truly a kids' pool, the Pine Grove Park wading pool was only three feet deep, making it the only area in the city for many years where a child could wade the entire length. It was removed in the 1950s for a water treatment facility.

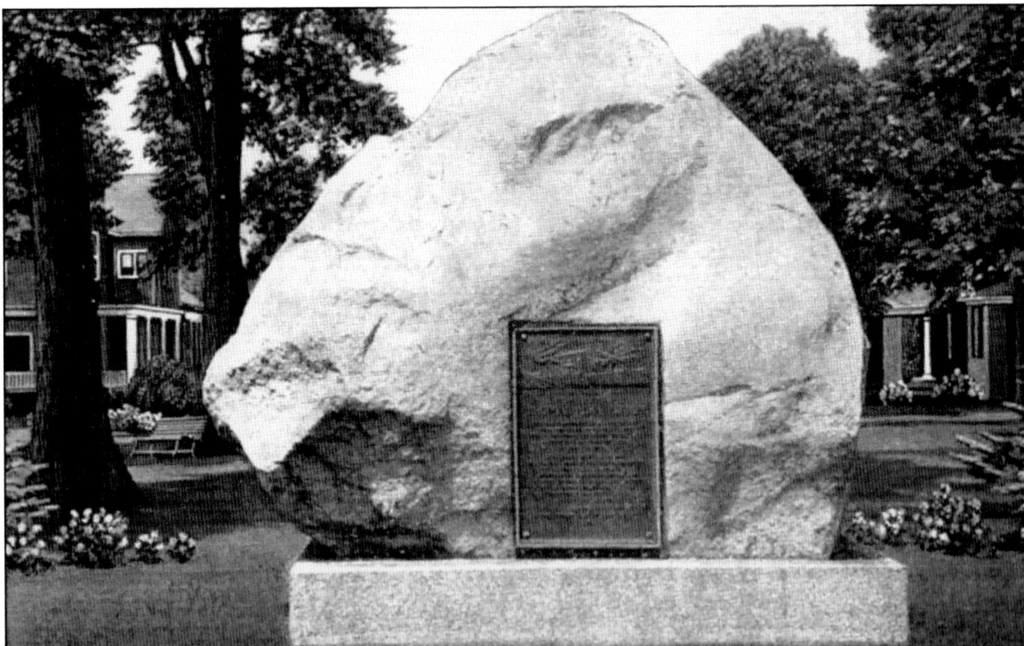

This monument commemorates the boyhood playground of Thomas Alva Edison. The boulder was obtained from a farm near Kinde and shipped via flatcar on the Pere Marquette Railway to Port Huron. Dedicated and purchased by the Rotary Club of Port Huron, it was repaired and refreshed in 2004 to commemorate the 125th anniversary of the incandescent lamp. At the rededication was famed Hollywood actor Mickey Rooney, who last came to Port Huron in 1940 for the premier of the movie *Young Tom Edison*.

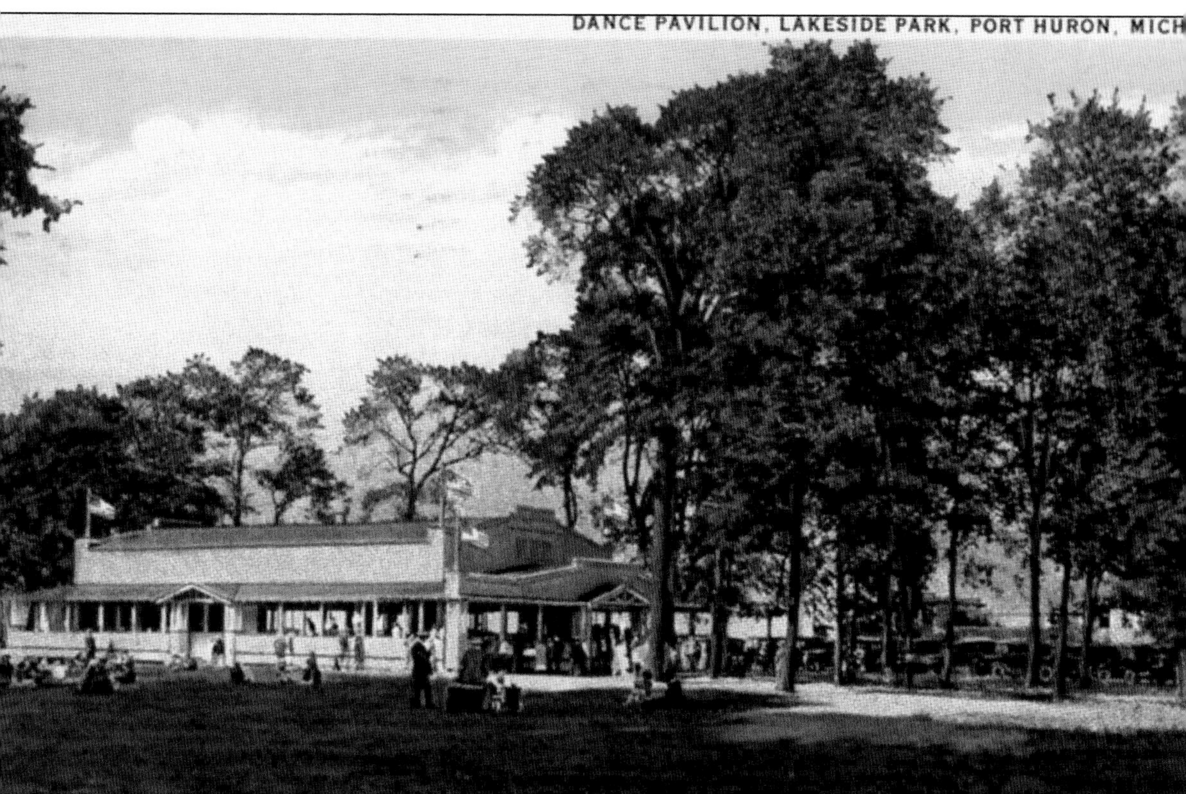


Warm summer breezes carrying the sounds of band music were once commonplace on the northern edges of Port Huron. Constructed at the start of the 20th century, the dance pavilion at Lakeside Park was once a popular entertainment venue. Including an equally ornate bathhouse, the park's facilities were some of the finest in the city and afforded easy access to Lake Huron for local citizens and visitors alike. Although the dance pavilion was removed after World War II, Lakeside Beach remains one of the most popular beaches in the Port Huron area.

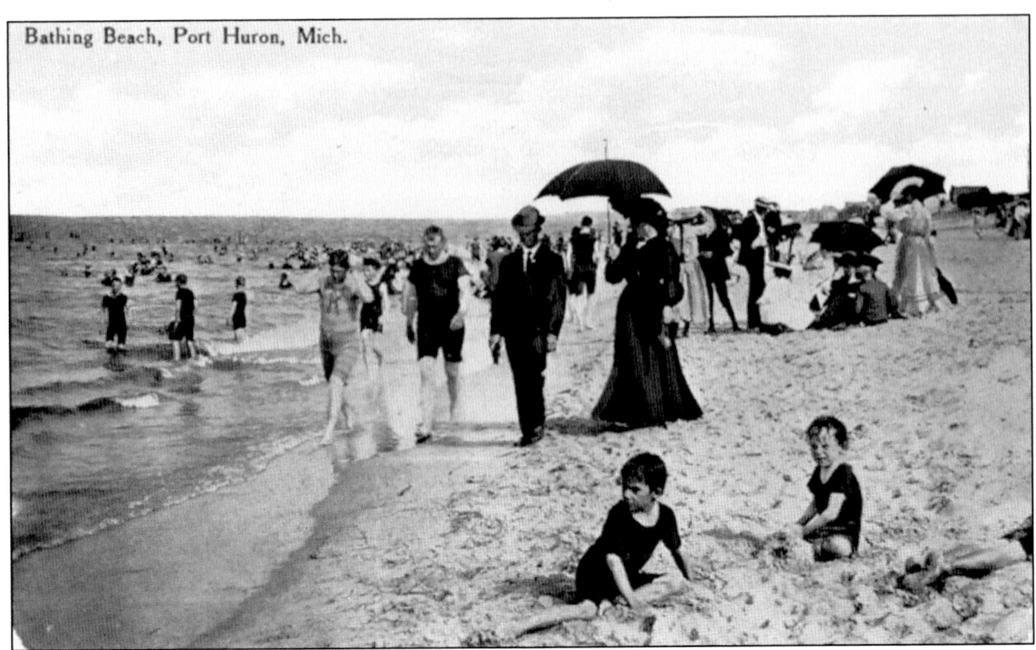


A bit farther down the beach from Lakeside was the Huronia Beach neighborhood, a popular area for those who came from Detroit and other areas to rent cabins and enjoy Lake Huron's fresh water. Children and adults alike enjoy the beach in the above *c.* 1900 image, although their outfits seem a bit conservative by today's standards. Unlike what many of us would consider a "cottage" today, these structures were quite ornate affairs, and although many did not have running water or electricity, they were well built and decorated, as evidenced by the ornate gingerbread porches in the Louis Pesha image below. Sadly, many of these ornate cottages have been replaced with larger homes lacking character.

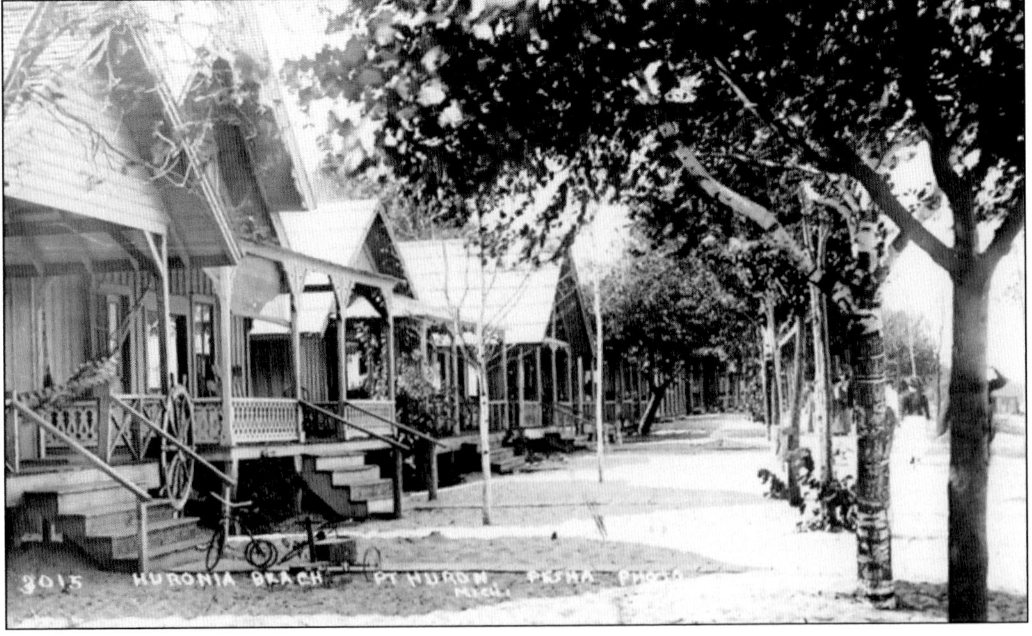

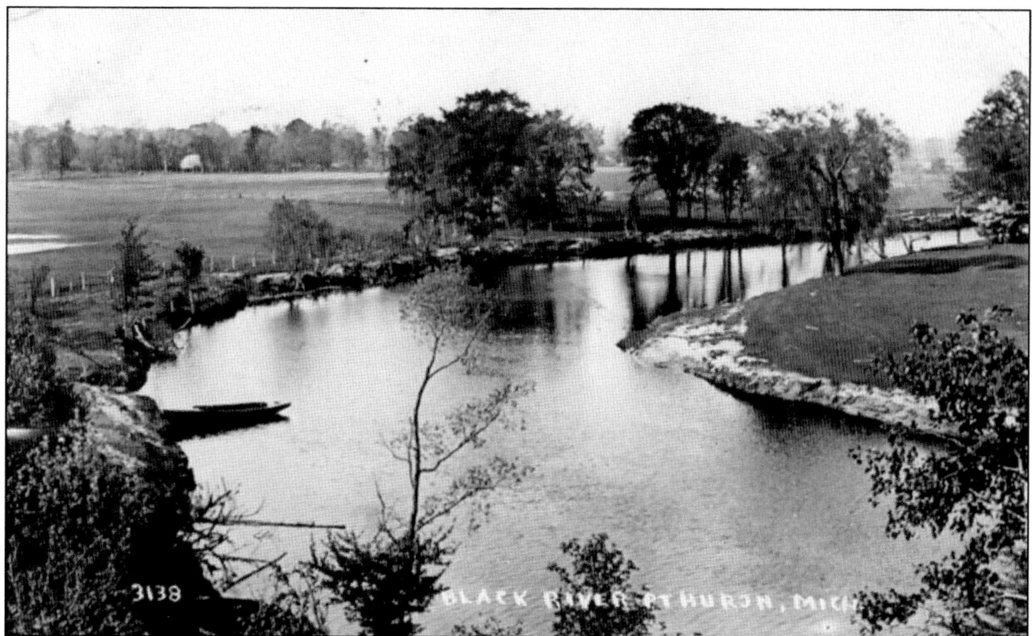


These two Louis Pesha photographs give a wonderful perspective of what once was the rural nature of Black River. Much of this area would be changed forever in the ensuing years, and homes, boat docks, and steel seawalls have since replaced much of its serene beauty. These images also provide a rare opportunity to note Pesha's style in consecutive images, as one is image number 3138 and the other number 3139. If one looks closely, the boat seen on the shore in the above view (first) is the same as that carrying a man in a bowler hat in the view below (second). The location may possibly be the Oxbow farm area just north of the city.

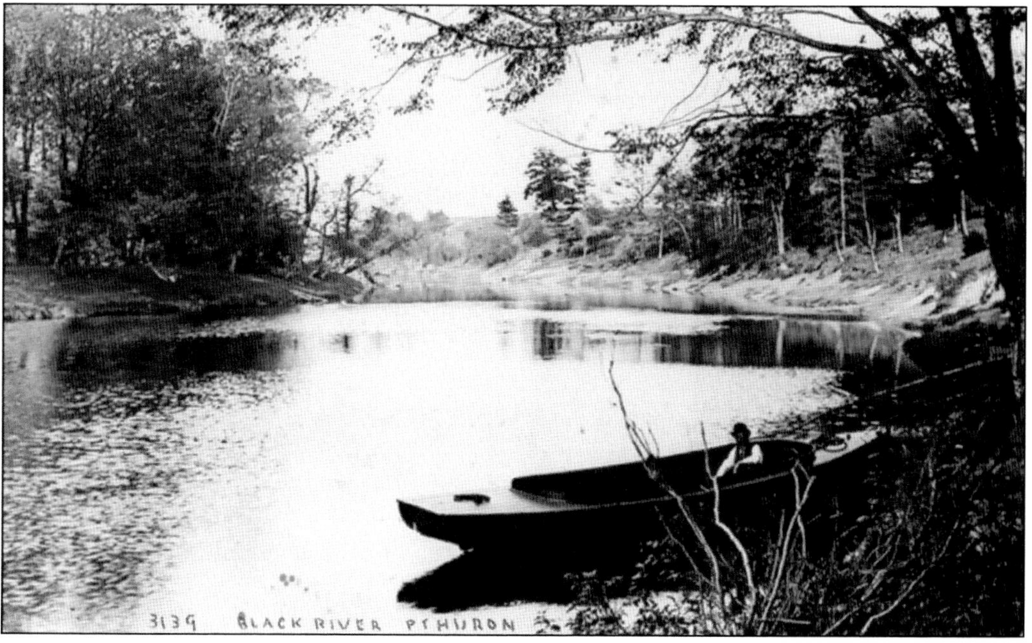

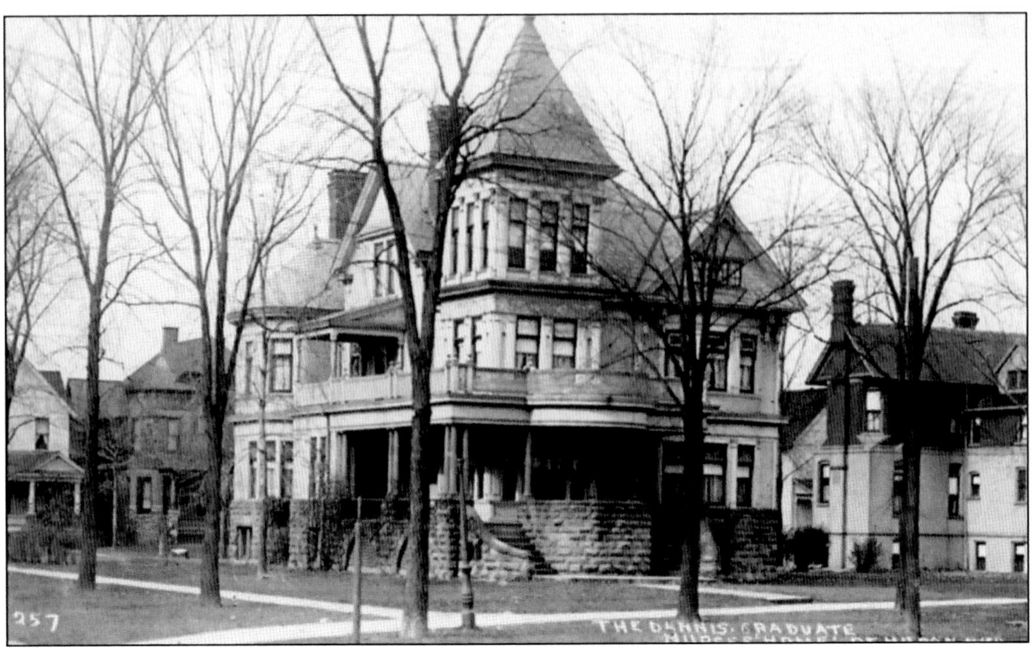


Although no longer a private home at the time of the Louis Pesha image above, this structure at Pine Grove Avenue, known today as Kearns Insurance Agency, deserves mention for its longevity. At the time of this photograph, the house was under the care of the Dennis Graduate Nurse's Home, which supplied nurses to Port Huron Hospital a mere block away. While many ornate homes similar to it once occupied the neighborhood, it now sits as a survivor on the fringe of a large medical office area. In 2006, the Kearns family began a much-needed restoration of the exterior of the structure, which now reflects and enhances its wonderful character.

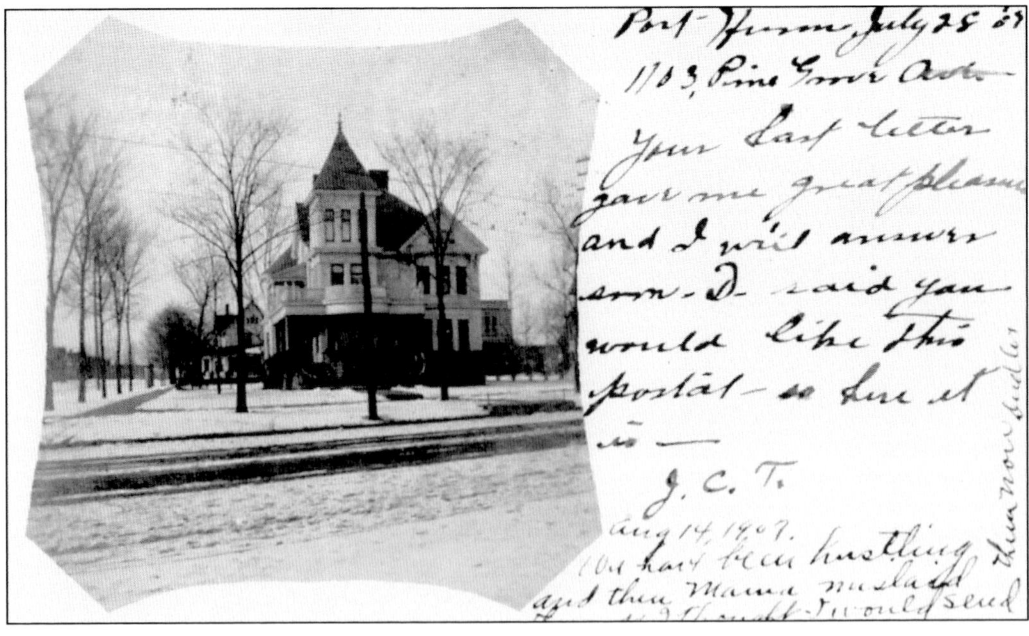

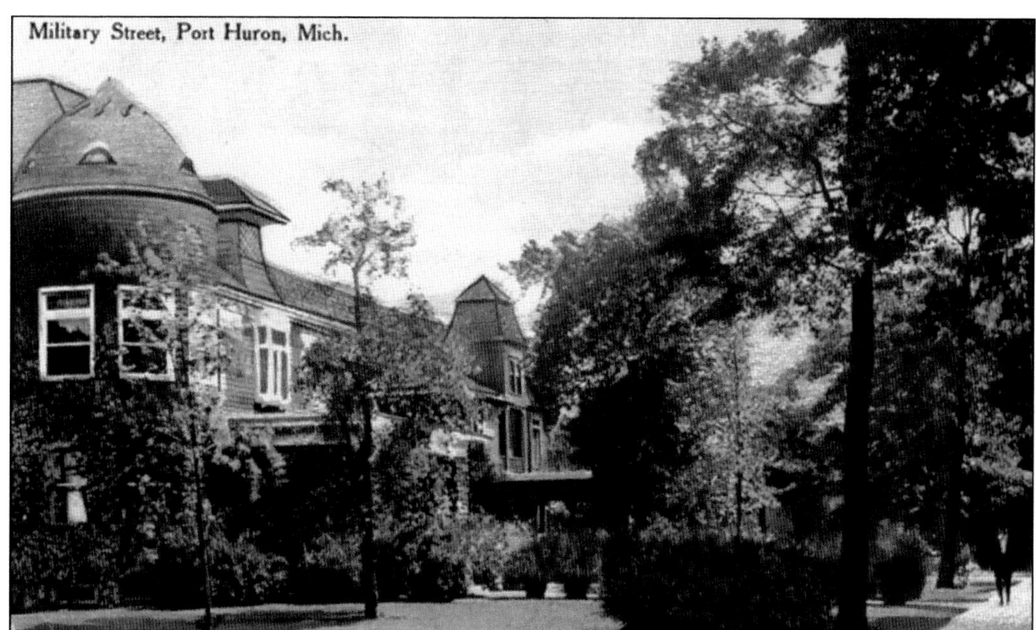


These different views show the heart of the Military Street residential area, once one of the wealthiest spots in the city. The above view, looking south to the Women's Life Insurance Society, includes a series of unique homes that no longer exist. The home on the far left is now the site of the Port Huron Post Office. One of these residences belonged to William Lee Jenks, a famed local historian and publisher of the widely regarded and referenced two-volume set *History of St. Clair County*. Published in 1913, it has become the bible for local historians wishing to better understand their heritage. The houses below happily share a better fate. The green building with awnings (second from right) is known today as the Secory Home, named for Lynn and Lew Secory, who over a period of 40 years have lovingly restored it to its former grandeur. Much of the neighborhood seen in this image will become part of the Military Street Historic District.

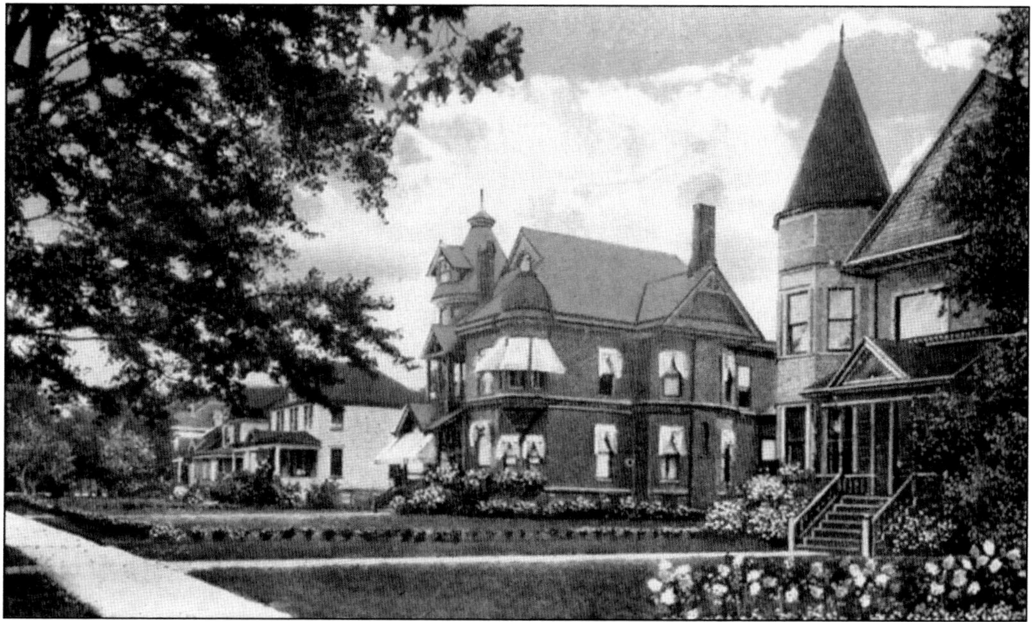

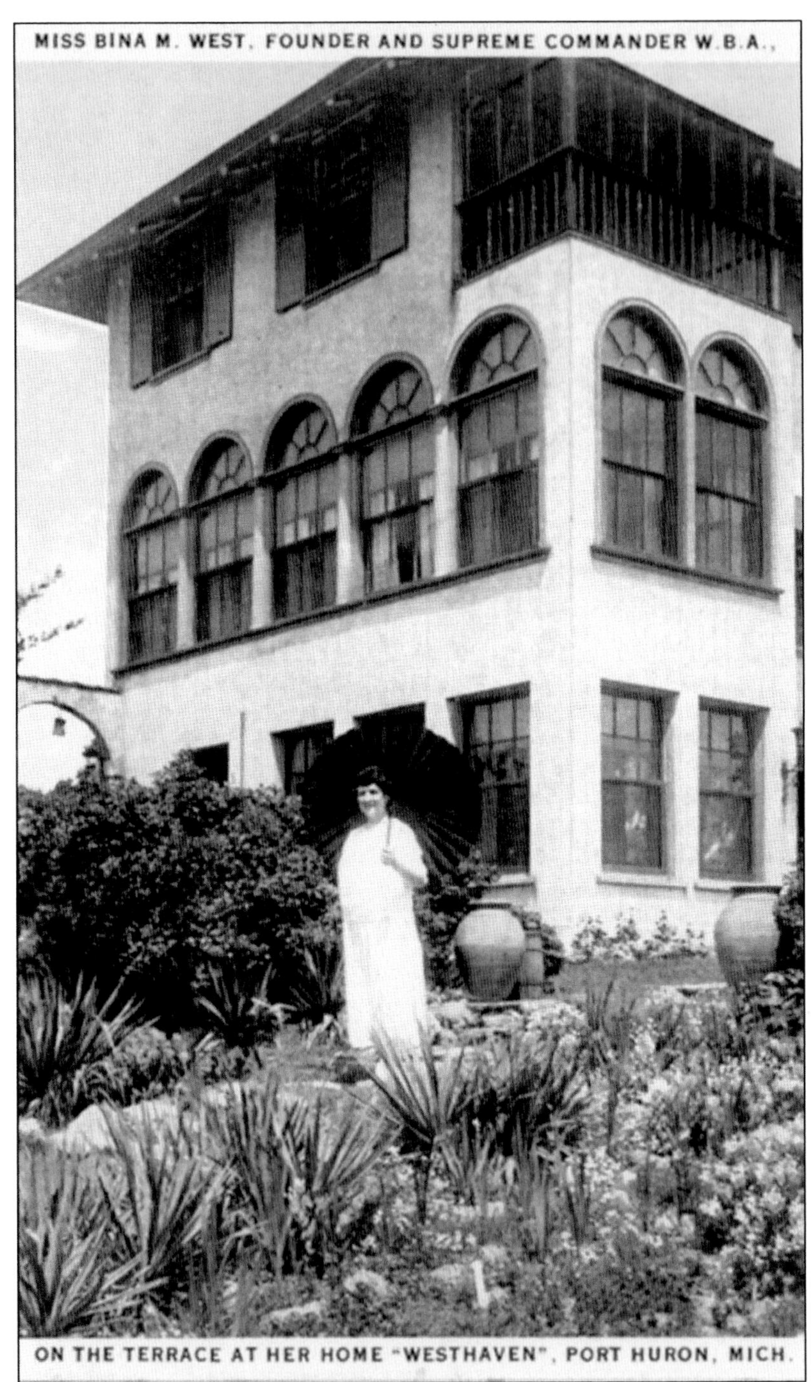


Bina Mae West-Miller, founder of the Women's Benefit Association, appears in the gardens of her home in Port Huron. Named Westhaven, the residence was designed in the Spanish style by local architect Walter Wyeth. West-Miller's passion for nature can clearly be seen; her gardens were at one time some of the finest in the area. With West-Miller's passing in 1951, the home was subdivided into apartments and fell into disrepair. It stands today, but as a shadow of its former beauty.

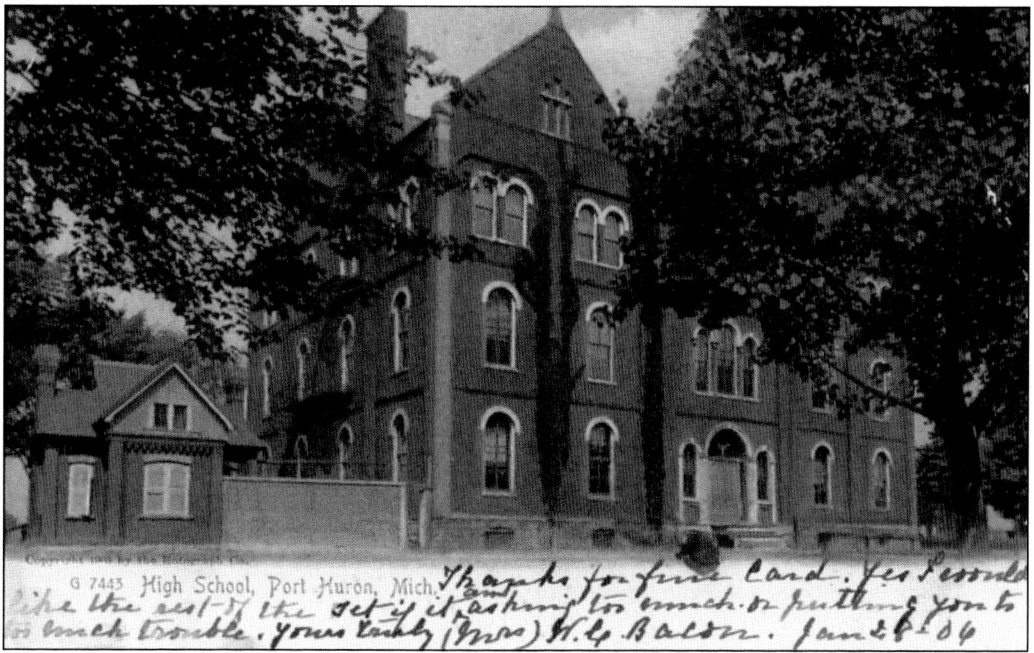


Two of the four buildings that have been home to Port Huron High School are pictured here. The above postcard view shows the 1880s school, built during a time of massive expansion for Port Huron Area Schools. This building served as a high school for many years until a fire destroyed it in 1906. Since the burnt structure was already aged and overcrowded, officials decided to build a completely new school. The image below shows that new high school building, completed in 1908. Like its predecessor, it was located on Erie Street, with a beautifully designed entryway flanked with pillars. This building became the first home of Port Huron Junior College, which occupied the basement until 1928, when it moved to a new location at the former Maccabee building. In 1957, the structure was vacated for a new high school on Twenty-fourth Street, and the junior college returned, this time to occupy its entirety. It remains the main building of that institution's successor, St. Clair County Community College.

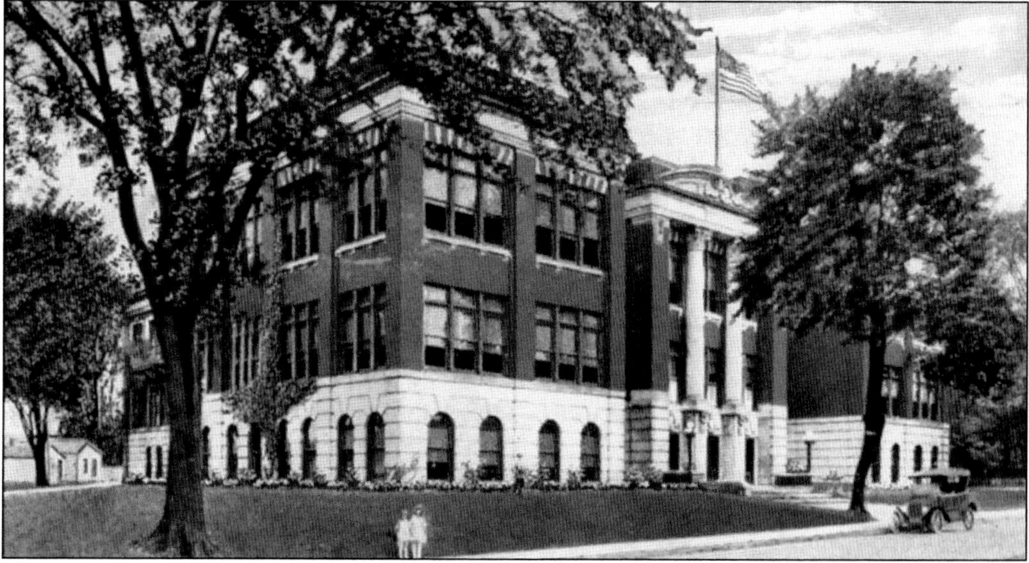

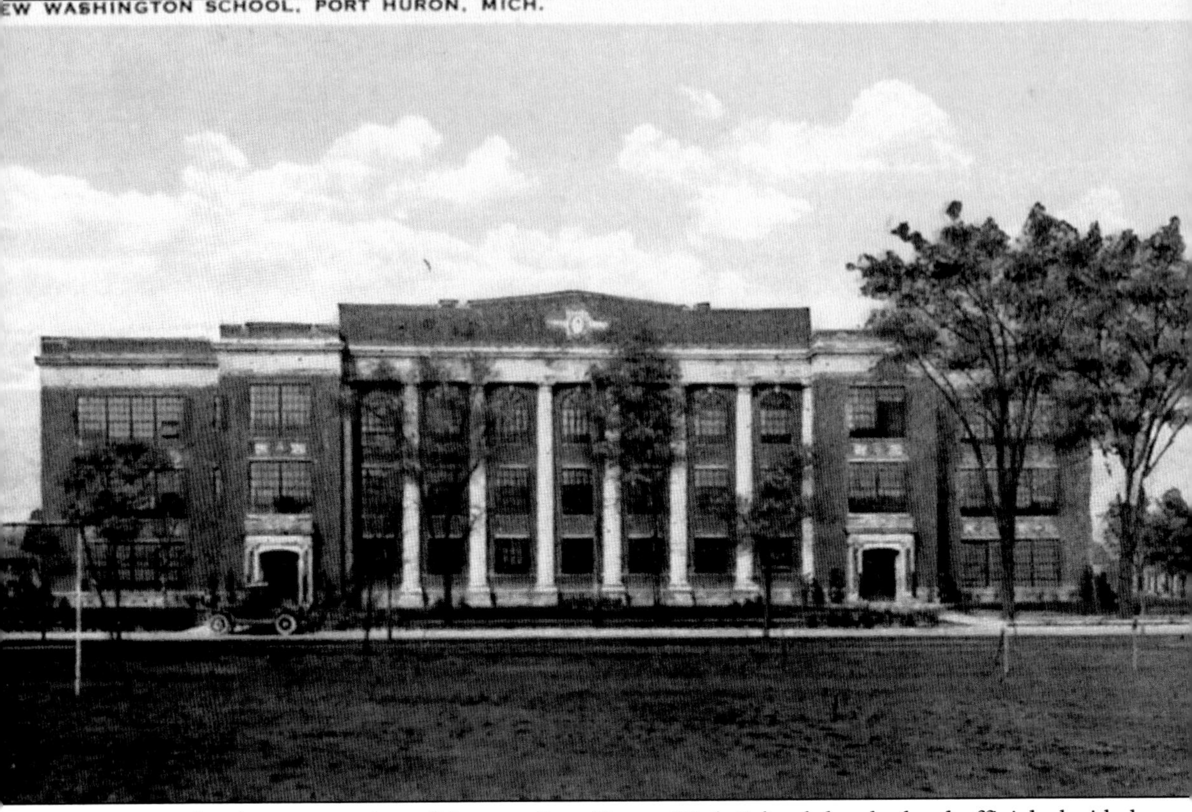


Soon after the construction of the new Port Huron High School, local school officials decided to replace an equally dated structure, Washington School. The first school, built in 1869, was located at the corner of Sixth and Wall Streets. By the early 1900s, it was nearly half a century old, and the necessity for a new junior high school was evident. The new school took the name of the old and was constructed around 1905 four blocks west on Tenth Street. It was similar to the high school, having a long front dotted with pillars. The building remained an active junior high school until the 1970s, when it was closed in favor of the newer Chippewa and Central Middle Schools.

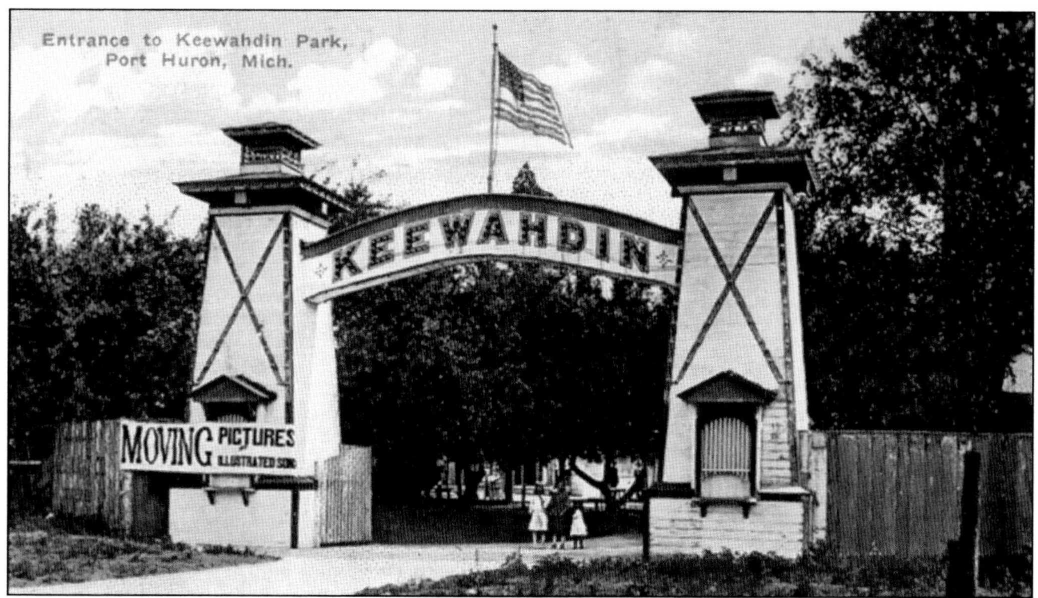


Children thrill at the possibility of seeing "moving pictures" in this *c.* 1910 scene. The massive entrance to Keewahdin Park, seen here, was itself a major landmark at the start of the 20th century. Created as a destination point for the city's electric streetcar system, Keewahdin was a thriving amusement for many years. Rides at the park included a Ferris wheel, carousel, and even a roller coaster that went out into Lake Huron. When the streetcar lines began to falter in the wake of the automobile in the asecond decade of the 20th century, Keewahdin Park was closed and the land became the home of the Gratiot Inn.

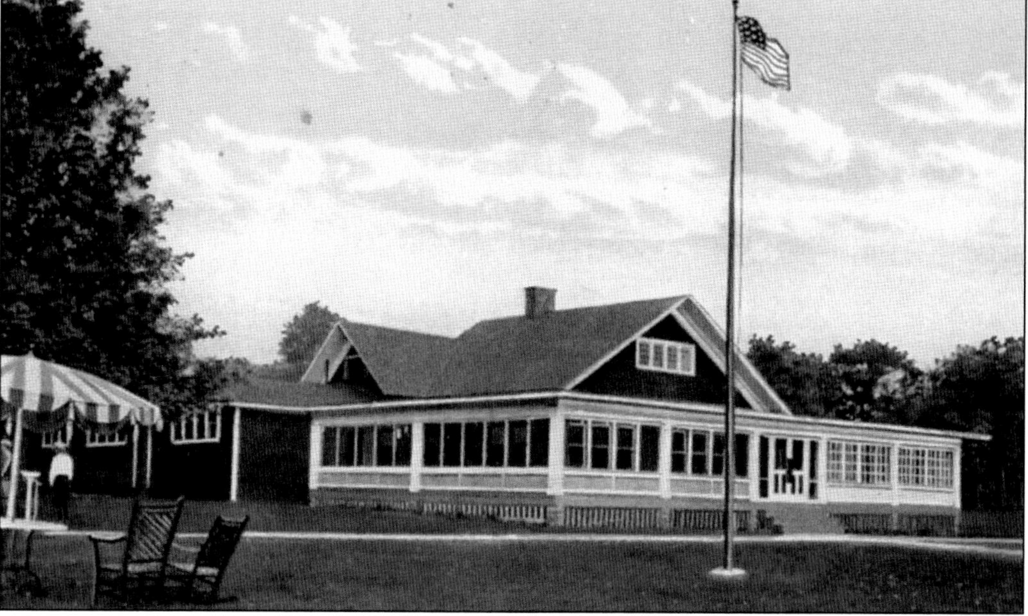

The Port Huron Country Club's first clubhouse is pictured in the 1920s. The original structure was a converted cottage, with the addition of extended porches and a larger kitchen and dining area. By the 1920s, the Port Huron County Club had become the Port Huron Golf Club, and the construction of an 18-hole course on nearby Fairway Drive was soon accomplished.

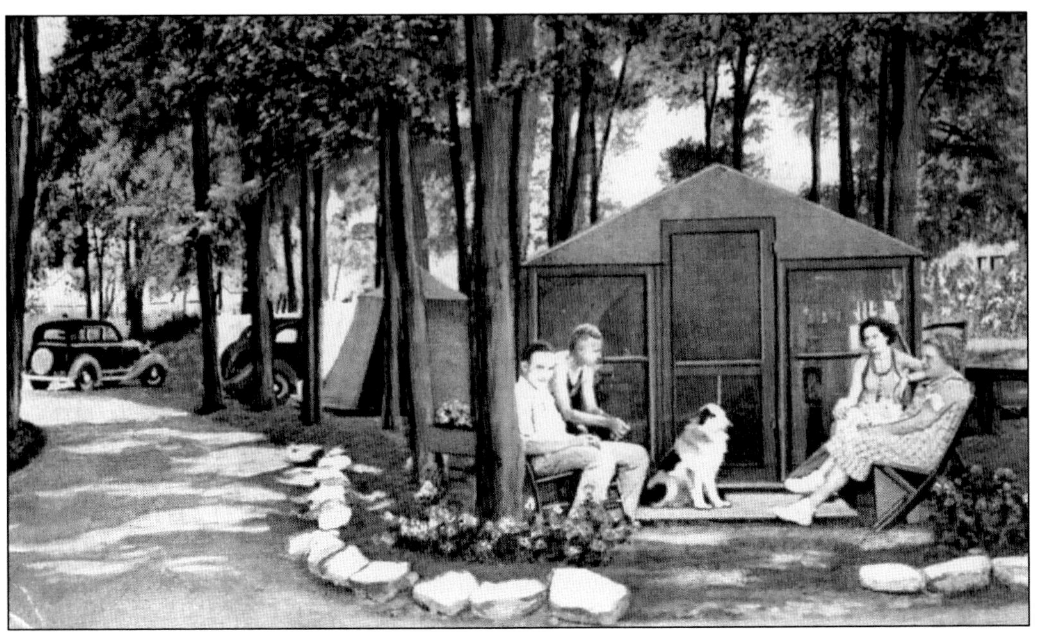

Couples lounge with their dog at one of the many tents in Lighthouse Park around 1930. Also known as the tourist park, Lighthouse served for many years as a place where one could place a tent for the weekend for a nominal fee. With the coming of the Depression, many of these "tourists" tended to stay for longer periods, which caused great consternation with many of the surrounding neighbors. By the 1950s, late-night fires and carousing had reached beyond the neighbors' tolerance, and overnight camping was no longer allowed. Although not an overnight venue, Lighthouse Park and Beach remain quite popular with locals and tourists alike.

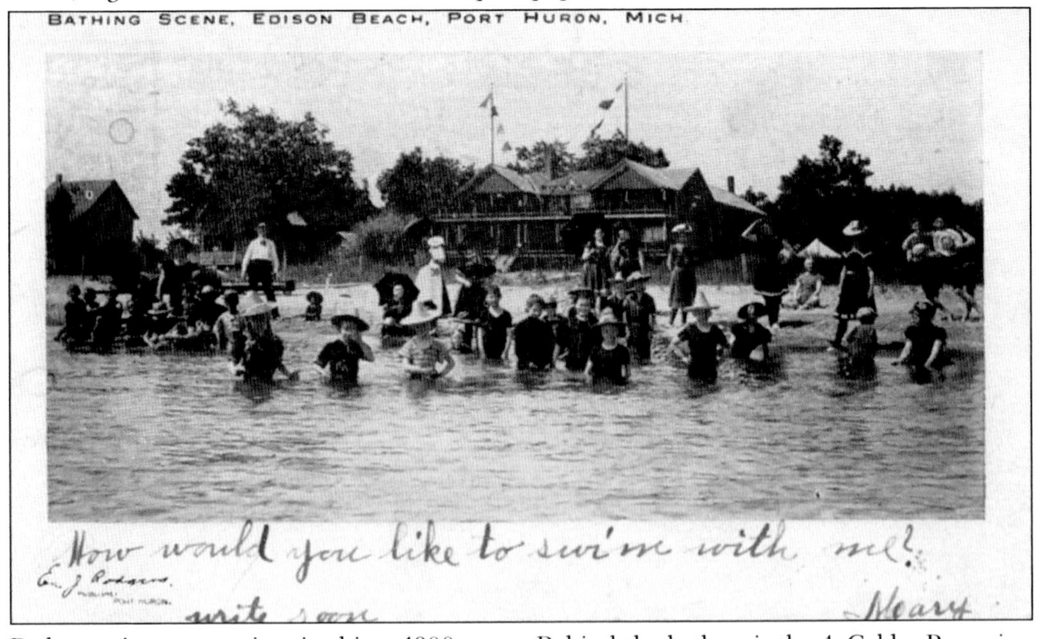


Bathers enjoy a great time in this *c.* 1900 scene. Behind the bathers is the 4-Gables Rooming House and Resort, one of many dotting the shoreline at the time. A unique postcard for its day, this one allowed the writer enough room to ask, "Would you like to swim with me?"

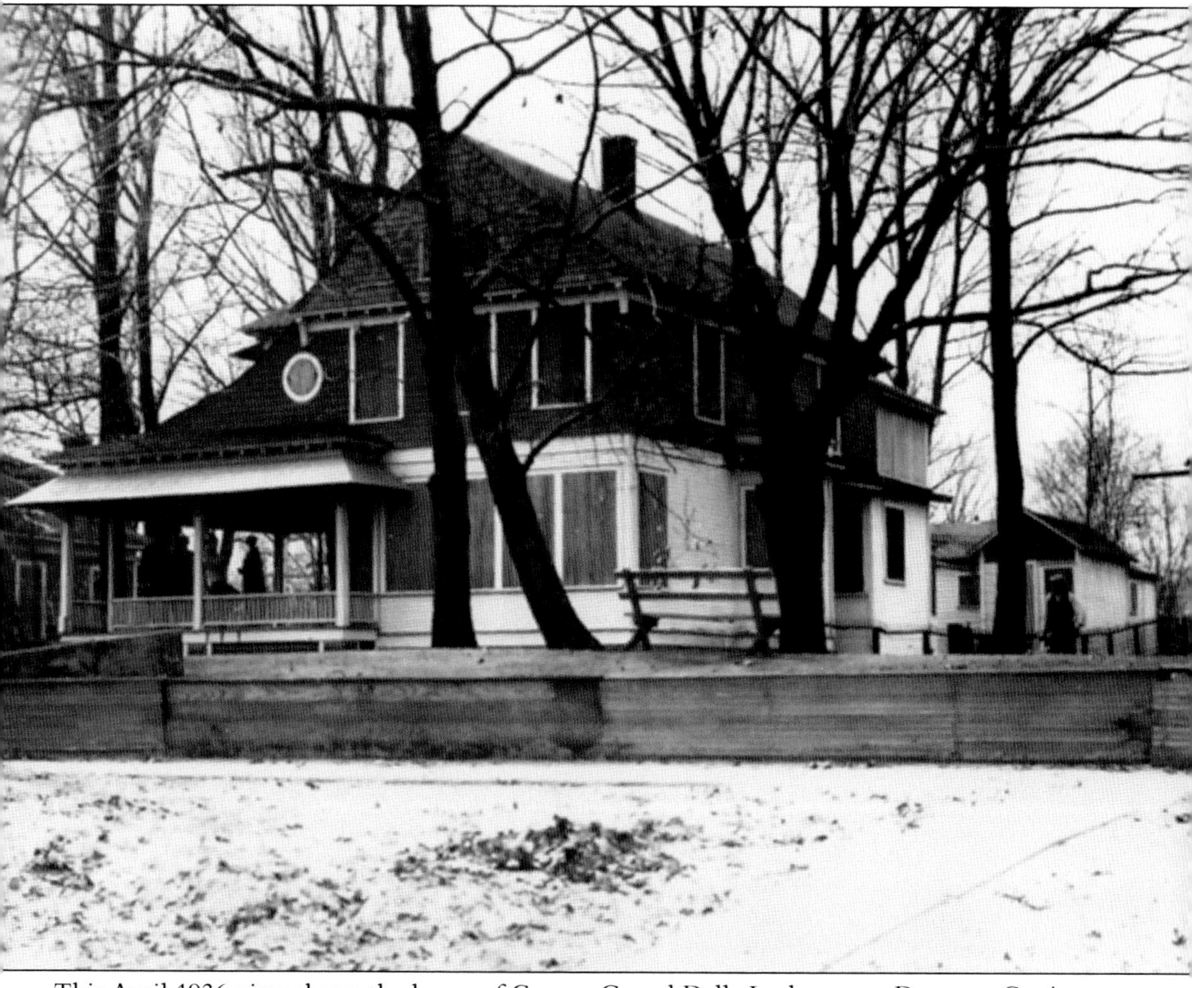

This April 1936 view shows the home of George C. and Della Laubengayer Dunn on Gratiot Avenue. One of the owners of the Dunn Paper Company, George Curtis Dunn purchased what had been a summer church camp and converted the lodge into a year-round home. Several of the smaller cottages were sold off and removed from the property. Though this was an unusual move at the time, the Dunns soon found that many of Port Huron's elite took to their idea and performed similar conversions. The Dunns continued to live in the home until the death of George in 1972. In 1974, George's great-niece Christine Bottomley Gaffney inherited the residence and made further renovations. The home continues to stand to this day, now owned by the Boyea family.

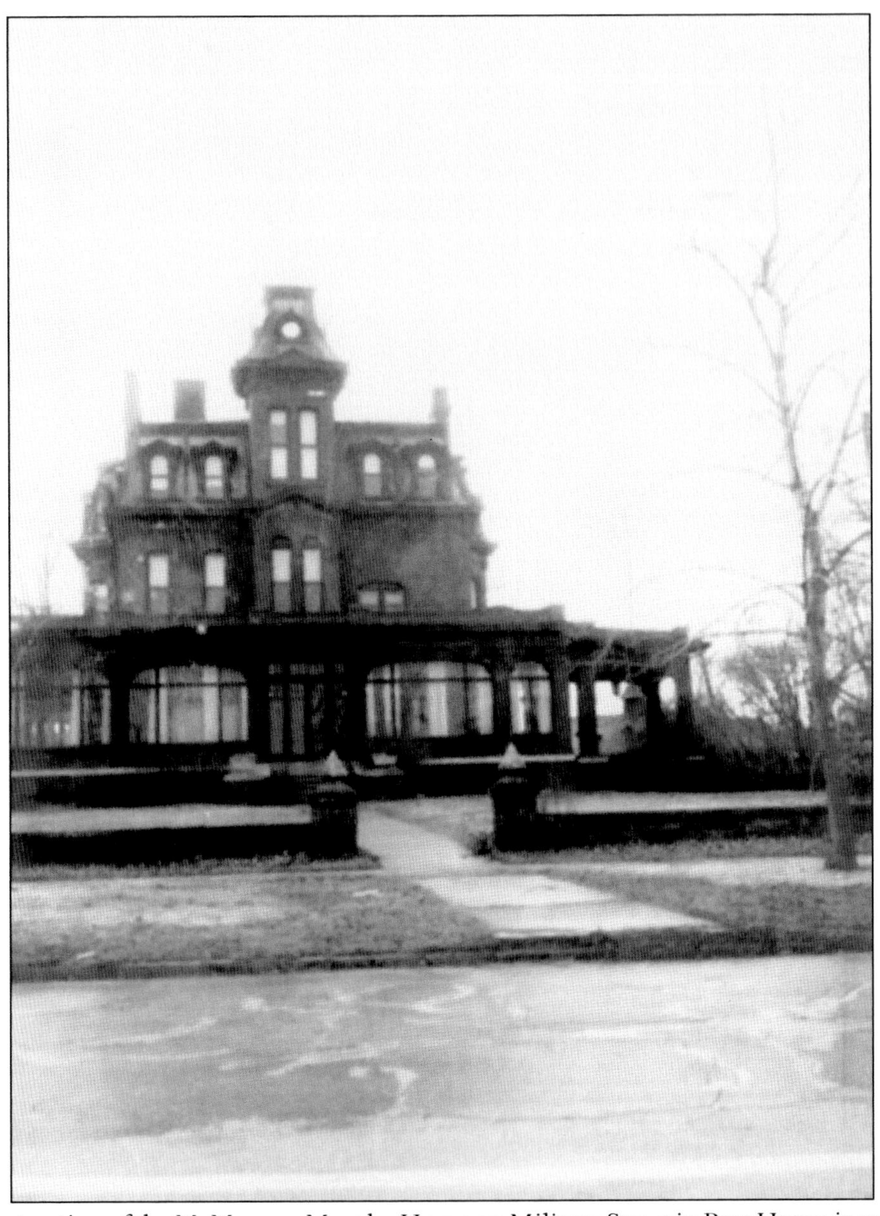

The destruction of the McMorran-Murphy Home on Military Street in Port Huron is an action that still baffles many preservationists. The residence was constructed in 1878 by Henry Gordon McMorran, a man who often described himself simply as "a capitalist." McMorran was involved in many aspects of business and industry, from railroads and shipping to milling and banking. Upon his death in 1929, his daughter Emma moved into the home with her husband, Andrew Murphy, and named it Deer Lawn. A true entrepreneur in his own right, Murphy had come to Port Huron from the Columbus, Ohio, area to improve the city's streets by paving them with bricks. Murphy was also an investor in the Havers automobile plant. At the time of his death in 1965, he was a major benefactor to the Sisters of Mercy and the city of Port Huron. Although the home was to be used for the sisters and nurses, the sisters decided that it did not fit their needs and tore it down in 1971. All that remains to this day is the brick and cast-iron fence, constructed in part from the bricks that made its owner his fortune.

Nothing says summer in Port Huron like the Port Huron to Mackinac Sailboat Race. Although run by members of the Bayview Yacht Club, the race is hosted at the start by the Port Huron Yacht Club, founded in 1923. Since the 1920s, the Mackinac Race has marked the height of the summer tourist season in Port Huron, and hundreds of sailors come from all over the world for this greatest of freshwater races. The crowded nature of the river can be seen in this overhead view, taken from the Pere Marquette Railroad bridge at the mouth of the Black River during the 1940s.

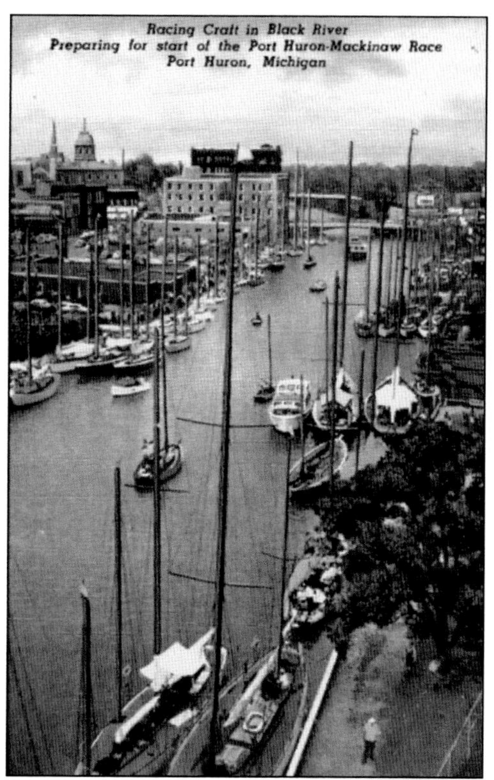


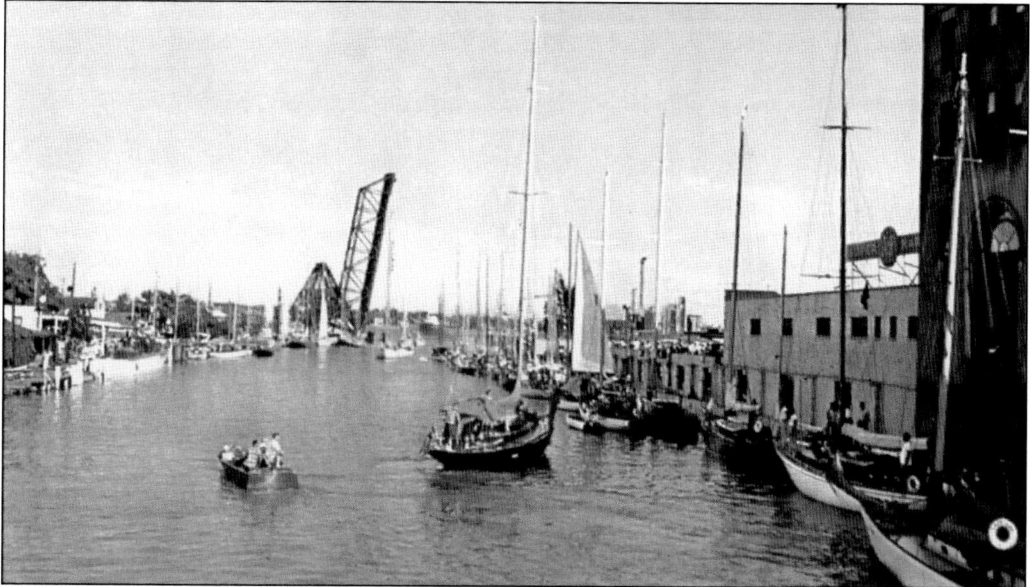

Roughly a decade later, this race view looks toward the Pere Marquette Railroad bridge from which the above photograph was taken. As the years have progressed, much has changed in the race. The sailboats, once made almost entirely of wood, are now primarily fiberglass. Even sailors of the 1950s would marvel at the strides made in the name of safety and speed, with carbon-fiber masts, inflatable life rafts, life lines, and GPS technology being the norms among today's racers.

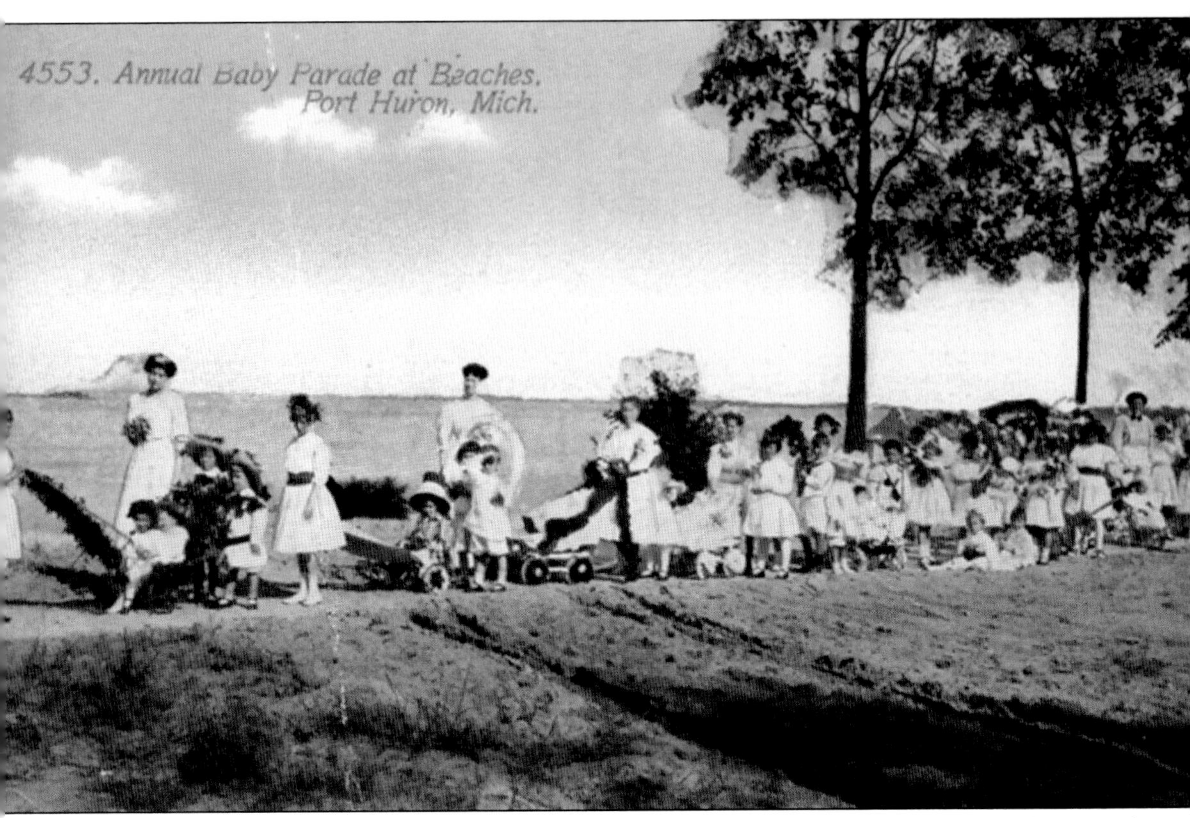


A veritable bevy of babies can be seen in this 1890s view. Once a rite of summer, the annual Baby Parade gave summer vacationers a chance to get away from their cabins and show off their progeny. No small affair, the parade awarded prizes in different age categories; as evidenced here, mothers and children were indeed dressed in their finest wares.

*Seven*

# Greetings and Salutations

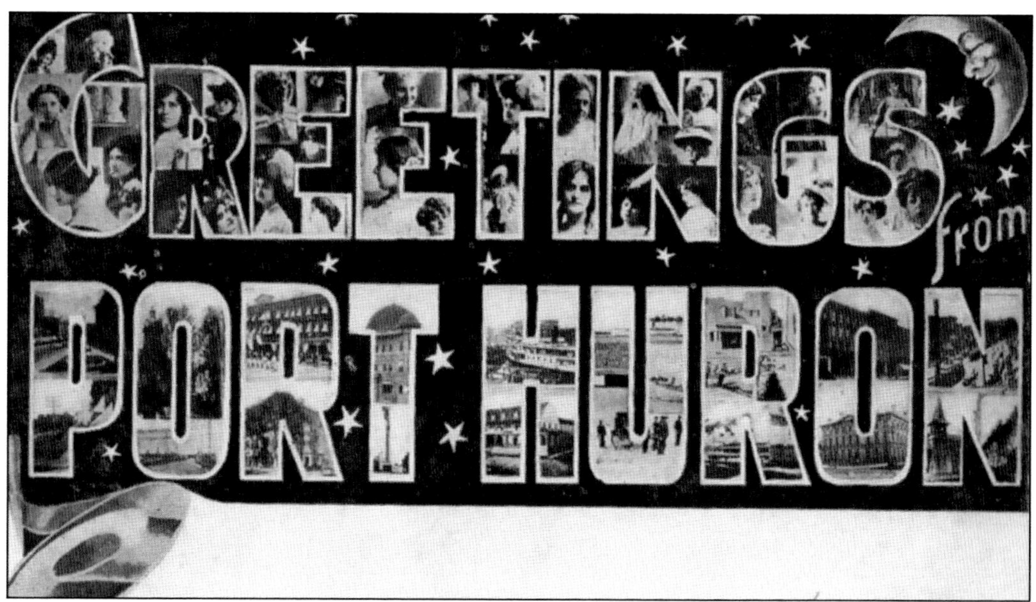


A popular postcard in its day, this composite image combines a series of photographs of women, possibly local, with important structures in the community. If looking carefully, one can find the following in the letters of "Port Huron": the post office; city hall; the Union Hotel; the Harrington Hotel; the Maccabee temple (Algonquin Hotel); the Windermere resort; the Lakeview Beach United States Life Saving Station; the steamers *Northwest*, *Omar D. Conger*, and *Tashmoo*; the Lakeside Cemetery Chapel; and Port Huron Hospital. Given the buildings shown in the image, it most likely dates to the World War I era.

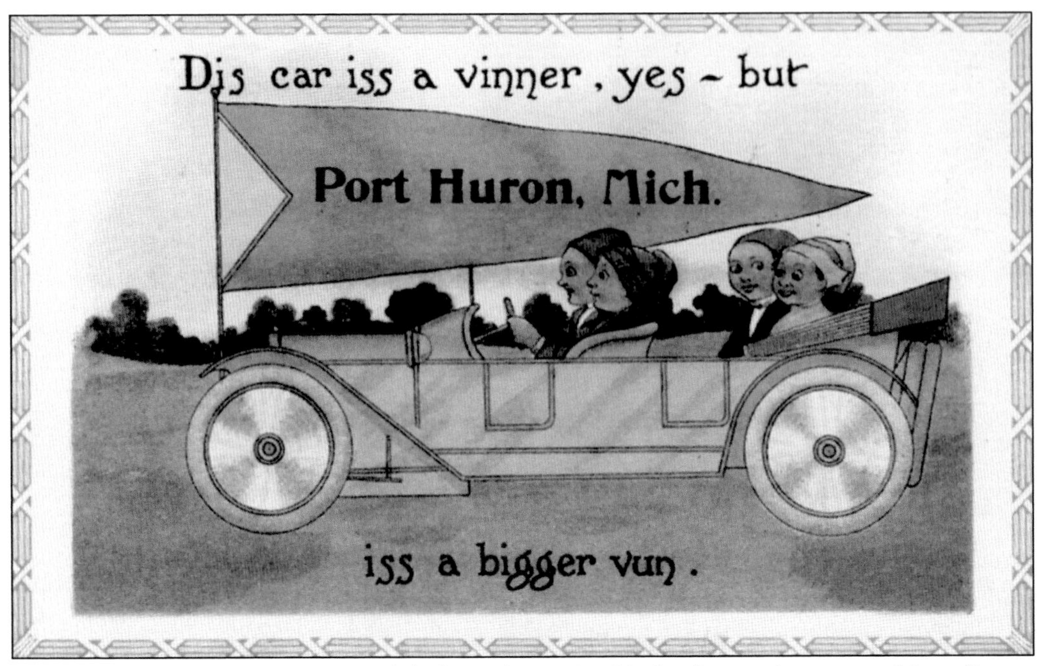


Revelers sit in an early open automobile from the 1910s. Obviously catering to an ethic audience, this postcard notes, "Dis car iss a vinner, yes—but Port Huron, Mich. iss bigger vun."

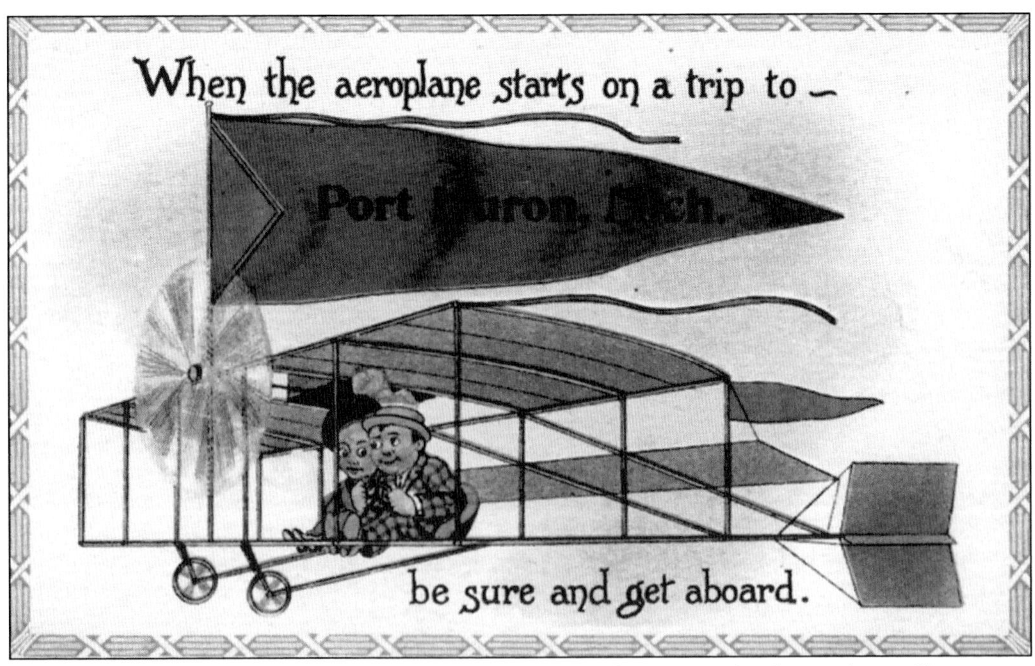


This popular card plays on the Wright brothers flight of 1903. It asks the reader to "be sure to get aboard." As is the case today, recent national events affected the way postcards were presented and printed.

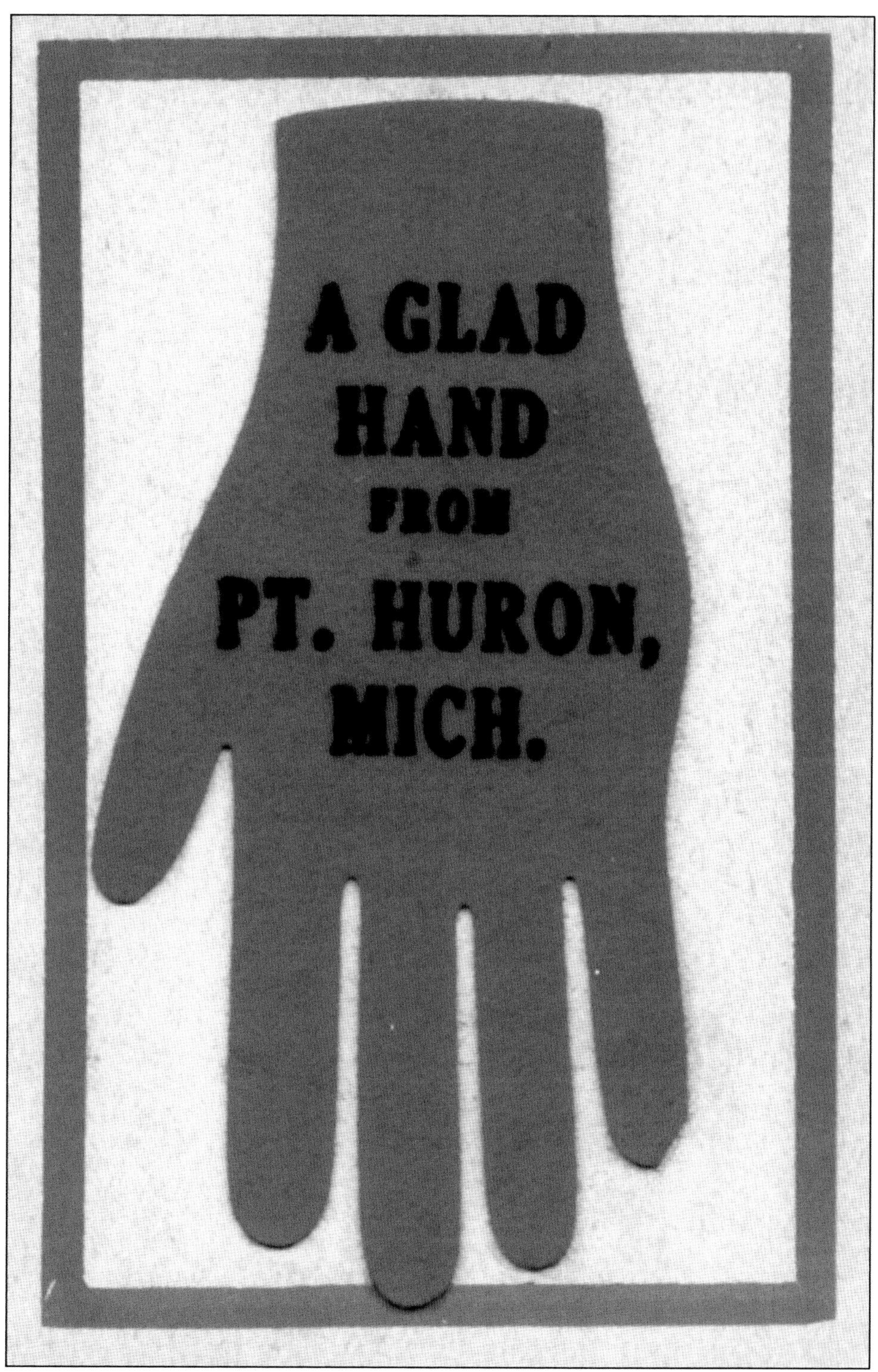


Yet another tongue-in-cheek reference, this postcard gives the reader "A Glad Hand" from Port Huron. Raised or two-dimensional cards were also quite popular, often using felt, cotton, or other materials to catch the eye of the prospective buyer.

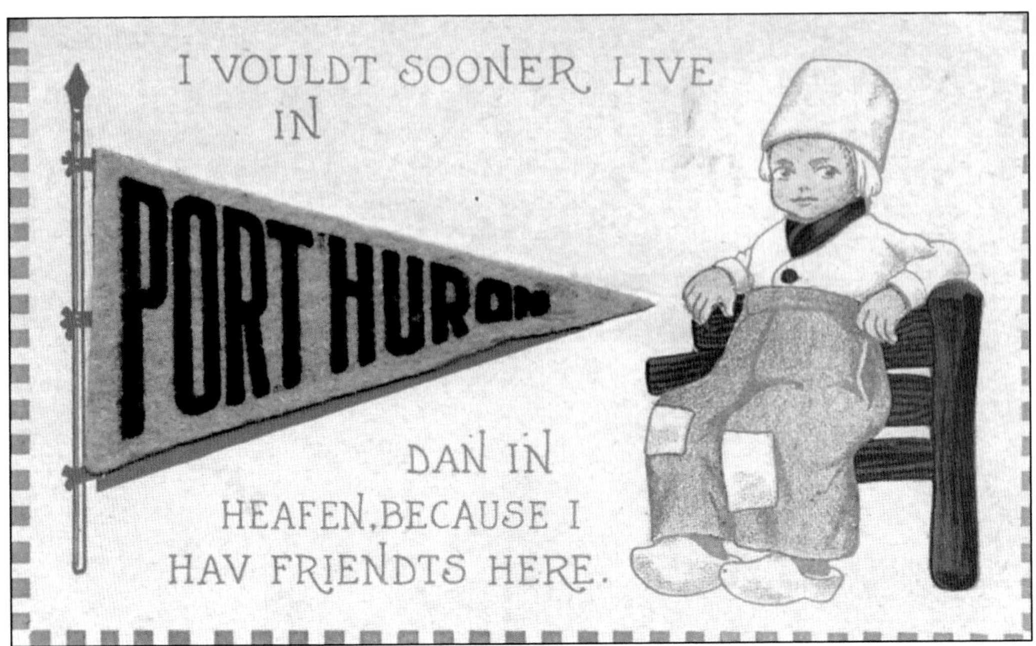


These two images use the raised addition to a postcard in a different format. The one above plays on the ethnic backgrounds of newly arriving immigrants, noting, "I vouldt sooner live in Port Huron dan in Heafen, because I hav friendts here." The below image takes more of a humorous edge: "I've monkeyed around 'bout long enough in Port Huron." It even goes a step further, making the extra interesting adage, "This is no place for a minister's son."

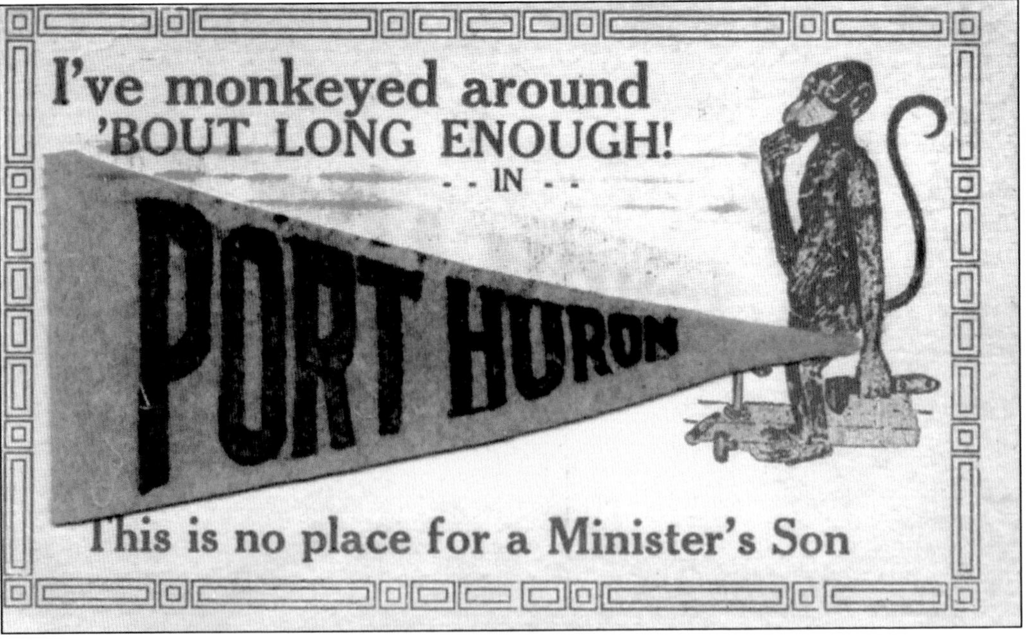

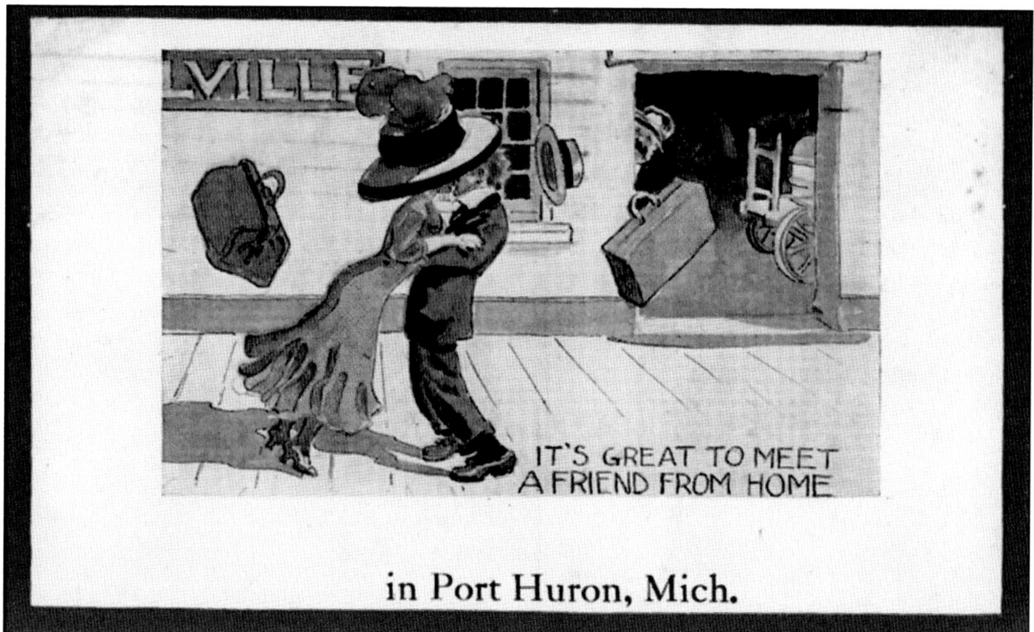


"It's great to meet a friend from home," reads this *c.* 1900 postcard. Unlike some of the other images shown in this chapter, this one uses more of an artist's rendering rather than a cartoon or real photograph to get its message across. The "lville" on the station sign allows the image to be a bit generic while still conveying the small-town feel.

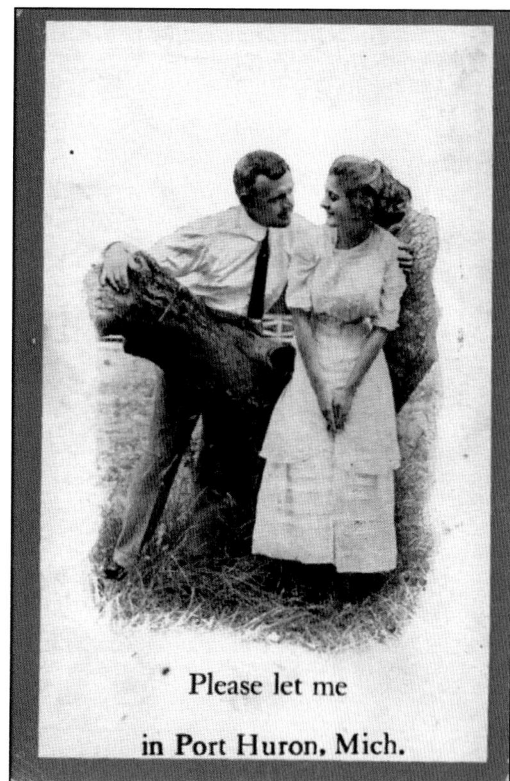


This image is from the same series as the one above, but with a bit different message. "Please let me" is definitely a bit risqué for the time in which it was written. Unlike the other image, it uses a real photograph of a couple.

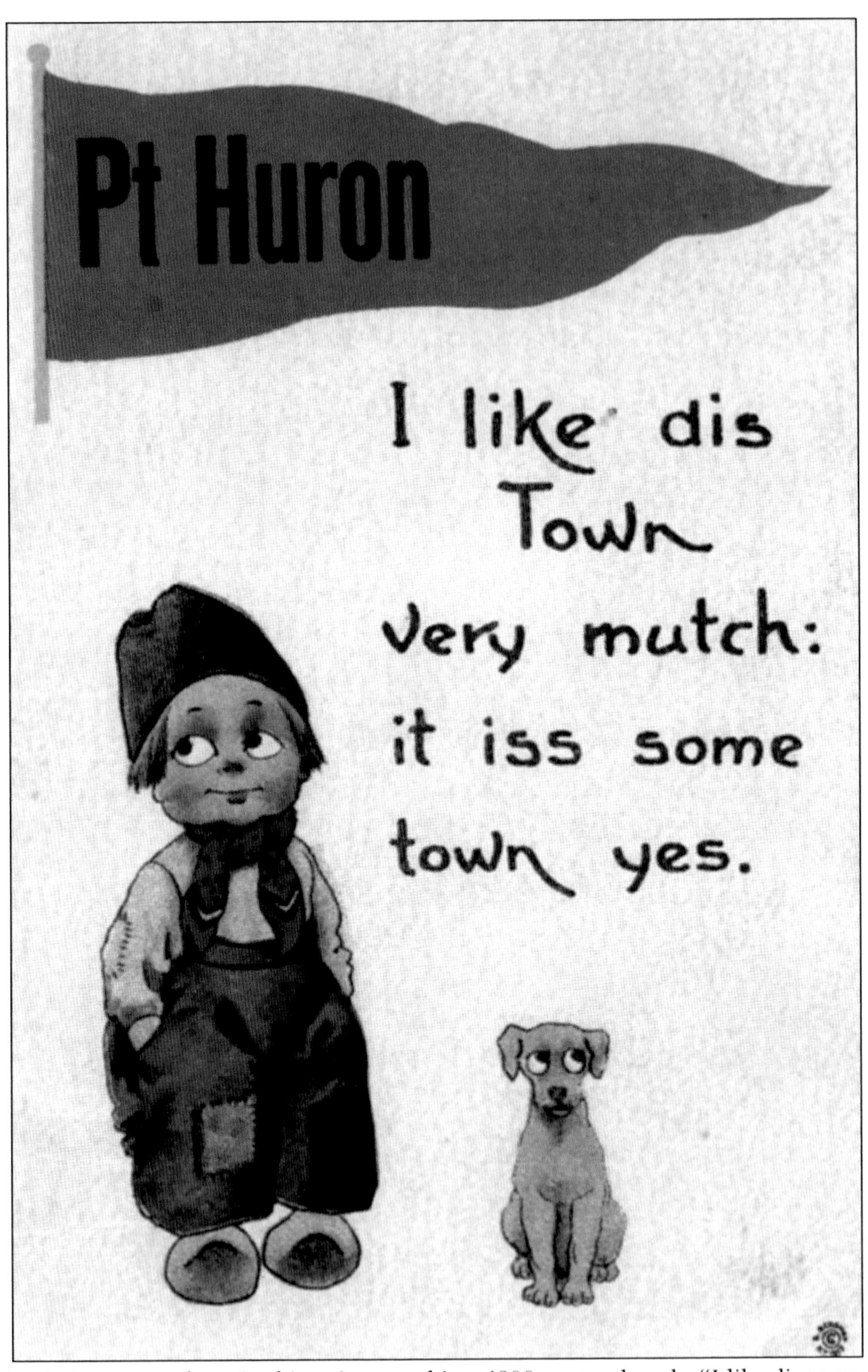


Again playing on newly arrived immigrants, this *c.* 1900 postcard reads, "I like dis town very mutch: it iss some town yes." The addition of a small dog and the popular pennant motif make it a bit more unusual.

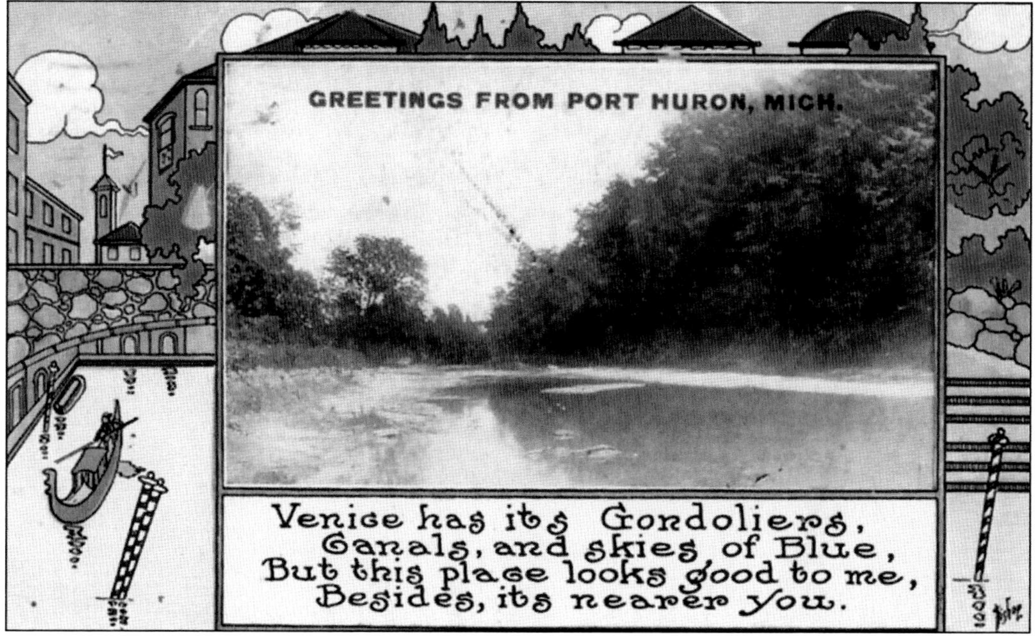


This postcard refers to a popular early-1900s reference to the St. Clair River being the "Venice of the United States." A real photograph set on a background of an artistic rendering of Venice itself helps grab the reader's eye. It notes, "Venice has its gondoliers, canals, and skies of Blue, But this place looks good to me, Besides, its nearer you."

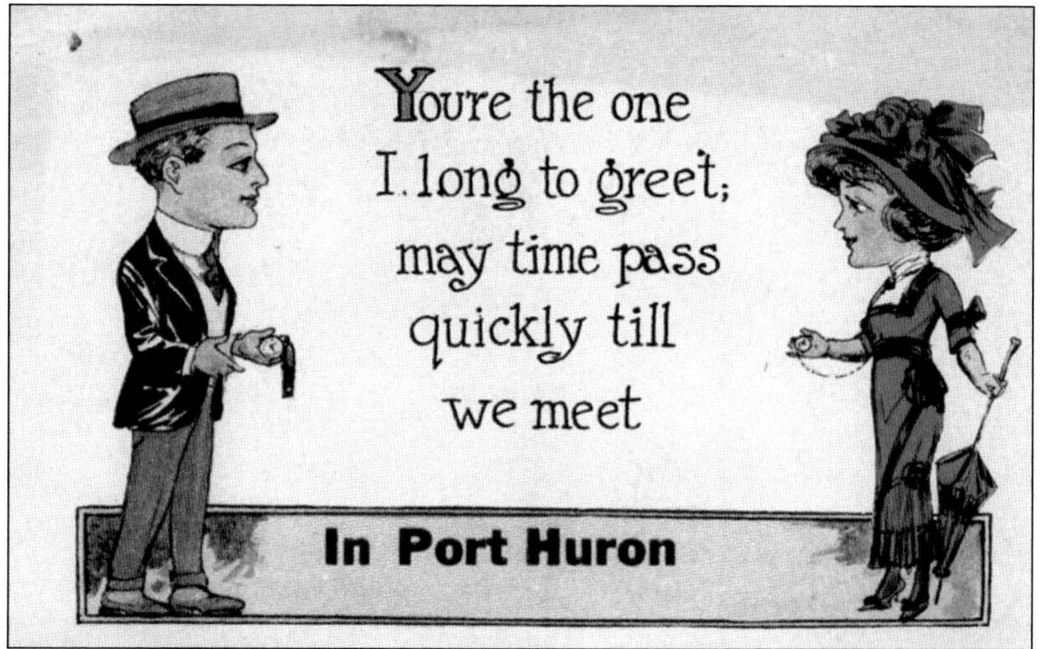


Cartoons have been popular for years, and in the era of the penny postcard, they often became a selling point. Here, a depiction of a young man and woman of the early 1900s plays this role while stating, "You're the one I long to greet, may time pass quickly till we meet."

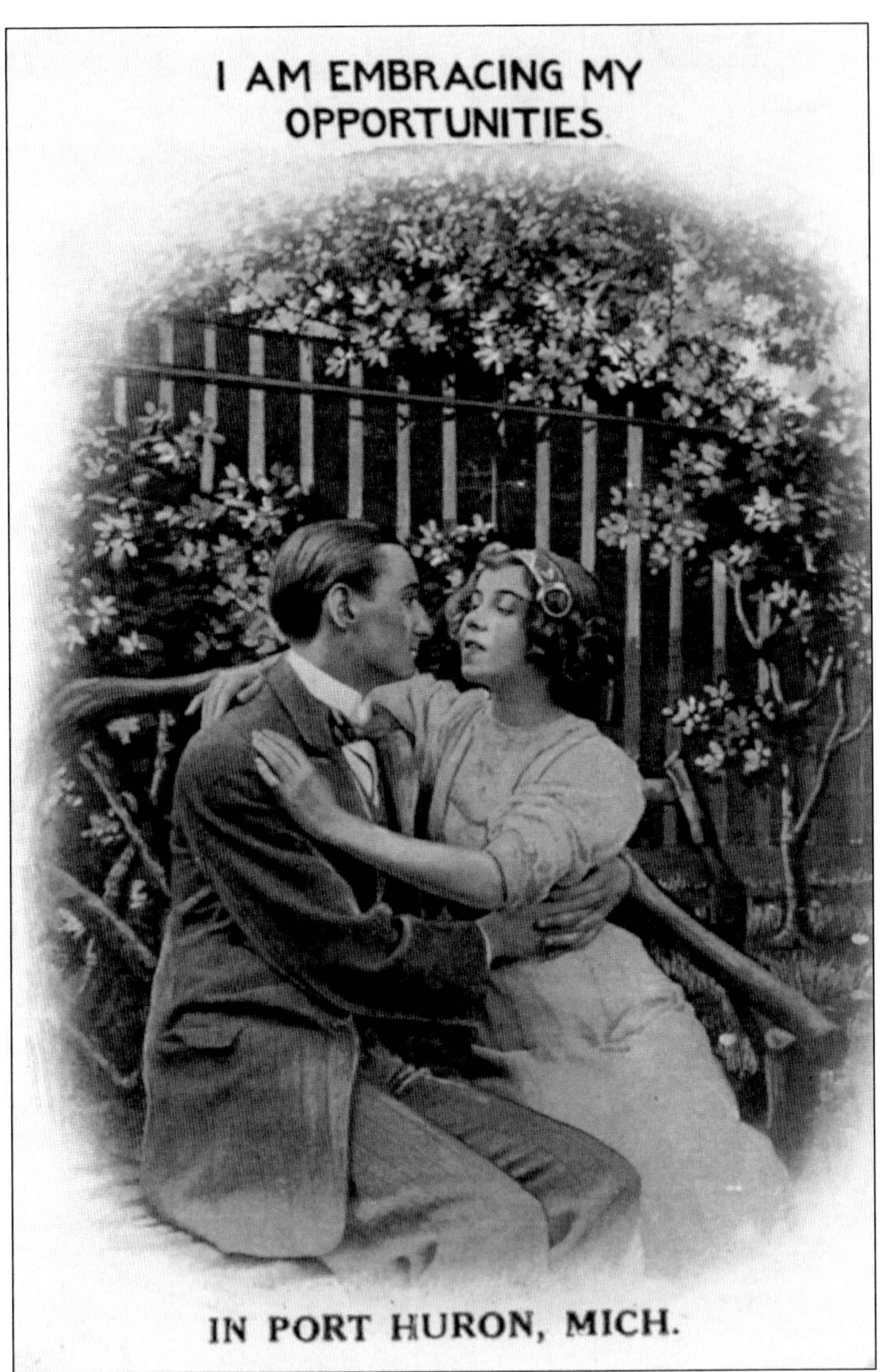


A real photograph plays the tongue-in-cheek role again on this postcard. "I am embracing my opportunities" takes on multiple meanings here. This particular card came from set or series No. 989 from T. P. and Company of New York. Like many in this section, this card could be purchased in a set or individually and was easily modified by adding a stamp with the name of the town.

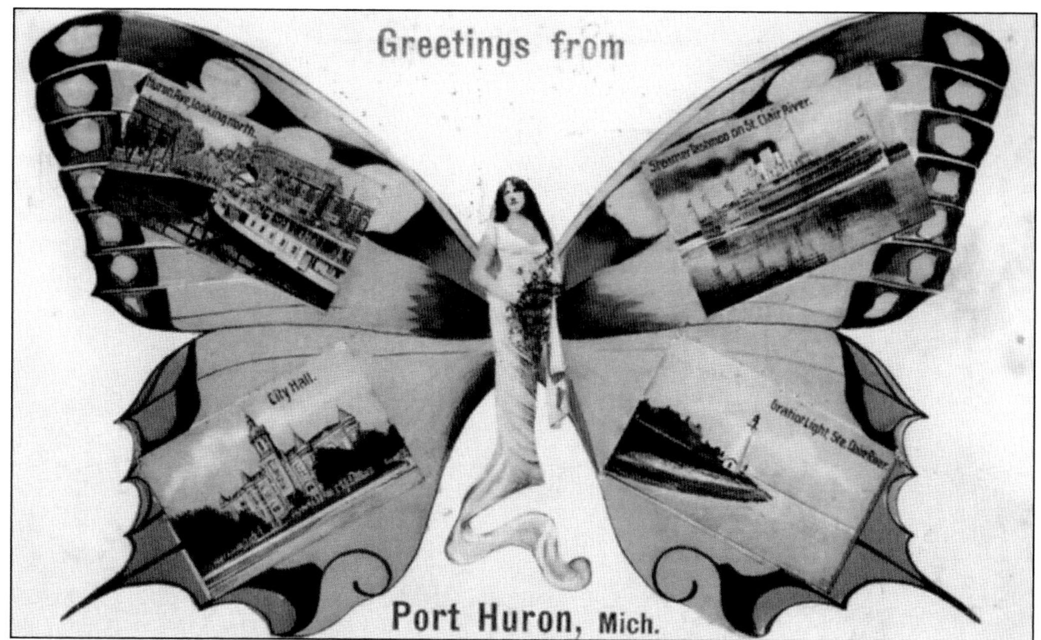


Another type of composite card is demonstrated here. This one is a bit unusual, as it takes real photographs and turns them into a composite view that looks like a butterfly. Within this card can be seen images of the following Port Huron landmarks: the Military Street Bridge (upper left), the steamer *Tashmoo* (upper right), Port Huron City Hall (lower left), and the Fort Gratiot Lighthouse (lower right). Created by the Souvenir Postcard Company of New York, this card was actually made in Germany under contract and then sent to the United States.

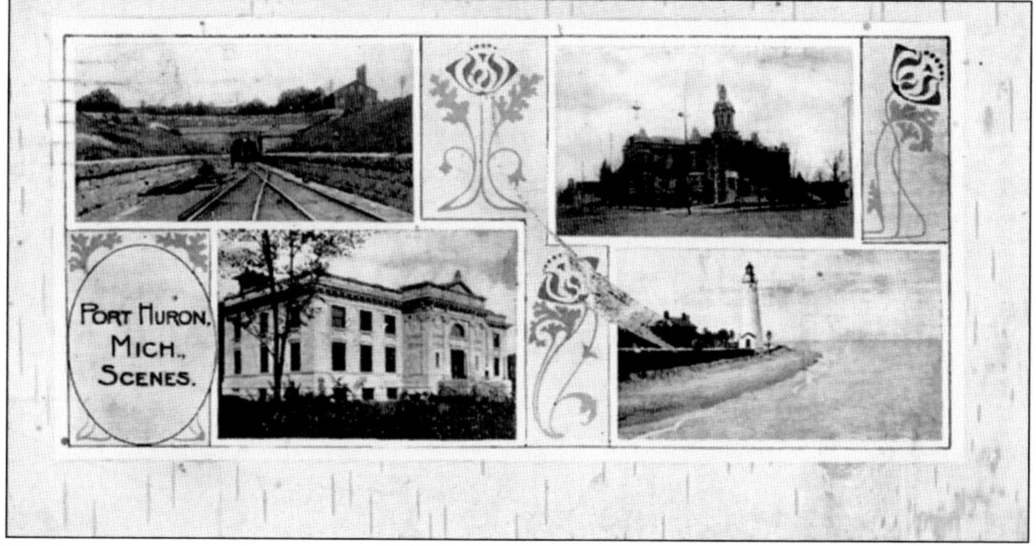


The Port Huron area's rich woodland and Native American heritage are touched upon with this particular postcard. While the images—which include the St. Clair River Tunnel (upper left), Port Huron City Hall (upper right), Port Huron Public Library (lower left, now the Port Huron Museum), and the Fort Gratiot Lighthouse (lower right)—are of more modern subjects, the birchbark nature of the card ties them with the more traditional arts of Port Huron's Native past.

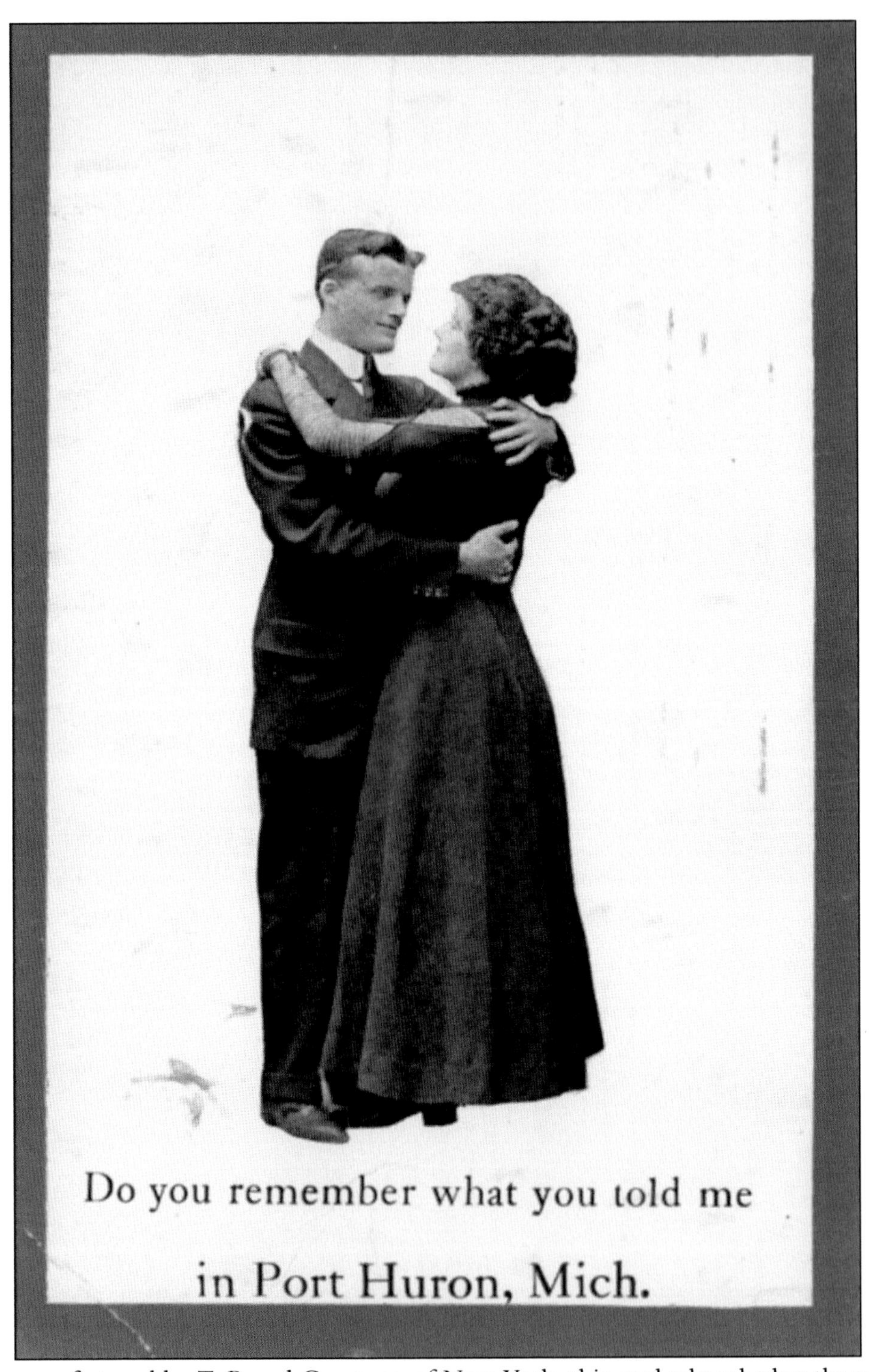


Also manufactured by T. P. and Company of New York, this card asks whether the reader remembers "what you told me" in Port Huron. One of countless similar views, the play on words and tongue-in-cheek nature was popular in the first and second decades of the 20th century. It was a much more innocent time, to be sure.

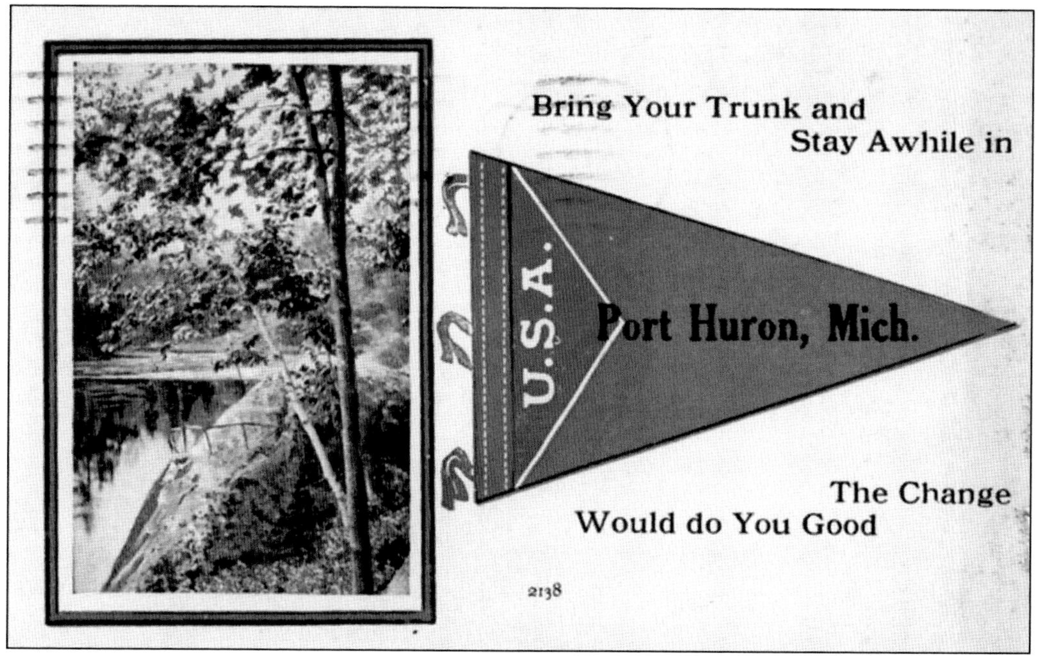


Although the producer of this card is unknown, it is obviously from a set. Note the 2138 in the lower middle of the image, recording its number within a series. A different sort of combination card, it uses the pennant and a photograph to help convey the message to "bring your trunk and stay awhile in Port Huron, Mich. The change would do you good." The Port Huron stamp is a bit too large for the stock spot on the pennant.

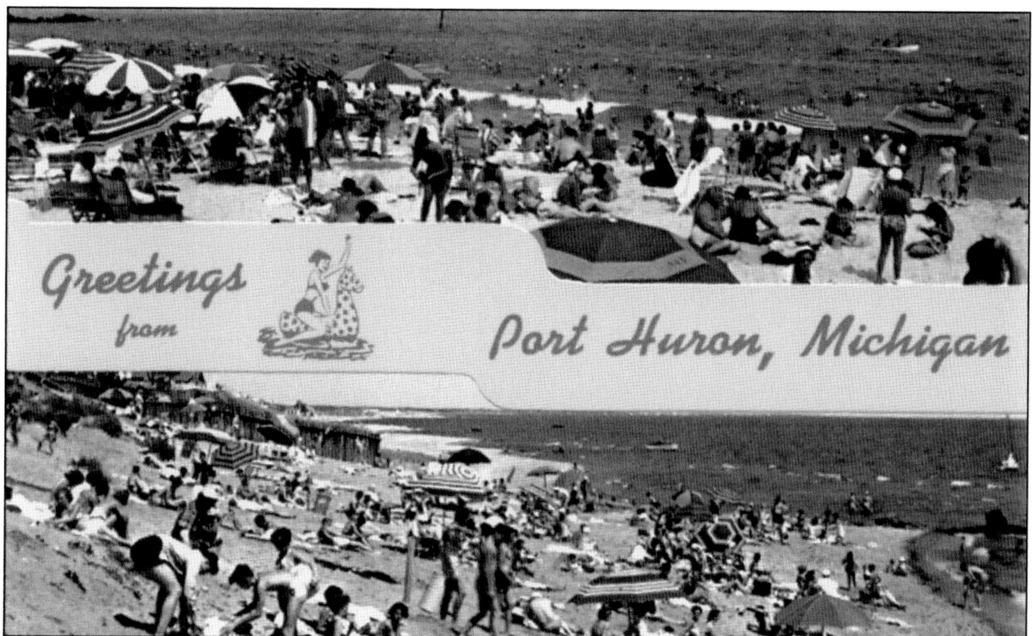


By the 1950s, advances in color photography and postcard production allowed for much more colorful cards. Manufacturers still found that stock images cut down on costs, however; it is doubtful that this photograph was actually taken in Port Huron.

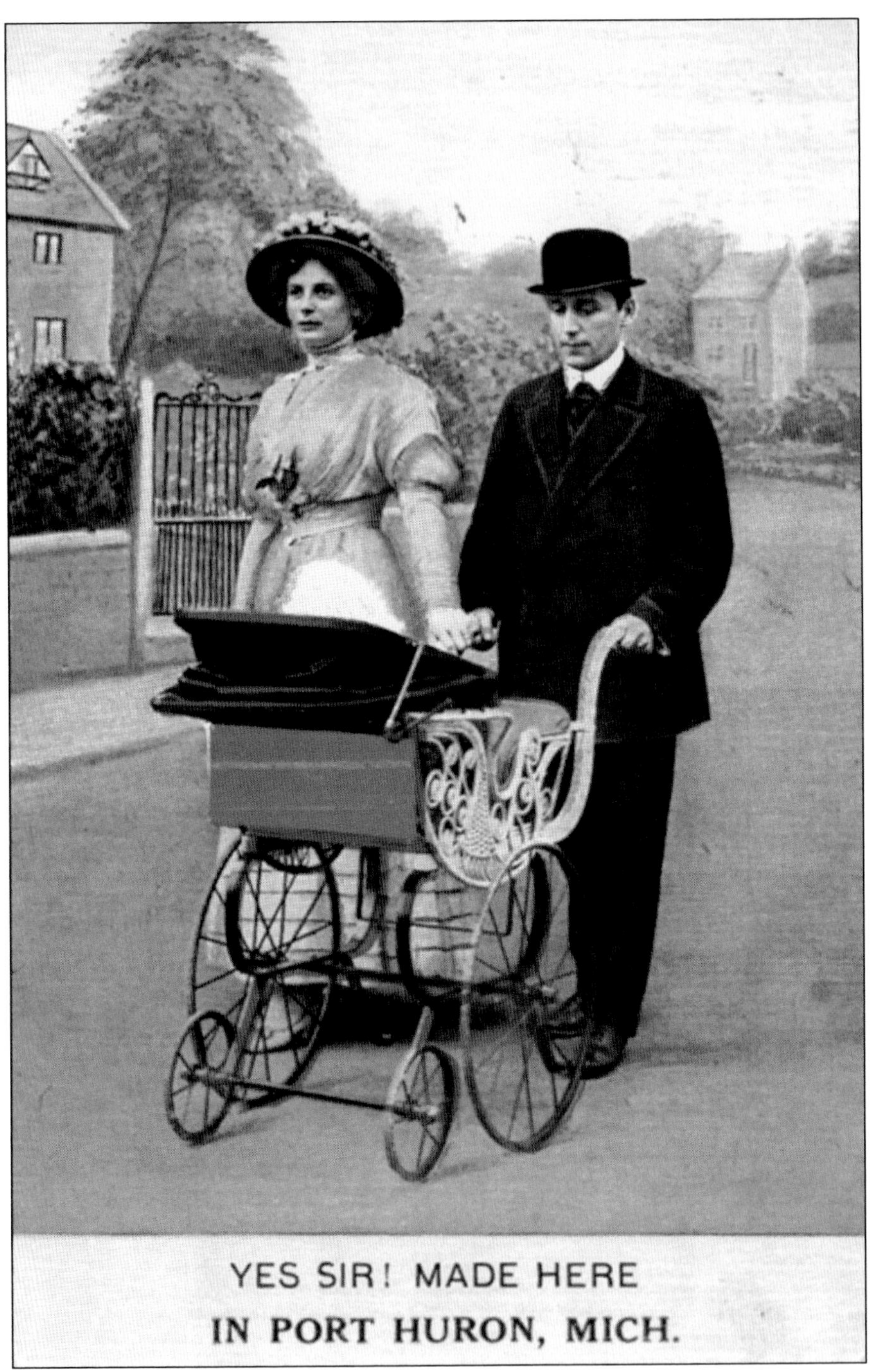


"Yes Sir! Made Here in Port Huron, Mich.," claims this card depicting a newlywed couple pushing a baby stroller. This was, by far, one of the author's father's favorite images; in a very real sense, it reflected his love and passion for his hometown. He loved this image so much that when the Mainstreet Port Huron organization opened its welcome center in the 1990s, he donated a framed poster-sized version for display. This image continues to greet visitors, who often chuckle at the humor of a simpler time.

# Index